This is the only empirical study of Lebanese political life viewed from the standpoint of its central force for change, the students. It will be an invaluable resource for students of the modern Middle East as well as for specialists in sociology, politics, and history. *Lebanon in Strife* has special relevance to problems of political change and development in the Third World countries, providing a sociopolitical model for the analysis of student politics in traditional and transitional societies.

Halim Barakat received his Ph.D. in social psychology from the University of Michigan in 1966. He has taught at the American University of Beirut, Lebanese University, and the University of Texas at Austin and is currently an associate professor at the Center for Contemporary Arab Studies at Georgetown University. Among his publications are *River without Bridges: A Study of the Exodus of the 1967 Palestinian Arab Refugees* (with Peter Dodd) and a novel, *Days of Dust*.

*Modern Middle East Series, No. 2*
Sponsored by the Center for Middle Eastern Studies at the University of Texas at Austin.

# Lebanon in Strife

*Student Preludes to the Civil War*

**Modern Middle East Series, No. 2**

*Sponsored by the Center for Middle Eastern Studies*
*The University of Texas at Austin*

# Lebanon in Strife

*Student Preludes to the Civil War*

by Halim Barakat

University of Texas Press
Austin and London

An earlier version of Chapter 3 was published as "Social and Political Integration in Lebanon: A Case of Social Mosaic." Reprinted, with permission, from the Summer 1973 issue of the *Middle East Journal*. This paper was originally published in Arabic in *Mawaqif* 1, no. 1 (1968).

Library of Congress Cataloging in Publication Data

Barakat, Halim Isber.
  Lebanon in strife.

  (Modern Middle East series; no. 2)
  Bibliography: p.
  Includes index.
  1. Students—Lebanon—Political activity. 2. Lebanon—Politics and government. 3. Lebanon—Social conditions. 4. Lebanon—History—Civil War, 1975–  I. Title. II. Series: Modern Middle East series (Austin, Tex.); no. 2
  LA1463.7.B37    378.1'98'109569    76-50046
  ISBN 0-292-70322-8

Printed in the United States of America

# Contents

# Tables

**Figure**

# Preface

This work is a witness and a study in anticipation of the Lebanese civil war in the making between 1967 and 1976. During this period I had been collecting documents on the polarizing confrontation, conducting surveys, observing demonstrations and strikes, discussing my findings and interpretations with my students and colleagues, comparing my data with those of similar studies in developed and developing societies, and rewriting previous drafts of the present book.

When the final version of my manuscript was delivered to the press in September 1976 with the understanding that I could not make any more changes, I felt a sort of letdown. It meant delivering a finished product which I saw as yet unfinished. The fact that the civil war itself continued to rage on added to the intensity of my exasperation. The dialogue that I had had with my friends and myself about improving the manuscript had to stop. Subsequent to my visit to Lebanon in late December 1976–early January 1977 I have formed a number of impressions, the following of which may be most pertinent: First, the Lebanese seem to have resumed their old ways and means of doing things without allowing themselves to reflect on previous orientations, including those that contributed to the civil war. Second, the Lebanese government has occupied itself with problems of reconstruction without the benefit of an overall vision for the future. Third, the Syrian forces seem to be in control of the situation, a fact which allows for relative stability in the immediate future but leaves a lot of questions unanswered in the long run. Fourth, while the Christian traditional leaders have been able to perpetuate themselves or even gain more power to the extent of guaranteeing the ascendancy of their children, the Muslim traditional leaders have lost much of their power and the vacuum waits to be filled. In fact, it became evident that the Muslim communities were represented by externally imposed leaders. To illustrate, the Speaker of the House, Kamil al-Assa'd, who supposedly represented the Shi'ites, sought refuge in the Maronite district of Kisruwan. Fifth, the problem of bridging the deep and wide gaps between the Lebanese communities constitutes the most urgent and challenging task. The psychological wound is so deep that a mental line continues to divide districts and neighborhoods. In the mind of each of the opposed factions, the other side has been dehumanized to the extent of abstraction and, thus, could serve as an easy target of hatred and cruelty without much remorse of conscience. Sixth, looting during the civil war was widespread, well organized, and even rationalized to the extent of legitimation. Along with the arms trade, it may well have contributed to the continuation of the war and determined the areas of engagement (e.g., the Beirut downtown commercial district). Seventh, the Lebanese tend to oversimplify issues related to explanation of the civil war. The general tendencies are to explain it in terms of one single factor; to blame events on the other side; to stress different or even conflicting factors on different occasions; to be immersed by local and immediate conditions; and to operate under constant pressure to project a false image of high morale. Simply, the ship continues to travel over stormy seas without a chart or sense of direction.

This study was profoundly influenced by a climate of political and social unrest following the June War of 1967 and began in response to several intriguing questions: What makes Arab society unable to face up to trying challenges? How can Arabs transcend their conditions? What makes Arab systems and institutions so repressive? How can they be changed? What is the role of youth in a changing society? What myths disguise reality?

My critical perspective must be traced to my identification with the uprooted, destitute, deprived, and humbled as well as to my affiliation with a transitional society struggling to transcend its underdevelopment. This is in no way a confession or an apology for my critical approach, but rather an explanation and a call for understanding.

My thanks go to the numerous friends who helped immensely in a variety of ways to bring about this work. I am thankful to Hanan Musallam, who assisted in the collection and processing of the data, and to Professor Robert Fernea for his valuable suggestions. I am also indebted to the valuable suggestions of the unknown reviewers of my manuscript for the University of Texas Press.

My special appreciation goes to Marilyn Duncan for the excellent job she did in editing the manuscript. I am also grateful to my editor at the University of Texas Press, Carolyn Cates Wylie, for her diligent work in the course of the latest revisions. My nephew, Bernard Doumani, has helped in preparing the index. I wish also to mention that my conversations with my friends Munir Bashshur, Peter Dodd, Hisham Sharabi, and several others have been a source of much of my speculation.

Finally, this book is dedicated to my wife, Hayat, for her constant contributions to the enrichment of my life, and to my students who gave their lives for what they believed to be true and just.

*H.B.*
January 1977

# Part I

# A Perspective on Youth and Change in a Mosaic Society

# 1. Introductory Statement:

*Youth and Change*

## Commitment to Change

The focus of this study on student politics in Lebanon is part of a more comprehensive concern with development and transformation in Arab society and with problems of political and social integration in mosaic societies in general. An attempt will be made to determine the nature of the relationship between the liberation of the young from socially corrosive traditional loyalties and their commitment to basic change.

Why the emphasis on change? Why youth or students in particular? What forces determine student political behavior and attitudes? To what extent is it possible for them to contribute to the historical task of human liberation? How do the student movements in Lebanon compare with those of other developed and developing societies? To what extent will a study of political youth in Lebanon allow for a comprehensive understanding of the civil wars that have eroded the very structure of the Lebanese society?

Such questions and others will be posed and responded to in the light of a theoretical framework of analysis of the society and the student movement. As a point of departure, I conceive of the student movement in Lebanon in the context of the ongoing confrontation between forces for change and forces for maintaining the established order. The year 1975 witnessed the eruption of this confrontation into a brutal civil war, which had caused about 40,000 deaths and 125,000 injuries by the end of the summer of 1976. This process of confrontation can be fully understood only on the level of the society as a whole and only in an international setting. The stratified mosaic social structure of Lebanon and the confessional political system based on it are explored for explanation.

This analysis begins with the premise that the established order resists changes, particularly those aimed at bridging the gap between the deprived and the privileged and at liberating man from dependency and conditions making for alienation. The very act of maintaining the gap between the privileged and the deprived is an act of violence. The irony is that violence is attributed to the process of initiating change rather than to the act of preventing it.

The basic rationale for the strong emphasis on change and liberation from the myths of the existing order lies in my assumption that the dominant systems, structures, institutions, and cultural orientations of Lebanon and other Arab countries are essentially opposed to human beings: opposed to their well-being, growth, self-realization, transcendence of misery, and creative involvement vis-à-vis themselves and their environment. People are rendered powerless, submissive, insecure, alienated, self-estranged, and obsessed with status symbols and superficial possessions. They are not at the center of their own activities and concerns. They think, but not of themselves. They achieve, but not toward promoting their well-being. They relate, but lack the courage to freely and critically relate to others and to themselves. They are not at the center of their existence. Instead, they survive on the fringes of the universe, always calculating the risks of falling. While everything around them is seen as being constantly enlarged, they feel like shrinking into insignificance. Not being at the center of one's activities is not the same as not being self-centered. People in such systems are self-centered to the core. In fact, they are self-centered precisely because they do not exist at the center, because they are pressured into conformity and crushed under the wheels of historical and daily events. The existing order opposes any change which might help them centralize their own powers of self-awareness.

The universities in Lebanon and other Arab countries are not qualitatively different from the other institutions and systems. As will be described later, they constitute another fortress of the established order. Their conditions do not promote free and critical learning, and students are being trained as elitists rather than as free thinkers and humanitarians. In entering the university and graduating from it, students are inserted like IBM cards into one end of the puncher and emerge at the other end with more holes.

The perpetuation of an inhumane, prohibitive status quo, then, is an active process carried on at all levels of that existing society, and the process of change must be initiated in the very substance of the prevailing structures, frameworks, and orientations.

## Why Students?

If the prevailing conditions call for action and if the required change is comprehensive, what historical agencies, groups, and strata are likely to be objectively and subjectively interested in the transformation of the established order?

The responses to these questions and to the question of the existence of a student movement in Lebanon are most often heavily influenced by subjective considerations, ideological orientations, and the extent to which political parties, trade unions, deprived strata, etc., have been effective in reforming the society under study.

A pessimistic perspective denies that the young constitute a significant agency for change and supports its claim by making the following arguments:

*Students do not constitute a social class.* Following a strictly Marxist-Leninist-Maoist doctrine, the argument is made that students are petit-bourgeois elements and uninvolved in the production process. Furthermore, students are privileged groups undergoing training to occupy elitist positions in the society.

However, the communist and socialist parties all over the world have shown great interest in the student body. Guido Martinotti notes that students were one of three major groups represented in the First International in Italy (the other two groups being urban proletariat and landless peasants). But Martinotti also points out that after World War I, students in Italy shifted to nationalism and universities became a stronghold for fascism.[1]

*Students or young people do not constitute an identity group in the sense in which sectarian, regional, religious, ethnic, or linguistic groups do.* As indicated by Herbert C. Kelman, "an identity group has its own culture and tradition, rooted in history and pointing to the future . . .; being young is not like being black or Flemish. . . . Youth is a commodity that is used up with time, not one around which a permanent identity can be built."[2]

*Studentship is a transitory role and therefore student activism is sporadic.* Regardless of social class origins of students, life as a student is a temporary stage during which there are great pressures to compete for grades and adjust to everyday problems. The norm in university life is to prepare oneself for the future rather than to engage actively in the present.

*Only a small minority of students are politically active.* While some such estimates are correct, these assertions tend to ignore at least two important facts. First, the dominant mood among university students, especially in developing societies, is one of alienation from the existing order. Constantine K. Zurayk points out that "student movements are now being led, as has always been the case in the past, by a small and determined minority. But this minority would have remained impotent had it not been sustained by the mood which is prevalent among youths."[3] My data, as will be shown in other chapters, reveal that feelings of alienation from politics, religious institutions, and the established order are highly pervasive and deep-rooted. The second important fact often ignored by the pessimists is that the small percentage of active students is the core and not the movement itself. In times of national crises, the proportion grows significantly and includes even those with grievances who could not in peaceful times afford to risk active political involvement. This expansion has been evident in the most recent civil war, as will be shown later in this study.

*The student movement lacks autonomy and is the instrument of groups outside its ranks—political parties, agents, and forces that promote ends and interests different from students' own.* Involvement in a more encompassing movement, however, is necessary if students are serious in their endeavor to transform the society or even reform the university. Yet it should be realized that the inability to transcend strict partisan interests and dogmas has often resulted in the fragmentation of the student movement.

An optimistic perspective, on the other hand, has its own arguments in support of the claim that the student movement constitutes a significant agency for change:

*In the past students have in fact played a very significant role throughout the world.* This has been frequently mentioned—sometimes with pride and often as a warning. The first reported major conclave of students in modern history took place in Germany in 1817. At a great festival on the Wartburge the student movement declared its intention to reform the nation. It also played a very important role in the 1848 Revolution. Friedrich Engels wrote that the working classes "and the students had borne the brunt of the fight . . . and the students, about 4,000 strong, well armed, and far better disciplined than the national guard, formed the nucleus, the real strength of the revolutionary force."[4]

In Tsarist Russia, schools were hotbeds of radicalism and "fortresses of criticism." The movement there is traced back to the student strikes and demonstrations of the 1850s. Such manifestations had become by 1887 almost annual (between 1894 and 1899 a total of 1,214 students were expelled from the University of Moscow) and reached a climax in 1905 when universities were closed by the government.[5]

In China, students played a role in the downfall of the Manchu Dynasty, supported Sun Yat-sen, rallied around the ideas of Professor Ch'en Tu-hsiu, shared in founding the Chinese Communist Party in 1921, demonstrated against Chiang Kai-shek, and resisted Japan. In fact, the Communist Party was founded and sustained by faculty and students (at least in its early stages). Similarly, the communist movement in Vietnam was founded by Ho Chi Minh from among young men who had escaped from the repression of the Hanoi student movement in 1925.[6]

In Latin America, students have been a significant force since the Córdoba Reform Movement of 1918 in Argentina. In Cuba, the Communist Party was founded by expelled students after a massive demonstration in the University of Havana, where Castro's movement began.[7]

In the Arab world, student strikes and demonstrations were reported as far back as 1882 and 1908 at the American University of Beirut, known then as the Syrian Protestant College, and in Egypt in 1919 and the forties and early fifties. On February 9, 1946, the Egyptian police raised the Abbas Bridge in order to break student demonstrations flowing to the center of Cairo; several dozen students were killed and several hundred wounded. The cabinet was compelled to resign.[8] Under Nasser and Sadat, students were the first to show resistance. The Algerian general student union launched a great campaign to enlist international support for the Algerian Revolution. Similarly, the Tunisian students played a crucial role in the struggle for independence. After independence, the Moroccan students under the influence of Ben Barka attacked the monarchy and the royal armed forces. Since 1964, they have participated in political strikes, demonstrations, rioting, and violent clashes at Rabat, Fez, and Casablanca. In 1965 student movements in Morocco were brutally suppressed at the cost of hundreds of lives.[9]

Most student activism is directed toward reform and rarely directly involves the masses. In their struggle against Gómez's rule in 1928, the Venezuelan students were surprised that the masses took to the street to support them. After their initial shock, the students "realized that they had been pursuing an elitist political policy."[10] The notable exception to this general division between students and the masses occurs during times of national crises, when a common cause brings them together in a common struggle. This has been the case in the Lebanese civil war, as will be shown later.

Historically, then, students have played active roles in political change, despite their relatively isolated and elitist social position.

*Students and alienated intellectuals constitute an alternative historical agency for radical change.* The disillusionment experienced by some socialists and radical intellectuals with the working classes in Western countries has resulted in shifting their attention to students and alienated groups. The American sociologist C. Wright Mills is critical of leftist writers who continue to "cling so mightily to the working class of the advanced capitalist society as the historic agency . . . in the face of the really impressive historical evidence that now stands against this expectation."[11] Similarly, Herbert Marcuse points out that the "Marxian theory soon recognized that impoverishment does not necessarily provide the soil for revolution, that a highly developed consciousness and imagination may generate a vital need for radical change in advanced material conditions."[12]

Influenced by Mills and Marcuse, the New Left has asserted that "students are the new working class" or that they "constitute the beginnings of a new historical class."[13] The French sociologist Alain Touraine talks of a new society with new forms of conflicts and class struggle which are no longer confined to factories. He notes that students are in a class situation similar to that of skilled workers, i.e., a situation of domination and exploitation.[14]

It should be noted, as will be shown later, that the objective conditions of deprived groups and strata do not necessarily lead into leftist political activism. There is ample evidence to support the argument that many deprived groups and strata in present and past societies all over the world have reconciled themselves to their deprivation, coexisted with their oppressors, submerged themselves in a culture of silence, and lived in-themselves rather than for-themselves.

In the developing countries, such as Lebanon, students do not represent a class, but they tend to serve as catalysts precipitating protests, to carry over the specter of change to the deprived classes, and to participate in violent encounters.

### The Moral Upsurge and Liberalism

Considering both the optimistic and pessimistic arguments, i.e., those for and those against the claim that student movements constitute a historic agency for change, one may assert that students at least represent a pioneering moral upsurge against injustices. There is ample evidence in modern times that students are often the sensitive radar that picks up and responds to the first signals of injustices and contradictions in their societies. They are often, in the words of P. G. Altbach, "in the vanguard of the political and social movements of their nations, and their actions frequently reflect sensitivity to social reality rather than immaturity."[15]

In developing countries of the Third World, students have often taken the initiative in political struggle. Kevin Lyonette, an observer of students' politics in Latin America, wrote in 1966, "In fact in the last 20 years almost all political movements posing a radical alternative to repressive or unrepresentative governments have originated in the universities and have found their first expression through student organizations."[16] In countries under military rule, student political activism is eliminated, but now and then students surprise the government and the people by launching massive uprisings, as was the case in Egypt in February 1968, November 1968, January 1972, and January 1973, and in Greece in the fall of 1973.

Students may represent a moral upsurge and they could constitute a vanguard movement, but there are many indications that the liberators need to be liberated from the traditional loyalties prevailing in their societies. In the case of university students in Lebanon, it will be shown, contrary to what some wish to believe, that they have not yet detached or liberated themselves from traditional ties and that liberalism is still the dominant trend among the political activists.

The basic thesis of this study is that vertical loyalties continue to constitute a highly significant force relative to horizontal loyalties in determining student political behavior and attitudes in Lebanon. *Vertical loyalty* is defined as grouping, organization, or solidarity on a non–social class basis; i.e., loyalty to or identification with groups whose members belong to various social classes, joined on the basis of religious, ethnic, regional, or tribal ties. *Horizontal loyalty*, on the other hand, refers to grouping on the basis of social class; i.e., members of the same socioeconomic class identify with one another and have a clear social class consciousness.

This thesis is based on the assumption that traditional and post-traditional societies such as Lebanon continue to be characterized by religious, sectarian, ethnic, kinship, regional, communal, and other forms of vertical loyalties, constituting the basic patterns of social organization as well as social cleavages. Though these vertical loyalties could be explained in socioeconomic terms, they do overshadow, conflict with, and undermine social class consciousness. Though they emerge from specific socioeconomic conditions, they do gain some independent and externalized power which undermines national unity and class struggle. This power is highly visible in Lebanon and could account for its recurring civil wars.

A question of much relevance in the present study is the extent to which traditional loyalties influence student politics in Lebanon. It is often assumed that university students and intellectuals in general are more likely to be detached or liberated from traditional ties than other segments of the society. While this may be true, one may argue that traditional loyalties still prevail among university students in Lebanon and constitute the most significant predictors and differentiators of their political behavior and views as well as explain their involvement on the opposite sides of the confrontation.

In this study, it is argued that religious and kinship affiliations are highly significant as determinant forces of student political orientations in Lebanon. For instance, it is hypothesized that traditional loyalties are key variables in determining (1) leftist-rightist orientations, (2) political alienation, (3) attitudes toward the Palestinian resistance movement, and (4) socialist-capitalist inclinations.

In spite of their lack of liberation from traditional loyalties, students in Lebanon have continued to actively agitate for change and to represent a pioneering moral upsurge against injustices.

## Plan and Perspective of the Study

The aim of this study is to seek evidences for the above hypotheses and claims in the context of the prevailing socioeconomic conditions through (1) analysis of empirical data collected in the early seventies at the American University of Beirut (AUB), Saint Joseph University (SJU), and Lebanese University (LU); (2) a historical examination of the development of the student movement in Lebanon since the inception of higher education in the country more than a century ago; and (3) in-depth case studies of student strikes.

Part I addresses the task of providing a framework of analysis for a perspective on the student movement in Lebanon. It includes this introductory chapter and two others. The second chapter deals with reasons for student revolts sought in the society in its international setting, the social institutions, the cultural value orientations, the university situation, etc. The aim here is to expose purely psychological interpretations by relating them to a conservative ideology antagonistic to students and threatened by calls for change, and to suggest a sociological model for understanding student behavior.

Chapter 3 addresses problems of social and political integration among the various communities and groups of which Lebanon is composed, its social class structure, and forms of conflicts dominating the Lebanese scene. It also focuses on the educational system and shows how it reflects the mosaic structure of the society.

Part II presents the empirical data that show the influence of religious affiliation, family, and social class origins on several aspects of student politics, including leftist-rightist orientations, nationalistic loyalties, support of the Palestinian resistance movement, voting patterns in student elections, and political involvement. The general overriding argument is connected with the issue of fragmentation and how vertical and horizontal loyalties influence the above aspects of student politics. It is shown here that religious, ethnic, kinship, regional, communal, and other forms of vertical loyalties continue to constitute highly significant forces undermining the student movement as an agency for basic social and political transformation.

Part II also deals with forces determining political alienation and leftist radicalism. Comparison is made between leftists, liberals, and rightists as well as between the politically alienated and nonalienated on the basis of their socioeconomic backgrounds and the extent of their social liberalism.

Part III deals with the development of the student movement since its inception in the last quarter of the nineteenth century by presenting some analytical case studies of student strikes and demonstrations. The purpose here is to deepen our understanding of the student movement, the educational system, and the established order as a whole, as well as the forces determining student behavior. The analysis reveals each group's basic concerns, their reactions to conflict situations, their means of resolving conflicts, and their goals in doing so. An attempt is made to identify some repeated patterns in the behavior and attitudes of those involved, and to interpret those patterns in the light of my basic theses.

Finally, a special epilogue attempts to show how the ongoing confrontation between forces for change and forces for maintaining the established order erupted in 1975 into a brutal war that ripped the country apart and continued unabated at the time of final revision of this book at the end of the summer of 1976. The purpose is to explore the social origins and prospects of this civil war in an effort to offer an explanation of why it took place at this juncture of the country's history.

## The Approach of the Study

This study is basically empirical in nature, but it attempts to account for the contemporaneous situation through a historical survey of the development of the student movement and by close observation of, and continuous dialogue with, active students and others.

The empirical data on which the study is based were collected through a self-administered questionnaire in three universities in Lebanon (AUB, SJU, and LU). This questionnaire (see Appendix) was designed to measure several aspects of student politics and social backgrounds. It consisted of questions covering general background information, political and social beliefs and opinions, political activism, social and political liberalism, revolutionary attitudes, leftist-reformist-rightist orientations, and alienation from politics, religion, family, school, and the world. The questionnaire was administered first in English at AUB in the spring of 1970, in French (in revised form) at SJU in the fall of 1970, and in Arabic (also in revised form) at LU in the spring of 1971. The revisions were made in order to avoid repetition, to improve some questions and condense others, or to pose new ones. These surveys were preceded in 1969 and followed in 1972 by briefer forms to check on certain specific aspects and groups. Information on the samples of interviewed students and other methodological issues is presented in Part II.

As a critical and analytic endeavor, this study does not dismiss quantitative investigation or see it as conflicting with speculative and historical exploration in depth. Much of what might be considered insight into student behavior was inspired by empirical facts. Similarly, it should be pointed out that much of the data collected through self-administered questionnaires would not have made sense without constant contact, observation, and dialogue with students, along with a historical survey of the contemporaneous situation. Some of the data may appear to validate only the obvious. However, they may be significant in at least three ways: First, such data not only familiarize us with existing orientations, but also show to what extent they exist, what forms they take, and under what conditions. Second, empirical results may lead to cross-examination of some interpretations and inspire new ones as well as suggest other ways of seeing the obvious. Third, empirical findings can undermine tendencies toward denial, mystification, rationalization, suppression, and resistance. In other words, such findings strip us of our defenses and force us into face-to-face confrontation with reality.

This study is also intended to follow a social interactional approach. Social phenomena such as violence are seen as related to and emerging out of certain specific situations in which different individual groups and communities, having conflicting and yet complementary interests, are in a state of constant interaction and are in pursuit of their goals under specific socioeconomic conditions and organizational setups.

Finally, this approach reflects a special fascination with dilemmas. While dilemmas constitute a great source of inspiration for literature and social philosophy, empirical sociology and experimental psychology have avoided them as unmanageable, ambiguous, and unmeasurable areas of study. Here, dilemmas related to student politics are examined within the context of the integrative and alienative forces in the society as a whole and are given a dominant position in attempts at analytical discussion and theorizing. Simply, it will be demonstrated that students are exposed to conflicting pressures and are in pursuit of contradictory goals for themselves and for the groups, communities, or classes with which they identify. With that in mind, we move to explore reasons for student revolts.

# 2. Reasons for Student Revolt:

## A Sociological Model

Attempts by scholars to explain student political activism are strongly influenced by their ideological orientations and relative positions in the existing socioeconomic and political structures. Interpretations vary, as different analysts trace student activism to different sources and focus on different sets of reasons, assumptions, premises, hypotheses, and implications.

### Conservative Interpretation

A conservative interpretation often seeks the roots of student unrest in individual psychology, assuming the problem lies in the person rather than in the system or the society. Thus, we are told by Lewis S. Feuer that "the distinctive character of student movements arises from the union in them of motives of youthful love, on the one hand, and those springing from the conflict of generations on the other."[1] He focuses more, however, on the "obscure unconscious workings of generational conflict"[2] and conceives of student movements as "born of vague, undefined emotions which seek for some issue, some cause to attach themselves, a complex of urges . . . [that] searches the social order for a strategic avenue of expression."[3]

S. M. Lipset and P. G. Altbach examine the assumption that the student movement represents an expression of generational conflict and point out that studies of "the activists indicate that the opposite, if anything, is true."[4] Richard Flacks made a detailed comparative study of activists and nonactivists and concluded that the activists showed strong antiauthoritarianism and antidogmatism tendencies and that their parents were more liberal and permissive and placed greater stress on involvement in intellectual, humanitarian, and esthetic pursuits than the parents of the nonactivists. Thus, his data reveal continuity rather than conflict between the culture of youth and that of their parents.[5] F. Solomon and J. R. Fishman argue that protestors are living up to the values in which their parents believed.[6] Similarly, Kenneth Keniston notes that "activists are not, on the whole, repudiating or rebelling against explicit parental values and ideologies. On the contrary, there is some evidence that such students are living out their parents' values in practice."[7] As will be reported in later chapters, data on Lebanese student leftists confirm this parents-children continuity hypothesis rather than the generational-conflict assumptions.

Another psychological interpretation is proposed by the American diplomat and foreign-policy analyst George Kennan, who asserts that "the decisive seat of evil in this world is not in social and political institutions, and not even, as a rule, in the ill will or iniquities of statesmen, but simply in the weakness and imperfection of the human soul itself."[8]

Conservatives find special comfort in those psychological interpretations that conceive of political activism as a mechanism of escape from personal maladjustments. Such a conception views advocacy of and involvement in radical change as a response to inner urges and complexes. Thus, the student movement is seen as an attempt to resolve personal rather than socioeconomic and political problems.

The conservative interpretation also subscribes to notions and hypotheses that are complementary to or derived from the above psychological perspective:

*It subscribes to the conspiracy theory by constantly referring to agitators outside the student ranks.* Thus, Charles Malik of AUB warns that "Certain tendentious movements which have nothing to do with the justified complaints and demands of the student body have infiltrated student activism. These movements make use of the students for their own extraneous ends."[9]

*It undermines the student movement and its genuine concerns by contending that it is "controlled by a small group of students."* This contention does not consider the questions of how and for what reasons a small minority could control the student body. The prevailing conditions of alienation (and the failure of the system to generate enthusiasm for itself and socialize its members to identify with it) are not accounted for and are in fact totally kept outside the picture.

*It maintains that the university is solely "a place for study and training."* Thus, Malik warns that "whatever students do, obviously they must not jeopardize their chances of perfecting their own academic pursuits. There is such keen competition today that society later on will employ and shower its favors only upon the best doctors, engineers, lawyers, economists, and other experts and specialists. A student is only harming his future prospects for a useful and creative career if he attends to activism at the cost of his studies."[10]

## Liberal Interpretation

A liberal interpretation of student activism admits that there are some basic limitations in the system or legitimate sources of discontent in the society, but liberals address themselves to centers of power; overstress problems of emotionalism; call for reform from within the prevailing systems; confuse the prescriptive with the descriptive or the ideal with the actual; and seek reasons for activism within and outside the university as separate rather than as integral forces.

*The liberals direct themselves to centers of power.* They warn them that frustration and violence will increase if they do not try to understand the student protest and if they refuse to consider the moderates' viewpoint. Repressive measures are condemned by the liberals not because they are wrong and degrading to humanity and the creative search but because they render the student activists more radical and push the liberal students into the camp of the activists.

*Though the liberals admit that there are some basic limitations in the system, they overstress problems of student emotionalism.* Thus, students are constantly warned against the dangers of "sheer negativism"; "falling prey to outside pressures"; indulging "in activism as an escape from more rigorous duty," as a way to "self-adulation" or the "satisfaction of one's ego"; irrationality and amorality; and lack of clear purposefulness.[11]

*The liberals see the limitations of the educational system and the society as resulting from inefficient administration;* thus the cure lies in changing leadership and policies. In their view, the system is structurally sound and can be improved by planned series of partial reforms.

*The liberals confuse the ideal with the actual.* We are told by some liberals that the university "is a locus of rational discussion" and is characterized by its cultivation of "intellectual and moral excellences," "nobility of character," "zeal for truth," "free and responsible search for knowledge," etc.[12] We are told that these are abiding truths rather than ideals that do not necessarily exist in the actual, everyday operation of the university. As a result of this lack of distinction between the prescriptive and the descriptive, liberal proposals are often rejected by both parties of the conflict.

*The liberals seek reasons for student activism within and outside the university as separate rather than as integral forces.* Though liberals explore reasons for student activism both in the university situation and in the society as a whole, they do not try to show how the two sets of forces could be highly related. We are told that the basic problems of the university are "its inability to meet the surging and broadening aspirations of society for higher education; the depersonalization of the teaching process and the decreasing degree of attention given to students; and the university's slowness in adapting its structure, its programs, and its procedures to the changing political, economic, social, and cultural conditions." As to *why* the "inability," the "depersonalization," and the "slowness," we are told very little indeed. Reference is often made to lack of foresightedness or to "causes which lie beyond the means and control of the university."[13]

## Radical Interpretation

A radical interpretation based on comprehensive sociological analysis sees student activism in the context of the established social order and its socioeconomic and political structures. Adoption of a sociological approach means that the roots of student activism are sought in the prevailing socioeconomic and political structures of the society as a whole and in its international setting. Specifically, reasons for student revolts inside and outside the university and the country are related, and are sought mostly in (1) the gaps between the developed and developing or underdeveloped societies; (2) the gap between the privileged and deprived within the society; (3) the institutionalized mechanisms for maintaining the status quo; and (4) conditions and situational factors allowing for consciousness of and sensitivity to human suffering and injustice.

Change, as defined in this radical approach, is not seen as a state of mind but as a state of the society and its institutions and groups. In order to transfer a society from a state of underdevelopment to a state of development, it is necessary to start on the level of systems and structures, i.e., the political, social, and economic structures of the society. It is neither sufficient nor efficient to try to change mentalities, values, motives, parts, roles, or particular aspects of the social order. It is necessary to change the substructures which give rise to mentalities, parts, roles, aspects, values, and motives. Change in the mentality of traditionalism is almost impossible without changing the prevailing structures in underdeveloped societies, because these structures not only give rise to traditionalism but also insistently and deliberately continue to cultivate it through control of education, religious institutions, mass media, and other agencies of socialization.[14]

### Gap between Developed and Underdeveloped Societies

Among the most visible facts in the twentieth century is the existence of developed and underdeveloped societies in the world. A wide gap separates the two types of societies and renders the latter highly dependent on the former and almost totally stripped of their rights to determine their private destinies.

Underdeveloped and developing countries have been subjected to all types of infringements on their rights, lands, resources, and even their existence as nations. In their vulnerable positions they are the favorite prey of colonization powers who have humiliated them and deliberately attempted to destroy their self-esteem. Recognition of the need for change is the first step toward liberation, whether it be liberation from one's own system or from an outside oppressor. The struggle of the people of the Third World for independence constituted the most significant impetus for the emergence of the student movement in these countries.

Psychological interpretations do not take account of the whole phenomenon of close association between student activism and national crises. The fact that student movements in the Third World emerged in times of national struggle for independence and subsided in several countries afterward can be explained neither by the generational-gap theory nor by reference to individual dislocation or search for adult roles. Students in Lebanon have been most active in times of national and political crises, namely in the early fifties following the Palestine war of 1948–1949, in the late sixties following the June War of 1967, and in the Lebanese civil war of 1975–1976.

*Gap between Privileged and Deprived Strata of the Society*

The gap between strata within a society may be characterized as a miniature of the gap between developed and underdeveloped societies. The same kind of conditions and relationships prevail. As will be shown in the next chapter, underdeveloped societies are characterized by pyramidal social class structures, meaning that the majority of the people are poor, some are middle class, and very few are well off.

Again, the relationships between the privileged and the deprived are characterized by conflict, domination, and exploitation. Furthermore, the privileged groups are actually linked to the colonizers; their mutual interests result in various forms of implicit and explicit cooperation. The colonizers maintain control over underdeveloped and developing societies by supporting the privileged segments of these societies, and the privileged maintain their control over the deprived through the protection of the colonizers. The cycle is vicious and difficult to break.

Students become aware of these conditions even in their own immediate environment. The universities are highly stratified and inequalitarian, and their patterns of student recruitment are highly selective on the bases of such factors as social class, rural-urban residency, race, ethnic background, religious affiliation, and sex.

At this stage, it might be suggested that those students who come from deprived communities are more likely to become political activists. Thus, while the Palestinian students have constituted the core of the student movement at AUB because they have been the victims of the colonizers, the Shi'ite students have been found in this study to be the most radical at LU because they are the victims of deprivation. The Palestinians suffer most from the first kind of gap (between the developed and under-developed); the Shi'ites suffer from the second kind of gap (between the privileged and the deprived).

*Institutionalized Mechanisms to Maintain the Status Quo*

The university cannot be separated from the outside world, even for purposes of analysis. The university is a reflection, an extension, and an agency of the society and its centers of power. The accuracy of this statement is most clearly demonstrated in the area of university involvement in politics. It is a myth that universities are objective and value-neutral institutions that are solely interested in learning and character building. Available evidence and data show that several institutions of higher education have been engaged in such political activities as conducting research both for the military, in support of warfare and counterinsurgency throughout the Third World, and for industry, to manipulate workers and prevent strikes; serving international corporations; promoting production and consumption commodity systems; firing critical-minded professors and promoting conservative ones; firing staff members for trying to form unions; and granting honorary degrees to dictators and rulers who serve colonization and exploitation.[15]

In view of the direct and close ties between universities and centers of power on both international and local levels, scholars should be able to explain more accurately some of the conditions prevalent in universities which contribute to student activism. I have identified the following conditions as promoting activism by serving as mechanisms to maintain the status quo:

*Centralization of power.* Students in Lebanon are becoming increasingly aware that power in the university system, as in the society, is concentrated in a few top positions, and decisions are being made with total disregard for those most influenced by these decisions. From the moment they join the university until they graduate, they are coerced to fit into the system, to follow orders, to comply with decisions, to obey instructions, and to adjust to rigorously planned curricula that do not take into account their real needs and problems. They are passively rather than actively involved in the education process. Caught in the IBM-card syndrome, they find themselves urgently trying to change their conditions.

*Lack of free communication and dialogue.* It is intrinsically true that an authoritarian and stratified system does not provide for free and meaningful dialogue among its members, groups, and strata. Because of the authoritarian and stratified nature of the system, dialogue is characterized by suppression of true feelings and ideas, by the wearing of masks, by the filtering of information, by the distortion of facts, and by impression-making. Dialogue becomes instrumental rather than expressive. The aim is not to search together for meaningful answers and fair decisions; nor is it even to raise real and fundamental questions, as deliberate attempts are made to avoid or mystify the pertinent issues. The aims of communication are to further personal or group interests, to transmit already-made decisions, and to impress the other parties. Information flows down the hierarchical pyramid in the form of orders, decisions, instructions, warnings, condemnations, verdicts, demands. This flow is held to a minimum, to the degree it is necessary to help the receivers to follow instructions and carry on their duties.

The upward flow is also distorted. Those who occupy the lower status positions labor under the fears of punishment and/or the temptations of rewards. Thus, they try to release those kinds of information and messages that favorably impress the authority figures and to suppress those that may cause them trouble. This upward flow takes the forms of suggestions, appeals, reports, questions, requests, pleas, recommendations, and expressions of gratitude.

*Universities as centers for training.* The famous Arab classical historian Ibn Khaldun noted in the fourteenth century that, when Arabs founded their empire, the states needed clerks. Modern empires are no different. J. H. Skolnick writes that the student movement in the United States saw "the university as a factory whose goal is to produce: (1) trained personnel for corporations, government and more universities, and (2) knowledge of the uses of business and government to perpetuate the present system."[16] American scholars have described the university as "the marketplace of ideas" or "the corporation of learning," requiring expertise rather than critical knowledge, especially since the businessmen-trustees replaced clergymen as controllers of universities in the nineteenth century. In West Germany, as we are told by Jurgen Habermas, the "university is to serve as an instrument for the industrial development. . . . In addition, universities must not only transmit technically exploitable knowledge, but also produce it. . . . Thus, through instruction and research the university is immediately connected with functions of the economic process . . . ; research and instruction today have to do only with the production and transmission of technologically exploitable knowledge."[17] Similarly, the French sociologist Alain Touraine points out that the university "in this programmed society . . . becomes affiliated more and more with the new production apparatus it trains."[18] The result, as seen by Jacques Sauvageot of the French student movement, is that "Students are expected to have a certain critical intelligence, while their studies are such that they are not allowed to exercise it."[19]

In a sarcastic manner, the sociology students of Trento in Italy described the role of the university as follows: "The university is one of the productive institutions of this social system, which is a mercantile system (i.e., a system of dealing in commodities). As such it produces man as a commodity, that is as skilled (graduate) or semi-skilled (nongraduate) members of the labor force. The goal of this productive institution—the university—is to supply the labor market with such a commodity. There it will be sold and thereafter consumed in the cycle of social reproduction."[20]

In Lebanon, students are trained to supply the business corporations and governments in the area. As pointed out by former AUB president Bayard Dodge, students during his presidency or earlier were "essential for civil and military posts in Egypt and the Sudan, where British rule required a knowledge of English."[21]

The above institutionalized mechanisms in the university situation are extensions of those prevailing in the society. As such, they bring into the open a basic contradiction: On the one hand, universities are supposed to be concerned with the cultivation of "intellectual and moral excellence," "nobility of character," "zeal for truth," "free and responsible search for knowledge," "maturity," "rational behavior," and so on.[22] Values such as creativity, honesty, and critical reflection are supposed to be central in any meaningful intellectual search. On the other hand, in reality, "universities have been institutions established by or supported by the authoritative centers of society—political and ecclesiastical—and they have been more integrated into the tasks of training young persons for careers connected with the central functions of society and culture."[23]

The gaps between ideal proclamations and actual behavior, between claims to democracy and real concentration of power, and between free search for knowledge and manipulative training are at the roots of students' alienation from the university.

A student movement becomes radical as a result of deep alienation from politics, society, and culture. Students gradually realize that the educational system is not a separate entity and that it cannot be changed without changing the political system and the society.

*Conditions and Situational Factors*

In trying to account for student political activism, some studies have failed to distinguish between the above forces and conditions at the root of student unrest and such facilitating, contributing, or situational factors as the following:

1. Large numbers of students exist in one central location, which facilitates the communication, organization, and spread of ideas.

2. Students are burdened with few adult responsibilities. They normally do not have to worry about earning a living and caring for dependent members of the family. Being unhampered by the practical concerns of everyday life, they can afford to follow their consciences and take risks.

3. As students are young people, some of their rebellious behavior could be interpreted as resulting from conformity to the norm of youth and intellectual nonconformity. In other words, youths are often expected to be idealistic and rebellious. Thus, student activism is relatively, and insofar as it can be contained, tolerated by society, the university, and even government. Active students are more tolerated than other nonconforming segments of society because they are viewed by adult members as children and/or as the young in heart and brain who do not know the hard realities of life.

4. In spite of all the limitations described earlier, the university is normally and relatively more favorable than other systems for search, reflection, raising questions, taking issues, and challenging the established order.

These situational factors do not explain student radicalism; they merely facilitate the process of alienation in taking its proper course of action. The objective forces making for radicalism already exist.

**The Process of Alienation**

Alienation is viewed here as a process consisting of three main stages: sources of alienation at the level of the socioeconomic and political structures prevailing in the society as a whole; alienation as a subjective experience of feelings of dissatisfaction and rejection of the established order; and behavioral consequences of alienation, namely, withdrawal, compliance, or revolt.[24]

Student revolt is thus seen as a behavioral consequence of deep and intense feelings of alienation from the established order. These feelings are traced back in turn to the gap between the developed and underdeveloped societies; the gap between the privileged and deprived strata of the society;

and manipulative institutionalization of mechanisms to maintain the status quo. This process is diagrammed in Figure 2.1.

Revolt, then, is seen as one of three major behavioral consequences of alienation from the established order. An alienated person either retreats from, complies with, or acts upon the social system from which he or she is alienated. On one end of the continuum are those alienated persons who tend to retreat from the social system. On the opposite end are those alienated persons who engage in spontaneous or organized activities aimed at changing the system. Somewhere in between is a third group of alienated persons who comply publicly but not privately with the demands and expectations of the system.

This explains why the activists, though small in number, often draw widespread support in times of crises—they are joined by alienated retreaters and compliers who are pushed into action.

## Conclusion

In this chapter, an attempt has been made to refute (or show the limitations of) the conservative psychological and liberal interpretations of student political activism and to propose a more radical comprehensive sociological interpretation. According to the latter model, student activism is explained in the context of the established order and its socioeconomic and political structures. By adopting a sociological approach, I seek to uncover the roots of student radicalism in the society as a whole and in an international setting, as well as in the process of alienation.

These expectations will be checked in later sections of this study by reference to empirical data and examination of student strikes.

**Figure 2.1. The process of student revolt**

*Sources of student revolt in the socioeconomic and political structures:*

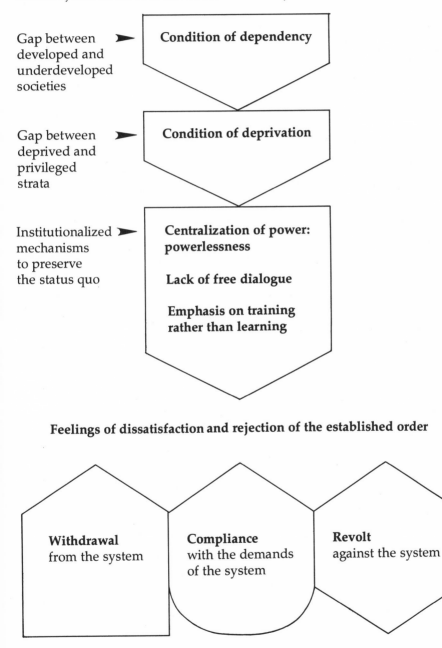

# 3. Social and Political Integration in Lebanon:

*A Case of Stratified Social Mosaic*

Despite its small extent (approximately 4,000 square miles) and population (2.5 million), Lebanon is a complex mosaic of social diversity. We must ask, however, whether this complex social diversity is an example of harmonious pluralism which can allow for change, or whether it is so rigid that it must be radically restructured to become secular and democratic. By posing this question and responding to it, I hope to explain Lebanon's recent history, marked as it has been by an uprising (1949), an attempted coup (1961), and two civil wars (1958 and 1975).

This chapter examines Lebanon's problems of integrating the various groups and communities of which it is composed. I argue, contrary to several political sociologists, historians, and other observers of the Lebanese scene,[1] that Lebanon is closer to a mosaic than to a pluralistic society. Traditionally, scholars have differentiated between homogeneous and heterogeneous societies without making further sharp distinctions within each of these two ideal types. Here, *pluralistic* and *mosaic* refer to two forms of heterogeneous societies. *Pluralism*, as used here, refers to harmonious relationships among several interest, religious, and/or ethnic groups within a unified social order. In a pluralistic society, there is consensus on fundamental principles, and provisions are made for a fairly balanced participation of its composite groups, so that no one group or small alliance of groups can monopolize rewards or hold a preponderance of power. A *mosaic* society, by contrast, consists of diverse groups interacting within the confines of a common structure without consensus by the groups on fundamentals. The relationships are regulated by some system of checks and balances but are generally characterized by an imbalanced distribution of rewards and powers.

Later in this chapter, a detailed distinction will be made between pluralistic and mosaic societies as applied to Lebanon. At this point, however, it is sufficient to note that each of these two types of societies is composed of diverse groups and that provisions are made to introduce some system of checks and balances among these groups. The distinction between the two types lies in the degree of harmony in relationships and in the kind of relationships which exist. The relative conditions of harmony and equality are based on the extent to which there is consensus among the groups on fundamentals, fair representation and distribution, extensive and open dialogue, and dominance of public interests over private interests. This distinction is made on a continuum which precludes any pretensions of the existence of either a completely pluralistic or a completely mosaic society within heterogeneous societies.

Two observations need to be introduced before expounding on the above argument. First, the most dominant cleavage in the Lebanese society is religious in form and socioeconomic in essence, but these two kinds of cleavages (the religious and the socioeconomic) have coincided, disguised one another, and prevented the development of clear social class consciousness. It is often repeated, though accurate statistics are lacking, that Lebanon is half Christian and half Muslim, and each half is in turn subdivided into several sects. The present political system is based on highly inaccurate estimates drawn from a French mandate census in 1932 which claimed that, among Christians, Maronites were the majority, presumably constituting about 30 percent of the total population, followed by the Greek Orthodox (10 percent) and the Greek Catholics (6 percent). Other officially recognized Christian communities and enclaves have included Armenian Orthodox, Armenian Catholics, Syriac Orthodox, Syriac Catholics, Eastern Nestorians, Chaldeans, Evangelicals, and Roman Catholics. Among Muslims, the Sunnis were thought to be the majority, presumably constituting 21 percent of the total population, followed by the Shi'ites (presumably only 18 percent), and the Druzes (6 percent). Other officially recognized Muslim sects have included Alawis and Isma'ilis. Finally, there has been a small, officially recognized Jewish community. The 1932 population census reported that Christians outnumbered Muslims by a ratio of six to five (total population—793,426). Since that date, representation in the parliament, cabinet, and other governmental bodies and agencies has been based on this ratio. For example, the 1975 Lebanese parliament was composed of ninety-nine seats allocated in the following manner: thirty seats for Maronites, twenty for Sunnis, nineteen for Shi'ites, eleven for Greek Orthodox, six each for Greek Catholics and Druzes, four for Armenian Orthodox, and one each for Armenian Catholics, Protestants, and other Christian minorities. Thus there were fifty-four seats for Christians and forty-five for Muslims (still in the ratio of 6:5). While it is highly probable that Muslims exceed Christians in numbers, the Christian elite has opposed conducting a population census, for fear of exposing the system's contradictions.

The second pertinent observation is that, during the last century and a half, relationships among the different religious communities in Lebanon have wavered between two stages. During the nineteenth century and almost through the end of the first quarter of this century, relationships among the various religious groups were characterized by outright conflict. These conflicts were manifest, open, direct, aggressive, and quite violent at some points. Around the beginning of the second quarter of this century, Lebanon began to pass from the stage of conflict into the stage of accommodation, in which groups coexisted in a relatively harmonious manner; now and then it lapses into violent conflict, as evidenced by the 1958 and current civil wars. After World War I, the Lebanese leaders began to realize that the various religious communities had to learn to accommodate themselves to one another, and that a policy of coexistence had to be adopted in order to achieve some measure of social harmony. It was hoped that such a policy would provide a system of checks and balances and encourage autonomous participation of all groups within a comprehensive and unifying social order. This tendency toward accommodation is most clearly reflected in the 1943 National Pact,[2] based in essence on the following tenets:

1. Lebanon is an independent and sovereign state.

2. Lebanon is an Arab state and follows a policy of cooperation with the rest of the Arab world.

3. Lebanon is a democratic country and all Lebanese are equal before the law.

To what extent do these tendencies toward accommodation make Lebanon a pluralistic society? Has the National Pact been successful in containing and moderating conflicts and in limiting the power of any one group or the alliance of few groups to dominate others? Has it provided for autonomous participation of all groups within a unifying social order and guaranteed a fair distribution of rewards and powers? Has it enabled Lebanon to transcend its status quo without real threats to its foundations? Finally, what are the prospects for assimilation and national unity?

In the light of the civil war that began in 1975, the responses to the above questions are categorically negative. Yet these questions could not have been raised before 1975 without causing annoyance to conservative groups in Lebanon, let alone the political elites and officials.

With these observations in mind, we proceed to the argument, adumbrated above, that Lebanon is closer to a mosaic than a pluralistic society. The evidence for this contention is sought in the following dominant characteristic features of the Lebanese society:

1. Lack of consensus on fundamentals.

2. Lack of extensive and open dialogue.

3. Domination of public loyalties and interests by private loyalties and interests.

4. Geographical concentration of different religious communities.

5. Nonseparation of religion from the state and legitimization of confessionalism.
6. Existence of conflicting reference groups.
7. Pyramidal social class structure.
8. Absence of a unified educational system.

## Lack of Consensus on Fundamentals

In order for a pluralistic society to maintain accommodation, there must be consensus among its various groups on fundamentals. This principle is advanced by both conservative and liberal political sociologists, including Alexis de Tocqueville, S. M. Lipset, W. A. Kornhauser, and others. Without such consensus a "pluralistic social organization tends to break down into a society torn by conflict."[3]

The Lebanese do not agree on governing fundamentals such as the constitution, the National Pact, confessionalism, and, above all, the national identity of Lebanon. They are divided as to whether or not Lebanon constitutes a complete nation. Some, predominantly Christian, conceive of Lebanon as an independent, separate, sovereign, and complete entity. For them, the sovereignty of Lebanon as a nation-state is not a temporary arrangement or a historical stage. In the words of Michel Shiha, Charles Malik, or Sa'id 'Aql, for instance, Lebanon is "eternal" and "everlasting." Several political parties, such as al-Kata'ib, the National Bloc, and the Party of the Free Nationalists (Hizb al-Watani'een al-Ahrar) of Ex-President Sham'oun, confess such beliefs and feelings.

On the other hand, there are those Lebanese who see the present arrangement as temporary. For them, the state of Lebanon in its present form was externally imposed by France on August 30, 1920, and was never accepted by the Muslim community. The majority of them see it as an integral part of the Arab nation. Kamal Junblat, head of the Progressive Socialist Party, leader of the alliance of leftist groups during the current civil war, and often a member of the Lebanese cabinet, expresses this view in the following manner: "This society is not a society in the real sense of the word, because there is no such thing as a Lebanese community. There is no Lebanese social unit. Lebanon is a collection of sects and socio-religious communities. Thus, it is not a society, nor a community, nor a nation. That is why the state in which the society reflects itself is very weak, so weak that it might collapse any minute. . . . There is no such thing as Lebanese nationalism. The dominant nationalism in the Arab world today is Arab nationalism."[4] A number of political parties in Lebanon, such as the Arab Ba'ath Socialist Party, and the Arab Nationalist Movement, call for a pan-Arab state. Still others, a small group of Christian and Muslim minority groups, see Lebanon as an integral part of greater

Syria or the Fertile Crescent (e.g., members of the Syrian Social Nationalist Party). This search for a national identity has continued to be at the root of existing conflicts (between isolationists and nationalists) but is increasingly coupled with struggle for socioeconomic and political reform. In other words, nationalist-versus-isolationist struggles and class struggles have increasingly overlapped and reinforced one another.

The lack of consensus on the national identity of Lebanon is accompanied by a number of social-psychological phenomena which, in turn, add to the intensity of present cleavages and probably help in creating others.

One such phenomenon is what might be called self-aggrandizement tendencies among some Lebanese isolationists. This is manifested in exaggerated descriptions of Lebanon's beauty and its role in the world. A familiar expression asserts that "Lebanon is the center of enlightenment and inspiration in the world." Statements to this effect permeate popular songs, poetry (especially poetry in colloquial Arabic, i.e., *zajal*), speeches, etc. The Lebanese *zajal* and popular songs are diametrically opposed to the protest songs in the West. To illustrate, a popular song says:

> Under the sky, there is nothing like Lebanon.
> Lebanon is the most beautiful face.
> Lebanon is the proudest forehead.
> . . . Lebanon is man's first home.

This might strike the non-Lebanese as empty bravado, but it is said with deep conviction by some Lebanese isolationists. The well-known Lebanese poet Sa'id 'Aql speaks of the need for "Lebanonizing" in the whole world. This self-aggrandizement tendency could be partly explained as a social-psychological reaction to the expressed doubt of a substantial number of Lebanese in the nationhood of Lebanon. There has been a threat from within to the Lebanese ego, and self-aggrandizement is an announcement of its existence in the face of such a threat. There has been an enduring challenge to the Lebanese ego, and consequently it has tended to proclaim itself loudly and assert its being. This reaction has in turn led to further rejection of nationhood by the disenchanted groups—each group's reaction, then, is fuel for the other's fire.

A second social-psychological phenomenon accompanying lack of consensus on the national identity of Lebanon is the feeling of relative lack of deprivation among some Lebanese isolationists. This refers, among other things, to the tendency to compare Lebanon with other Arab countries in worse condition and, consequently, to gain self-acceptance; to feel self-satisfied, overconfident, and proud about Lebanese accomplishments. Any criticisms directed against the Lebanese system are defensively countered by pointing out what is going on in the other Arab countries. This is usually followed by raising the accusing question to the critics: Do you want Lebanon to be like the rest of the Arab countries?

A third, but connected, phenomenon is resistance to the introduction of basic change out of fear of upsetting the political system. Evidence of this fear lies in the outdated public documents by which the country is ruled; the Lebanese constitution has not been structurally amended since it was drafted under the French mandate in 1926. Further evidence is in the previously mentioned refusal by Christian officials to take a census, even though planning, scientific research, development, and projects such as the social security plan are hampered by this refusal. Recently, however, a number of Lebanese isolationists have publicly admitted some of the political system's shortcomings and have expressed concern with governmental inefficiency and corruption. Even proponents of the system point out, as did Ex-President Fu'ad Shihab, that "the Lebanese political institutions and the practiced traditions in political behavior are no longer capable of allowing for developing Lebanon to the levels required by the seventies."[5] The prevailing tendency has been to admit the limitations of the Lebanese system and yet to defend it.

The results of one of my research studies on a representative sample of Lebanese students at the American University of Beirut in 1969 showed the following: 84 percent said they were dissatisfied with the political conditions at that time; 73 percent said they found themselves in basic disagreement with the general political trends and activities of the Lebanese government; 71 percent believed that the Lebanese political system was not really democratic; and 94 percent said there was a great deal of corruption and favoritism in the political administration. In spite of this high rate of alienation from the Lebanese political system, the majority believed that the change required could be gradual and peaceful. In response to a similar question, only 22 percent agreed that what was needed was revolution, not reform.

This ambivalence of Lebanese isolationists toward the existing system makes change doubly difficult to bring about—they acknowledge that the need for change exists, that the institutions are inefficient, corrupt and incapable of resolving severe conflicts from within or threats from without. Yet they still feel they have to defend the system and oppose change out of fear of upsetting the balance. Hence the decline in the capacity of the Lebanese establishment for institutional adjustment and the potential dilemma observed by Michael C. Hudson in discussing the problem of social justice in Lebanon: "To adjust to the new social justice and the newly politicized elements may lead to a derangement of the traditional balance of power, with its attendant instability; not to adjust may invite the total destruction of the political system."[6]

Lack of consensus extends to include less fundamental and enduring issues, especially those indirectly connected with the problem of national identity. Public opinion polls in 1968 and 1969, with samples of the population of Beirut and its suburbs, show that the religious factor is highly significant in determining support of the Palestinian commando movement and its activities. The data of 1968 show that 93 percent of the Muslims and 64 percent of the Christians said they strongly supported the commandos. The data of 1969, collected in early November immediately after the crisis between the Lebanese government and the commando movement, show that 73 percent of the Muslims, as compared to only 26 percent of the Christians, expressed strong support of the commandos. The majority of Christians (51 percent) expressed conditional support and about one-fifth (19 percent) expressed nonsupport. Only 25 percent of the Muslims expressed conditional support, and none expressed nonsupport. On a question as to whether or not the commandos should be allowed to operate within Lebanon, the gap becomes even wider. The majority of Christians (53 percent) said they did not support the idea of such operations, 31 percent said they supported it with reservations, and only 12 percent said they strongly supported it. By contrast, the majority of Muslims (56 percent) said they strongly supported it, 35 percent said they supported it with reservations, and only 6 percent said they did not support it. Another relevant item is degree of agreement on a political solution of the Palestine problem (such as United Nations Security Council Resolution 242 of November 22, 1967). The data of the 1968 public opinion poll show that the majority of the Christians (72 percent) agreed with it, while the majority of Muslims (64 percent) did not agree with it.[7] The gap between the two religious communities has increased on these issues and has partly contributed to the intensity of the current civil war.

In conclusion, the consensus essential for an effective pluralistic system is lacking in Lebanon. The behavior of the Lebanese, including the educated, is still largely determined by their religious affiliations. Such a condition tends to extend beyond fundamentals to temporary issues, especially those connected with the question of national identity. These general and basic disagreements put Lebanon into the category of mosaic societies, destined to chronic tension and civil war.

## Lack of Extensive, Deep, and Open Dialogue

Before the current civil war, very little sincere dialogue had been taking place on the Lebanese stage. Discussion of the relationships among the various religious communities had been hampered by labeling these relationships as very sensitive. The confessionalists themselves tended to publicly deny the existence of disunity and appeared to be offended when the issue was brought into the open. In fact, the ruling elites and their prop-agandists as well as leaders of confessional parties often asserted quite emphatically that there had been real unity among the Lebanese people regardless of their religious identification. Such façade building was what probably prompted the well-known journalist (and member of the cabinet during the current civil war) Ghassan Tueini to point out in a debate with university students that "the treatment of confessionalism should start with a confession of its existence. The Christians say two things and the Muslims say two things: what they say to themselves and what they say to others."[8]

An artificial, inauthentic, and hypocritical dialogue has been taking place. This situation is accurately described by the anthropologist Fu'ad I. Khuri: "the Lebanese is reserved in his communication with members of other sects, tactful, polite, and tolerant . . . , but once in the presence of members of his own sect, he forgets his tolerance and starts to exercise his cleverness in narrating jokes and stories that are harmful to the reputation of the other sects and critical of their ways of life. . . . The Lebanese has two faces."[9] In one another's presence, members of different sects may exchange positions, as in a social gathering of two friendly Christian and Muslim families that I witnessed. The Christian family, in order to please the Muslim family, praised Abdul Nasser as a liberator and nationalist leader working for the welfare of his people. On the other hand, the Muslim family, in order to please the Christian family, criticized Abdul Nasser as a dictator who interfered in the internal affairs of Lebanon and other Arab countries. Deep inside, each realized they were trying to accommodate one another, and neither was deceived by what the other had to say. Yet they exchanged positions in order to facilitate their relations without departing from their points of view.

The dialogue within these religious communities has not been much more open and useful. Insecurities bar self-criticism and self-examination. Neither group seems to be able to reflect freely on its situation. Lebanese Christians, including those of lower social class origins, tend to accept the status quo and show little concern about changing the political system, though they may admit some of its limitations. On the whole, they seem to share the feeling of Michel Shiha that "Living in Lebanon is a bliss which will continue unless the ideologists and reformers become strong enough to put an end to it."[10]

Lebanese Muslims, on the other hand, in general tend to reject the political status quo and concern themselves with problems of Arab unity, imperialism, redistribution of wealth and power, and wars of independence and liberation; but, at least before the civil war, they seemed to ignore problems of individual freedom, liberation from traditions, secularism and separation of religion from the state, the significance and rights of the individual, and other internal problems that plague the Arab society.

## Loyalty to the Part versus Loyalty to the Whole

Kinship, religious, and communal loyalties persist strongly in Lebanon. The typical Lebanese seems to be more attached to family, religion, and local community than to the country as a whole. Ample evidence is given by Hudson that religious, communal, and kinship cleavages have made Lebanon politically an area of traditional veto groups, and that the several primordial sentiments divide Lebanon and retard its political modernization.[11]

Confessionalism and familism constitute the most pervasive, diffuse, and enduring loyalties undermining nationalism in Lebanon. The confessions in Lebanon are autonomous and seem to constitute the most significant force affecting Lebanese politics. In fact, Lebanese nationalism can be explained as a manifestation of religious consciousness and identification. The loyalty of the Lebanese nationalist to Lebanon has been rooted in loyalty to a religious community. If the interests of Christians as a religious community are threatened, the nationalist's loyalty to present-day Lebanon is likely to diminish. Hence the nostalgic talk of a return to a smaller Lebanon (i.e., Mount Lebanon, which is inhabited mostly by Christians) as it existed before the French mandate. In fact, during the current civil war some Lebanese isolationists proposed partitioning the country to guarantee a national home for Christians in Mount Lebanon. This tendency was also evidenced in the tendency of the Christian Lebanese isolationists to see any basic sociopolitical change in the status quo as a potential source of disturbance of the sensitive balance. Thus, the Christians, and especially the Maronites, "are the group interested exclusively in Lebanon, it is they who have more frequently tended to feel responsible for national leadership."[12]

Familism is at least as significant as confessionalism in undermining nationalism in Lebanon and other Arab countries. In fact, familism is more subtle and more difficult to detect than confessionalism. The psychologists Levon Melikian and Lutfy N. Diab discovered that undergraduates at the American University of Beirut affiliated themselves with family first, ethnic group second, religion third, citizenship fourth, and political party fifth.[13] A more recent empirical study of a representative sample of the students of the same university showed that they were less alienated from family than from religion, university, and government. None showed a high feeling of alienation from the family, 5 percent showed a moderate feeling of alienation, 32 percent showed little feeling of alienation, and 63 percent were found to be fully integrated in their families. In comparison, alienation from religion was found to be much higher. The data showed that 17 percent were highly alienated from religion, 26 percent moderately alienated, 31 percent little alienated, and 25 percent nonalienated.[14] Another recent empirical study, a content analysis of the twenty elementary school readers recognized recently by the Lebanese Ministry of Education as the most significant readers currently in use, showed that the number of words denoting family names (such as *father, mother, brother, son*) was 1,238. The number of words denoting national names (such as *country, nation, people, government, state, society, independence*) was only 210.[15]

Familism at the expense of national loyalty is also diffuse and pervasive among other Arabs. In a research survey, Peter Dodd and I found family loyalty to be the overriding loyalty and showed that it contributed greatly to the exodus of the Palestinian refugees after the June War of 1967.[16]

An additional factor prohibiting development of nationalism is the individualism characteristic of Arabs. This individualism in the Lebanese is reflected by their lack of cooperation on broad social programs, by the widespread misuse of public properties and facilities, and by the weakness of voluntary associations.

Finally, two significant social-political phenomena reflect as well as reinforce loyalty to the part rather than loyalty to the whole.

First, political parties in Lebanon are not nationally based. None of the formally recognized political parties (about ten in number) is integrative and representative of the country as a whole. On the contrary, they represent and derive their support from their own communities. Furthermore, they were founded by traditional leaders and they continue as gatherings or blocs around these leaders. The Lebanese parliament is not composed of competing political parties having different ideologies or professed programs and goals for the society, but of blocs and temporary alliances headed by traditional leaders and revolving around personal, communal, kinship, and sectarian interests. The chairmanships of these parties are reserved for their founders, and in some cases they are inherited by their sons.[17] Ideological and integrative parties do not function as legitimate and integral parts of the Lebanese political system.[18] This is a major deficiency in the Lebanese democracy because, as S. M. Lipset pointed out, "a system in which the support of different parties corresponds too closely to the basic social divisions cannot continue on a democratic basis."[19]

The second of these social-political phenomena is the weakness of the central government, or dominance of private powers over public powers. In 1969 Lebanon lived without government for seven months. One may venture to say that if the Lebanese had not been constantly reminded by the press that there was no government, they would not have noticed the difference. The government has always had little control over powerful traditional leaders, who could proclaim their autonomy within their own local communities, provide protection to outlaws, and settle family feuds and other violations without interference of court or central authorities. In a study of cabinet politics in Lebanon, Elie Salem asserts that "the crisis of 1958 revealed beyond doubt that in the moment of truth local leaders and established families held greater control on their followers than did the central government. Each religious and ethnic group has its own pyramid of power and its own internal source of strength, and it is with these pyramids that the cabinet must deal and at times even negotiate."[20] The civil war of 1975–1976 has proved beyond the shadow of doubt that the central government has no role in times of crises. In fact, some cabinet members were simultaneously playing conflicting roles: the role of maintaining law and order, and the role of leading their own private militias in the ongoing war. Thus, Premier Rashid Karami accused Minister of the Interior Camille Sham'oun of being simultaneously "the guard and the thief"(*hamiha haramiha*).

As a result of its weakness, the Lebanese government follows policies of compromise, nonconfrontation, and quite often denial of the existence of challenging problems. Hence the rhetorical comment of Ghassan Tueini in an editorial of his paper, *an-Nahar*—"the government does not exist, and whatever part of it exists it has no authority, and whoever has authority it is not the government."[21] In short, the Lebanese political system is a unique form of nongovernment, and several states have always existed within the state.

### Geographical Concentration of the Different Religious Communities

Even in shape and form, Lebanon is mosaic. The different religious groups tend to live in and control specific and isolated geographical regions of Lebanon. The Maronites live almost to the total exclusion of others in the districts (*gada'*) of Zgharta, Batrun, and Kisruwan, and constitute the majority in Jezzin, Matn, and Ba'abda. The Sunnis constitute the majority in the districts of Tripoli (about 80 percent) and Akkar, about one-third of the districts of Beirut, and about a quarter of each of the districts of Rashaya and Zahlah; the Shi'ites constitute the majority in the districts of Tyre (80 percent), Ba'albek-Hermel (68 percent), Saida, and Marjayun-Hasbaya; the Greek Orthodox constitute the majority in Kura and about a quarter of Rashaya; the Greek Catholics make up about a quarter each of the districts of Zahlah and Ba'albek; the Druzes make up almost half the district of Aley, one-third of Rashaya, and more than a quarter of Shuf and Matn. Furthermore, in districts composed of several religious groups, one finds towns and villages inhabited by one group almost to the total exclusion of others. And even where different religious groups live in the same city, town, or village, they tend to live in separate neighborhoods. (This explains the emphasis on neighborhoods rather than streets.)

The tendency of different religious groups to dominate specific regions is reflected in their representation in the Lebanese parliament. So far as this tendency is concerned, the electoral districts (twenty-six in number) of Lebanon can be divided into five groups (see Table 3.1). First, eight of the twenty-six districts are represented only by Christian deputies. These are Batrun, Bsharri, Kisruwan, and Zgharta (represented by eleven Maronites); Kura (represented by two Greek Orthodox); and Beirut I, Matn, and Jezzin (represented by sixteen members of different Christian sects). Second, four districts are represented chiefly by Christian deputies. These are Aley, Ba'abda, Jubayl, and Zahlah (out of eighteen deputies representing these districts only seven are Muslims). Third, three districts (Akkar, Shuf, and Zahrani) are equally represented by Christians and Muslims (seven deputies each). Fourth, six districts are represented largely by Muslim deputies. These are Beirut II, Beirut III, Ba'albek-Hermel, Rashaya, Tripoli, and Marjayun-Hasbaya (twenty out of the twenty-seven deputies are Muslims). Fifth, five districts are represented only by Muslim deputies. These are Bint-Jubayl, Nabatiyyah, and Tyre (represented by eight Shi'ites); and Dinnieh and Sidon (represented by three Sunnis).

To add to the concentration and fragmentation, there have been regional imbalances in the distribution of rewards and powers. Beirut and Mount Lebanon show higher educational, industrial, and socioeconomic development than other regions. For instance, about 40 percent of children between the ages six and ten do not attend school in South Lebanon, compared to about 4 percent in Mount Lebanon. The Shi'ites are the most deprived religious community in Lebanon. For instance, while they probably constitute about one-fourth of the total population, the present empirical study shows that only about 8 percent of university students in Lebanon are Shi'ites. The Christians, especially the Maronites, do not seem to be concerned about these imbalances. On the contrary, there is a tendency among Maronites and some other Christians to believe that the Maronites are entitled to hold the larger share of power.[22] They rationalize this tendency by pointing out that "it is they who have more frequently tended to feel responsible for national leadership,"[23] and that the "Muslim Lebanese masses . . . are unprepared to appreciate the virtues of a liberal way of life."[24]

One could conclude, then, that the geographical concentration of the different religious communities and regional imbalances of power are likely to present, as Michael C. Hudson puts it, "a formidable obstacle to developing a positive national consensus, particularly since the outlying regions are predominantly Muslim."[25]

**Nonseparation of Religion from the State and Legitimation of Confessionalism**

Another condition that reflects the mosaic nature of the Lebanese society, contributes to its persistence, and probably even furthers fragmentation, is nonseparation of religion and state and the adoption of confessionalism as a legitimate and integral part of the political system. The different religious communities have the power to legislate and administer the laws of personal status and manage their religious courts. Consequently, legislation in the areas of personal status has become very diversified. Each of the officially recognized sects has its own laws, courts, and councils. Adding to the autonomy of these sects is the fact that the courts and legislation in some cases are governed by religious authorities outside Lebanon.

One of the basic consequences of nonseparation of religion and state is the lack of intermarriage between Muslims and Christians and even among different sects within the same religion. Some sects do not permit intermarriage at all; others, while they permit it, insist by tradition on marriage within the sect. This affects interpersonal relationships and communication among members of the different religious communities. In order for these relationships to become extensive and intimate and for dialogue to become open and authentic, the Lebanese will have to go beyond being just friends and neighbors and accept each other in marriage. Only through intermarriage are they likely to transcend the social and psychological distances that have separated them so long. Just as any move toward a pluralistic system would be almost in vain unless religion were separated from the state, no cultural assimilation will be possible as long as barriers to intermarriage continue to exist.

The National Pact of 1943 further institutionalized confessionalism by designating religious membership as the most important criterion for recruitment to public positions. That this arrangement was supposed to be temporary is shown in the cabinet statement submitted by Premier Riyad al-Solh to the parliament on October 7, 1943: "Unless the hearts of all people rally to the nation, a nation cannot long endure. . . . Sectarianism has often served to promote special interests and worked against the national interest. . . . The moment when sectarianism is eliminated is a moment of blessed national awakening." Nevertheless, sectarianism has increasingly become a permanent and legitimate political arrangement. Top as well as minor governmental positions in the executive, legislative, and judicial bodies continue to be distributed on sectarian bases. Even judges, public school teachers, and the faculty of Lebanese University have been recruited in accordance with the same formula as for members of parliament. In spite of ample evidence that sectarianism conflicts with rational

**Table 3.1. Sectarian distribution of deputies in the Lebanese parliament, 1964–1976**

| Electoral Districts | Christian Deputies Maronites | Greek Orthodox | Greek Catholics | Others | Total |
|---|---|---|---|---|---|
| **Group 1** | | | | | |
| Batrun, Bsharri, Beirut I, Jezzin, Kisruwan, Kura, Matn, Zgharta | | | | | |
| | 17 | 4 | 2 | 6 | 29 |
| **Group 2** | | | | | |
| Aley, Ba'abda, Jubayl, Zahlah | | | | | |
| | 8 | 2 | 1 | 0 | 11 |
| **Group 3** | | | | | |
| Akkar, Shuf, Zahrani | | | | | |
| | 4 | 1 | 2 | 0 | 7 |
| **Group 4** | | | | | |
| Beirut II, Beirut III, Tripoli, Ba'albek-Hermel, Rashaya, Marjayun-Hasbaya | | | | | |
| | 1 | 4 | 1 | 1 | 7 |
| **Group 5** | | | | | |
| Bint-Jubayl, Dinnieh, Nabatiyyah, Sidon, Tyre | | | | | |
| | 0 | 0 | 0 | 0 | 0 |
| **Total** | 30 | 11 | 6 | 7 | 54 |

principles of management and bureaucracy, the institutionalization of sectarianism continues at all levels and over broader ranges than before. This kind of balanced distribution is becoming more and more a part of the Lebanese way of life and is reflected even in popular songs:

> Where are the Dabki dancers?
> Where is Mahmud? [a Sunni name]
> Where is Ma'ruf? [a Druze name]
> Where is Ilyas? [a Christian name]
> Where is Husayn? [a Shi'ite name]

| Muslim Deputies | | | | Total Deputies |
| Sunnites | Shi'ites | Druzes | Total | |
|---|---|---|---|---|
| 0 | 0 | 0 | 0 | 29 |
| 1 | 3 | 3 | 7 | 18 |
| 4 | 1 | 2 | 7 | 14 |
| 12 | 7 | 1 | 20 | 27 |
| 3 | 8 | 0 | 11 | 11 |
| 20 | 19 | 6 | 45 | 99 |

By legitimization of sectarianism, differences between the religious communities have been accentuated, and this in turn has contributed to further polarization rather than assimilation.

## Conflicting Reference Groups

The different Lebanese religious communities identify with, and to a great extent model themselves after, different outside groups. On the whole, the Christian Lebanese, and more particularly the Maronites, have looked to the Western nations for protection, inspiration, and education. They have exposed themselves most willingly and freely to Western influence and have often uncritically adopted many Western views, value orientations, styles and languages. As K. S. Salibi puts it, Christian Lebanese have tended to see "Western nations as protectors rather than conquerors or masters. . . . Hence, when they westernize, they do so without apology. Although their understanding of Western ideas is frequently shallow, they nevertheless adopt them with enthusiasm."[26] Some Christian Lebanese have aspired to model Lebanon after Switzerland, others after France. There are also those who call for a Mediterranean unity and consider Arab unity an unrealistic endeavor. It is fair, however, to say that many Christian Lebanese have contributed to the rebirth of Arab culture and some of them are strongly alienated from the West. On the other hand, and on the whole, the affinities of Muslim Lebanese are with the Arab nation. They have identified with other Arab countries and adopted Arab causes as their own. They have sought from Arab countries, especially Egypt, direction, guidance, and inspiration on political and other matters. In addition, Muslim Lebanese have feared and mistrusted the West—not without reason. During the last half century they have encountered enough evidence to justify their fears and mistrust. The promises made to the Arabs during World War I were soon broken. Instead of helping to unite the Arab world, the West has further dismantled it and worked to fulfill its promises to the Zionists. As a result of such disappointments, reinforced by the coming of Westerners to the Middle East as crusaders, colonizers, and missionaries, Muslims have tended to reject the West. The West is to be held at least partly responsible for such a rejection. Morroe Berger points out that, by "deliberate policy and sheer example, the West introduced ideas and technology that considerably changed social relations in the Arab world and have had profound political effects as well. At the same time, however, the Western powers studiously pursued a conservative policy regarding political life itself, seeking in effect to prevent the social and economic consequences of their presence from altering political institutions. They introduced revolutionary conceptions, but tried to keep them from making a revolution in Arab political life."[27]

One basic consequence of this situation is that the nature of the relationships between the two reference groups has influenced the nature of the relationships between the religious communities in Lebanon. More specifically, conflicts between Egypt or Syria and the West have tended to reflect themselves in Lebanon. This fact explains to some extent the crises that have confronted Lebanon since 1943, especially the 1958 crisis. On the other hand, improvement of relationships between the West and Egypt would undermine the influence of the latter on Lebanese Muslims and improve its image among the right-wing Christians.

**Pyramidal Social Class Structure**

Underdeveloped societies are characterized by pyramidal social class structures. This means that the majority of people are poor, some are middle class, and very few are well off. This kind of structure may be contrasted with diamond-shaped social class structures, in which the middle classes constitute the majority of the people, in developed societies.

A Lebanese government-commissioned study of the needs and possibilities of development in Lebanon (1960)[28] indicated that about 50 percent of the families were poor or miserable (i.e., their average yearly income was £L 2,000, £L 1,000 respectively), and another 32 percent had an average yearly income of £L 3,500, which was considered moderate. In other words, it was estimated then (see Table 3.2) that about 82 percent of the families in Lebanon earned £L 5,000 (poverty level) or less annually. The rest of the Lebanese families were considered "well-to-do" 14 percent), with an average yearly income of £L 10,000, and "rich" (4 percent), with an average yearly income of £L 40,000. The rich families, constituting only 4 percent of the Lebanese population, received about one-third (32 percent) of the gross national product, while 82 percent of the Lebanese families received about 40 percent.

Societies characterized by pyramidal social class structures show high resistance to development if left to evolutionary change. The great majority of the people who are poor are too powerless to be able to change their condition. Opportunities for social mobility, education, political involvement, exposition to technology, contact with the outside, etc., are highly limited. Most of the poor remain submerged in their culture of silence and reconcile themselves to misery, deprivation, and powerlessness. Here, it should be observed that the social class split cannot be separated from the religious split. The two conditions intimately and intricately overlap, coincide, and interconnect to the extent that each reinforces and transforms the other in its very essence. The Muslims, and particularly the Shi'ites, suffer most acutely from poverty and low social and political status. The Christians as a whole occupy the most significant positions in the socioeconomic and political structures in Lebanon. This way the Lebanese society is transformed into a vertical mosaic constructed from communal groups arranged in a power structure of haves and have-nots or privileged and deprived communities.

**Educational Systems in Lebanon: A Reflection of the Stratified Social Mosaic**

The stratified social mosaic nature of the Lebanese society is clearly reflected in its educational systems. There have been as many systems and

**Table 3.2. Income distribution in Lebanon**

| Income Strata | Percentage of Families | Average Annual Income (£L)[a] | Percentage of GNP |
|---|---|---|---|
| Miserable | 9 | 1,000 | 2 |
| Poor | 41 | 2,000 | 16 |
| Moderate income | 32 | 3,500 | 22 |
| Well-to-do | 14 | 10,000 | 28 |
| Rich | 4 | 40,000 | 32 |

*Source:* République Libanaise, Ministère du Plan, *Besoins et possibilités de développement du Liban,* 1:93.
[a]£L 3 = $1.00

philosophies of education as there have been religious communities, for each sect has its own autonomous private schools. There are private and public as well as national and foreign schools, using different languages as media of instruction (mainly Arabic, French, and English) and patterning their programs after French, Anglo-American, or mixtures of both programs.

About two-thirds of the students in pre-university education attend private schools of diverse programs, philosophies of education, and languages as media of instruction. The rest, mostly poor and Muslim, attend public schools, which have much lower standards than private ones.

The confessional nature of these schools is clearly reflected in the backgrounds of the students they recruit. Statistics (1960) on the distribution of students in Lebanese elementary public schools according to religious affiliation showed that about two-thirds were Muslims (27 percent Sunnites, 27 percent Shi'ites, and 11 percent Druzes). In public junior and high schools, 62 percent were Muslims (40 percent Sunnites, 18 percent Shi'ites, and 4 percent Druzes). Thus, Muslim students are more likely to go to public schools, and Christians are more likely to go to private schools. Data on some private schools show that the great majority of the 126,482 students who attended Catholic schools in 1967–1968 were Catholic (76 percent). Similarly, the great majority of the 17,830 students who attended the Maqasid school system in 1965 were Sunni Muslims.[29] Statistics on sectarian distribution have been collected yearly by the Ministry of Education but kept strictly confidential.

Student enrollment in pre-university schools has been increasing rapidly at a yearly rate of 9.6 percent in elementary schools and 24 percent in secondary schools since the mid-fifties, but at differential rates among the districts. The rate of increase in Mount Lebanon (Christian majority) has been 18 percent in elementary schools and 57 percent in secondary schools, while in the South (Shi'ite majority) the rates of increase have been 8 percent in elementary schools and 16 percent in secondary schools. This reflects the differences in opportunities for education and the fact that the gap is not decreasing. Furthermore, the proportion of students in private elementary and secondary schools increased between 1954–1955 and 1967–1968 in the Beirut district from 66 percent to 86 percent, and in Mount Lebanon from 58 percent to 78 percent, while in other districts the proportion of students going to private elementary schools remained the same (about 40 percent). The proportion of those going to public secondary schools increased from 37 percent to 64 percent in the North, from 26 percent to 67 percent in the South, and from 22 percent to 62 percent in al-Biqa'.[30] Simply, the proportion of students attending public schools has decreased in Mount Lebanon and Beirut, and increased in the other districts. Thus, the qualitative gap is not decreasing either.

The private schools are becoming extremely expensive and thus destined to serve only the well-to-do, while the lower and lower-middle classes can only afford to send their children to public schools.

In short, schools in Lebanon have been as diverse as its religious communities, and their diversity has contributed to further social fragmentation, national disunity, and cultural disintegration. The educational systems reflect as well as maintain the established stratified confessional order.

University education is an extension of secondary and elementary education. The same conditions, processes, and philosophical orientations prevail on all three levels. Similarly, universities in Lebanon recruit their students from certain specified communities and graduate them back into their communities of origin. The contacts among the different educational systems are rare and accidental.

The graduates of secondary schools following Anglo-American programs are destined to continue their studies, if they can, at the American University of Beirut or in Britain and the United States. The graduates of schools following a French program must continue their studies, if they can, at Saint Joseph University (founded in 1875) or in France. Those students who graduate from public schools and certain private schools and who are able to continue their studies are destined to join Lebanese University or Beirut Arab University. The number of students at LU (a state university founded in 1953) has ranged between ten thousand and fifteen thousand since the late sixties, but the majority are external students who do not attend classes but merely sit for the examinations. Beirut Arab University (BAU) was founded by Egypt as an extension of Alexandria University in 1960. The number of its students is estimated to range between fourteen thousand and twenty-five thousand. Again, the majority of students do not attend classes.

In demonstrating the stratified mosaic structure of Lebanon's educational system, it is perhaps most useful to describe the composition of students in the four universities by religion, social class, nationality, sex, and rural-urban background.

*Religious Composition*

Seeking homogeneity in their religious composition, SJU and BAU recruit their students almost exclusively from Christian and Muslim communities respectively. AUB and LU, on the other hand, recruit or attract their students from diverse religious backgrounds and may be described as being religiously heterogeneous.

The great majority of students (about 85 percent) at SJU have since its opening been Lebanese Christians. My sample at SJU in 1970–1971 showed almost exactly the same percentage: 84 percent Christian. Forty-one percent of the total student body were Maronites, 20 percent Catholics, 16 percent Orthodox Christians, 10 percent Sunnites, 4 percent Shi'ites, 2 percent Druzes, and 7 percent others. At BAU it is estimated that 90–93 percent of the students have been Muslims, with nearly half coming from private Muslim schools. At LU it is estimated that about 54 percent of students have been Christians. My roughly representative sample (1971) showed that 29 percent of the students were Maronites, 27 percent Sunnites, 15 percent Shi'ites, 14 percent Orthodox, 6 percent Catholics, 5 percent Druzes, and 4 percent other Christians. At AUB in 1973 it was estimated that about 56 percent of students were Christians, 42 percent were Muslims, and about 2 percent were of other religious affiliations. A highly representative sample of Arab students at AUB in 1970 (Arab students then constituted 78.4 percent of the total student body) showed that 38 percent were Sunnites, 6 percent Shi'ites, 3 percent Druzes, 19 percent Orthodox, 10 percent Armenian Christians, 8 percent Catholics, 7 percent Maronites, 6 percent Protestants, and 2 percent others.

AUB official statistics (1972–1973) showed that about 57 percent of the total student body (4,258) were Christian, and about 42 percent Muslim. The greatest proportional increase since the thirties has been in the case of Maronites, Roman and Greek Catholics, and Gregorians. These statistics are shown in Table 3.3.

*Social Class Composition*

In social class composition, AUB and SJU are highly homogeneous and elitist. The majority of their students come from upper and upper-middle

**Table 3.3. Student distribution at AUB by religion**

|                    | 1933–1934 | 1961–1962 | 1971–1972 | 1972–1973 |
|--------------------|-----------|-----------|-----------|-----------|
| Sunnites           | —         | 1,023     | 1,362     | 1,411     |
| Shi'ites           | —         | 298       | 211       | 227       |
| Druzes             | —         |           | 143       | 151       |
| **Total Muslims**  | 457       | 1,321     | 1,716     | 1,789     |
| Greek Orthodox     | 281       | 488       | 750       | 827       |
| Protestants        | 237       |           | 388       | 393       |
| Maronites          | 74        |           | 347       | 406       |
| Gregorians         | 62        | 1,008     | 342       | 326       |
| Roman Catholics    | 38        |           | 247       | 262       |
| Greek Catholics    | 30        |           | 111       | 132       |
| Other Christians   | 49        |           | 60        | 63        |
| **Total Christians** | 771     | 1,496     | 2,245     | 2,409     |
| Jews               | 157       | 136       | 6         | 7         |
| Other religions    | 96        |           | 48        | 53        |
| **Grand total**    | 1,481     | 2,953     | 4,015     | 4,258     |

class families. My data on representative samples at AUB, SJU, and LU are presented in the Tables 3.4 and 3.5 and in the Appendix. As shown, at AUB only about 11 percent said their parents' total yearly income was £L 5,000 or less, 18 percent said that the occupations of their fathers were skilled, semiskilled, or unskilled (manual workers and farmers were considered unskilled), 9 percent said their fathers had no formal education, and only 2 percent ranked their families as belonging to lower classes relative to their own society or community. Taking father's occupation and education and family income into consideration, I estimate that about 10 percent of the students at AUB belong to the lower classes which constitute more than 80 percent of the population in Arab society.

A similar social class composition exists at SJU. My roughly representative sample of students at this university in 1970–1971 showed that about half said their parents earned £L 15,000 or more a year. Only 7 percent said their parents earned £L 5,000 or less a year, 11 percent said their fathers' occupations were manual, 3 percent said their fathers had no education,

**Table 3.4. Estimates of family yearly income of students (% for 1970–1971)**

| Family Yearly Income | AUB | SJU | LU |
|---|---|---|---|
| £L 5,000 or less | 11 | 7 | 26 |
| £L 5,000–10,000 | 17 | 14 | 26 |
| £L 10,000–15,000 | 15 | 22 | 18 |
| £L 15,000–20,000 | 11 | 14 | 11 |
| £L 20,000–35,000 | 20 | 24 | 11 |
| £L 35,000 or more | 18 | 11 | 5 |
| Don't know | 8 | 8 | 3 |

**Table 3.5. Level of education of students' parents (% for 1970–1971)**

| Level of Education | AUB (N=213) | | SJU (N=318) | | LU (N=219) | |
|---|---|---|---|---|---|---|
| | Father | Mother | Father | Mother | Father | Mother |
| No education | 9 | 14 | 3 | 6 | 13 | 30 |
| Elementary | 24 | 29 | 32 | 40 | 49 | 47 |
| Secondary | 33 | 40 | 38 | 46 | 28 | 17 |
| University | 33 | 13 | 23 | 6 | 8 | 2 |
| Don't know | 1 | 4 | 4 | 2 | 2 | 4 |

and only 4 percent ranked their families as belonging to lower classes relative to their society or community.

The social class structure at LU shows that about half of the students come from the lower and lower-middle classes. Fifty-two percent of the students there said their parents earned £L 10,000 a year or less, 62 percent said their fathers had elementary or no education, 26 percent said their fathers were manual workers or small-landed farmers, and 25 percent said their fathers were small-scale or middle-scale shop owners. However, only 12 percent ranked their families as belonging to lower and lower-middle classes relative to their own society or community. The majority (61 percent) ranked their families as belonging to middle-middle classes, and 25 percent as belonging to upper-middle and upper classes.

*National Composition*

Among the four universities in Lebanon, only AUB has shown a heterogeneous national composition.[31] At least 90 percent of the students at SJU have been Lebanese (the figure for the academic year 1973–1974 was more than 93 percent). The stratified quota sample that I took in the fall of 1970 showed that roughly 93 percent were Lebanese. Similarly, at least 80 percent of the students of LU have been Lebanese (the figure for the academic year 1973–1974 was only about 9 percent non-Lebanese).

The students at AUB have been recruited from over fifty countries in Asia, Africa, Europe, and North and South America. The percentage of Lebanese students ranged between 40.5 percent and 43.9 percent in the sixties. In 1970–1971 this percentage increased about 5 percent, to 47.1 percent, and in 1971–1972 it increased another 4 percent, to 51.2 percent, and in 1972–1973 AUB official statistics showed that 54 percent of the students were Lebanese. Because this increase accompanied increasing political activism in the University, it is often speculated that AUB is making an effort to recruit Lebanese students from private schools following a French program.

The number of other Arab students has been constant for the last ten years. There was a slight increase in the number of Kuwaitis, Moroccans, and Bahrainis, coupled with a slight decrease in the number of Palestinians and Sudanese. By 1960 the Palestinians were largely listed as Jordanians.

As for changes in the number of non-Arab students during the last ten years, there has been an increase in the number of students from Cyprus, Turkey, Pakistan, Afghanistan, Europe (especially the United Kingdom), and the United States and a decrease in the number of Africans. The statistics are shown in table 3.6.

*Sex Composition*

About one-fourth of the university students in Lebanon at present are females. The enrollment of women students at AUB hit a record high of 28 percent in 1971–1972 and has remained constant to present. During the academic year 1973–1974, the percentages of female students were about 34 percent at SJU, 27 percent at LU, and 19 percent at BAU. Coeducation officially started at AUB in 1925, when seven women enrolled in the School of Arts and Sciences.

The women students are more likely than men students to come from rich families. For instance, in the present survey 48 percent of the female respondents at LU, as compared to 20 percent of the males, said their par-

**Table 3.6. Distribution of AUB students by nationalities**

|  | 1933–1934 | 1960–1961 | 1965–1966 |
|---|---|---|---|
| Lebanon ⎱ | 752 | 974 | 1,479 |
| Syria ⎰ |  | 219 | 265 |
| Palestine | 242 | 185 | 150 |
| Iraq | 130 | 41 | 76 |
| Jordan | 12 | 397[a] | 390[a] |
| Egypt | 87 | 28 | 14 |
| Sudan | 14 | 118 | 85 |
| Saudi Arabia | 1 | 27 | 69 |
| Bahrain | — | 14 | 23 |
| Kuwait | — | 4 | 36 |
| Other Arab countries | — | 21 | 72 |
| **Total** **for Arab countries** | 1,238 | 2,028 | 2,659 |
| Cyprus | — | 22 | 27 |
| Iran | 48 | 121 | 156 |
| Turkey | 16 | 3 | 11 |
| **Total** **for other Middle** **Eastern countries** | 64 | 146 | 194 |
| Afghanistan | — | 33 | 47 |
| Pakistan | — | 119 | 66 |
| Other Asian countries | 9 | 8 | 40 |
| **Total** **for Asia** | 9 | 160 | 153 |
| Africa | 4 | 118 | 91 |
| Europe | 92 | 72 | 74 |
| United States | 64 | 124 | 175 |
| Others | 19 | 34 | 23 |
| **Grand total** | 1,490 | 2,682 | 3,369 |

[a]Includes Palestinians carrying Jordanian citizenship.

| 1970–1971 | 1971–1972 | 1972–1973 |
|---|---|---|
| 1,944 | 2,056 | 2,289 |
| 292 | 270 | 259 |
| 143 | 137 | 145 |
| 75 | 62 | 56 |
| 453[a] | 432[a] | 440[a] |
| 35 | 35 | 36 |
| 32 | 25 | 19 |
| 66 | 57 | 58 |
| 54 | 63 | 67 |
| 54 | 61 | 56 |
| 75 | 55 | 70 |
| ——— | ——— | ——— |
| 3,223 | 3,253 | 3,495 |
| 68 | 67 | 69 |
| 66 | 63 | 68 |
| 46 | 50 | 38 |
| ——— | ——— | ——— |
| 180 | 180 | 175 |
| 61 | 64 | 66 |
| 151 | 106 | 105 |
| 50 | 25 | 20 |
| ——— | ——— | ——— |
| 262 | 195 | 191 |
| 32 | 23 | 32 |
| 124 | 104 | 113 |
| 243 | 198 | 205 |
| 65 | 58 | 65 |
| 4,129 | 4,011 | 4,276 |

ents earned an annual income of £L 15,000 or more. Similarly, while 57 percent of the women said their fathers had secondary or university education, only 29 percent of the men said so. The data also show that while 39 percent of the women ranked their families as belonging to the upper and upper-middle classes relative to their communities or societies, 21 percent of the men did so. Almost the same trends were found at AUB and SJU. In the former, for example, 62 percent of the female respondents said their family yearly income exceeded £L 20,000 as compared to 40 percent of the males. Again, 46 percent of the women and 29 percent of the men said their fathers were big businessmen. Finally, 69 percent of the women respondents at AUB in comparison to 40 percent of the men ranked their families as belonging to upper and upper-middle classes.

*Rural-Urban Composition*

All universities in Lebanon are located in Beirut. The present data on AUB Arab students show that 58 percent have lived most of their lives in big cities (a population of 300,000 or more), 22 percent in small cities (population ranging between 50,000 and 300,000), 11 percent in towns (10,000–50,000), and only 8 percent in villages.

The educational systems in Lebanon, then, neatly correspond to the existing religious and ethnic communities in the society. Schools, colleges, and universities recruit or attract their students from specific communities, socialize them into the cultures of these communities, and prepare them to serve the elites. Education does not constitute a liberating force—it provides an environment for perpetuating tradition. Such patterns of socialization prevail throughout Lebanon's institutions—home, school, church, government, and university. These are complementary rather than conflicting agencies of socialization. They reinforce each other, maintain the status quo, and preserve the culture of silence.

**Conclusion**

While any one of the eight characteristics adduced in this chapter might not be sufficient alone to prevent the development of harmonious pluralism, the existence of all of them concurrently creates a stratified mosaic society.

Unity and assimilation into a unified national order remain a prospect only. As long as the above conditions continue to be unchallenged in a systematic and rational way, Lebanon will remain a stratified mosaic society with dim prospects for stability and national unity and, thus, threatened at its very roots. The communal groups of Lebanon are arranged in a power structure of haves and have-nots. The privileged communal groups subscribe to a policy of isolation from the other Arab countries and dissociation from Arab causes. The deprived communal groups, on the other hand, subscribe to a nationalistic ideology and socioeconomic and political transformation.

The current civil war is an eruption or culmination of the confrontation that has been building up between these groups at least since independence. It has been a confrontation between forces for change and forces for maintaining the established order against all odds and, quite often, in opposition to the professed principles. This process of confrontation has been gaining momentum and polarizing the society into two opposed camps.

A review of statements and reports on the current civil war in Lebanon will reveal that it has been characterized variously as a religious war between Christians and Muslims, as a confrontation between the isolationists and the nationalists, and as a confrontation between the deprived and the privileged, i.e., as a form of class struggle. According to the present framework of analysis, the Lebanese civil war is described as a complex and intricate fusion of the sectarian loyalties, isolationist-nationalistic tendencies, and deprived-privileged struggle.

In order to develop this argument and to check on the basic thesis, the empiral data collected in 1970 and 1971 will now be presented and analyzed. The data will allow an exploration of the causal and contributing forces making for radicalism and alienation, and consequently, for the current civil war.

# Part II

## Sources of Radicalism and Political Alienation:

*The Influence of Religion, Family, and Social Class*

## Vertical and Horizontal Loyalties

The basic thesis of this study, that vertical loyalties continue to constitute a more significant force than horizontal loyalties in determining student political radicalism and alienation in Lebanon, is demonstrated by empirical data. As pointed out in Chapter 1, vertical loyalty refers to grouping on the basis of religious, kinship, ethnic, regional, and similar ties, whereas horizontal loyalty refers to grouping on the basis of social class.

The empirical data demonstrating the influence of religion, family, social class, and other variables on student radicalism and alienation were collected through a self-administered questionnaire at AUB, SJU, and LU (see Appendix).

The first survey was conducted at AUB in the spring of 1970 with a random sample of 363 students representing all Arab students (2,903 at the time). The random sample was chosen by the university computer by shuffling the IBM cards of all Arab students so that they were not arranged in any systematic order; then every eighth card was extracted for inclusion in the sample. To check on the representativeness of this sample, the distributions of the universe (i.e., total Arab students), sample, and respondents were compared according to religious affiliation, nationality, sex, and college or field of specialization as shown in Table II.1. The distributions, as evidenced in the table, were found to correspond closely, and I am fully convinced that the sample was highly representative of Arab students at AUB.

The second major survey was conducted in the fall of 1970 at SJU and the Ecole des Lettres, an affiliated institution following a similar program. It was impossible to use the same procedure in selecting the sample because a complete list of the total student population was not available. Instead, a stratified quota sample was selected by taking the classroom (rather than the individual student) as the basic unit. In other words, classrooms as a

**Table II.1. Comparison of population, sample, and respondents for AUB (%)**

|  | Population N=2,903 | Sample N=363 | Respondents N=213 |
|---|---|---|---|
| **Religious affiliation** |  |  |  |
| Christians | 55.7 | 51.7 | 53 |
| Muslims | 44.3 | 48.3 | 47 |
| **Nationality** |  |  |  |
| Lebanese | 56.3 | 56.4 | 52 |
| Other Arabs | 43.7 | 43.6 | 48 |
| **Sex** |  |  |  |
| Males | 73.54 | 72.45 | 68 |
| Females | 26.45 | 27.54 | 32 |
| **College** |  |  |  |
| Arts and Sciences | 63.1 | 63.9 | 60 |
| Engineering | 15.8 | 16.2 | 14 |
| Others | 21.1 | 19.9 | 26 |

whole were chosen at random from a list of offered courses, and all students in the chosen classes were asked to fill out the questionnaire, with the consent of their instructors. The total number of respondents at SJU and Ecole des Lettres (hereafter all will be considered SJU) was 318.

The third major survey was carried out at two colleges of LU in the spring of 1971. In the College of Law and Political Sciences, the same procedure was used as at SJU (again because of the nonavailability of a list of the total student population). The number of respondents in this stratified quota sample was 108. In the College of Education it was possible to select a simple random sample representing the total population of students. A list of all students was available, and every fourth name was chosen to represent the student body in the first, second, third, and fourth years in all fields of specialization. The sample amounted to 167 and the number of respondents was 111 (about 66 percent of the total sample).

In reporting the data, it should be noted that nonrespondents to specific questions were discarded. This accounts for the continuously differing total number of respondents. In some other instances, such as in the case of tables presenting data on Lebanese national identity, the small number of non-Lebanese students (mostly at AUB) were excluded. It should be noted also that when categories of some tables were collapsed after computerization, the Chi square and coefficients were not recomputed, but original ones were used to determine the degree of statistical significance. It should be further noted that percentages were rounded off, which accounts for the fact that totals do not add up to exactly 100 percent in some instances.

# 4. Religion and Student Politics

The basic concern of this chapter is to assess the influence of religious affiliations as well as religiosity on several aspects of student political behavior and attitudes, such as leftist-rightist leanings, support for the Palestinian resistance movement and advocacy of violence and popular armed struggle, and identification with Arab, Lebanese, or Syrian nationalism. These aspects are highly pertinent to any serious attempt at understanding the latest Lebanese civil war. Furthermore, since religious affiliation and religiosity are inseparable from prevailing socioeconomic conditions, comparisons will be made between the Lebanese students and the Jordanian-Palestinian students with regard to the influence of the religious factor on their political behavior and attitudes in order to uncover some of the intricacies and complexities of the above relationships. In this way, it will be possible to demonstrate that certain religious communities contribute disproportionately to the cause of revolutionary change and others to the cause of conservatism and continuity of the status quo. It will also show that this disproportion is possible because Lebanon is a vertical mosaic society composed of communal groups arranged in a hierarchical economic and power structure.

The influence of religious sectarianism in the political lives of students has been explored in such societies as India, Latin American countries, and the United States. For instance, P. G. Altbach shows that deep religious, linguistic, and caste divisions have played an important role in shaping the student movement in India, and that modern education has not diminished the magnitude of such an influence.[1] The study by Liebman, Walker, and Glazer on university students in Latin America shows how closely the church has been allied with the rightist groups and especially the landed oligarchy and the army. Their data on university students in Colombia, Mexico, Paraguay, Puerto Rico, and Uruguay "reveal that in every case the most religiously involved, as measured by a scale of religiousness, are the ones most likely to be conservative in their political ideology. . . . As religiousness increases . . . the percentage of rightist students also increases."[2] In another study, on university student politics in Chile, Myron Glazer found that "those who defined themselves as practicing Catholics had a strong tendency to identify with the Christian Democratic Party and to indicate little preference for the FRAP (Frente de Acción Popular—socialist-communist dominated). Conversely, students who had no religious affiliation, and who were politically involved, tended to give their support to the FRAP."[3] Similarly, Moore and Hochschild discovered that in Morocco, "the less religious a student is—as is indicated by his observance of Ramadan and daily prayers and by his own self-evaluation—the more likely he is to be interested in politics."[4] Research findings on student politics in the United States such as those of Solomon and Fishman,[5] Keniston,[6] Flacks,[7] Braungart,[8] and others show that leftist activists came disproportionately from Jewish backgrounds.

In the present study, the relationship between religion and politics is expected to be highly significant. The data checking on this relationship will be presented in three sections: religious affiliation and student politics; religiosity and student politics; and religion, religiosity, and socioeconomic conditions.

## Religious Affiliation and Student Politics

As expected, the data on Lebanese students in all three universities (AUB, LU, and SJU) show that sectarian affiliation is the single most significant determinant of a whole range of political behavior and attitudes.

### Religious Affiliation and Leftist-Rightist Tendencies

The data on the relationship between religious affiliation and leftist-rightist tendencies are shown in Tables 4.1, 4.2, 4.3, and 4.4.

Students at AUB, LU, and SJU were asked to indicate whether they thought of themselves as (1) leftist, revolutionary, and recommending the use of violence if necessary; (2) leftist, revolutionary, but nonviolent; (3) reformist, nonrevolutionary, moderate; (4) rightist, antirevolutionary, and antileftist; (5) satisfied with the status quo and having no particular political position; or (6) of other inclinations (which they were asked to specify).

The data in Table 4.1 show that Muslim students were much more likely than Christian students to think of themselves as leftists. Among the Muslim students, the Shi'ites were most inclined to consider themselves leftists (61 percent in comparison to 45 percent of the Sunnites and 35 percent of the Druzes). While the Shi'ites tended toward being revolutionary leftists, the Sunnites and Druzes showed high tendencies toward leftist reformism.

The Lebanese Christian students, on the other hand, showed a strong inclination to think of themselves as reformists but exhibited a marked tendency toward the right.

Comparisons across universities show that the Shi'ite students at LU were more likely to consider themselves leftist than Shi'ite students at SJU (72 percent at LU versus 50 percent at SJU). The Sunni Muslims registered the same percentage in both universities. However, while at LU they tended to think of themselves as leftists who believe in violence when necessary, the trend was reversed at SJU, where they were more inclined to think of themselves as nonviolent leftists.

Table 4.2 presents the data showing the degree of relationship between religious affiliation and agreement with the following statement: "What is needed [in the Lebanese political system] is revolution, not reform." Again, the Muslim students showed a greater tendency to agree. About two-thirds of the Shi'ite students (68 percent) expressed agreement with the statement. The Sunni and Druze students were almost equally divided between the two alternative courses to change. The overwhelming majority of the Christian students (about three-quarters of them) disagreed, usually strongly, with the statement.

The data in Table 4.3 provide further information on leftist-rightist tendencies. Students were asked to indicate which of the following forms of government they preferred for Lebanon: communism, socialist democracy, liberal democracy, capitalistic democracy, or other forms. Muslim students showed a greater tendency than Christian students to prefer communist and socialist forms of government. Consistently with previous findings, the Shi'ite students expressed the greatest preference for socialism (60 percent) and communism (21 percent); at LU about two-thirds of them preferred socialism. Both the Sunnites and the Druzes also preferred a socialist form of democracy (42 percent and 53 percent respectively), but, unlike Shi'ites, their next preference was liberal democracy rather than communism. The Christian students, on the other hand, tended to prefer liberal democracy, and their next inclination was toward socialist democracy. In this case, some differences could be observed among Christian students: the Orthodox showed the greatest preference for socialism (38 percent), followed by Catholics (34 percent), and Maronites (26 percent). The latter professed some liking for capitalism (22 percent), more so than any other religious group. In short, most students in all groups seemed to reject both communism and capitalism; but, while Muslims indicated most interest in socialist democracy, the Christians preferred liberal democracy.

Table 4.4. provides another set of information on socialist-communist tendencies. Students were asked to indicate to what extent they agreed with the following statement: "Ultimately, private property should be abolished and complete socialism introduced." More than two-thirds of the

**Table 4.1. Religion and leftist-rightist tendencies among Lebanese university students (%)**

| Political Tendencies (*Students Consider Themselves*) | Sunnites N=92 | Shi'ites N=49 | Druzes N=20 | Maronites N=197 |
|---|---|---|---|---|
| Leftist | 22 | 45 | 30 | 11 |
| Nonviolent leftist | 23 | 16 | 5 | 9 |
| Reformist | 46 | 29 | 50 | 55 |
| Rightist | 3 | 4 | 0 | 17 |
| Apolitical | 0 | 0 | 0 | 3 |
| Other | 6 | 6 | 15 | 5 |

$X^2$ = 99.12; contingency coefficient = .3840; corrected con. coe. = .4102.

**Table 4.2. Religion and degree of Lebanese university students' agreement with the statement "What is needed in the Lebanese political system is revolution, not reform" (%)**

| Degree of Agreement | Sunnites N=89 | Shi'ites N=51 | Druzes N=21 | Maronites N=183 |
|---|---|---|---|---|
| Strongly agree | 30 | 39 | 24 | 12 |
| Agree | 20 | 29 | 33 | 12 |
| Disagree | 34 | 20 | 33 | 38 |
| Strongly disagree | 16 | 12 | 10 | 38 |

$X^2$ = 75.03; contingency coefficient = .3426; corrected con. coe. = .3836.

| Orthodox N=105 | Catholics N=71 | Others N=38 | Total N=572 |
|---|---|---|---|
| 13 | 11 | 8 | 17 |
| 11 | 14 | 5 | 12 |
| 50 | 46 | 34 | 48 |
| 15 | 21 | 29 | 14 |
| 5 | 1 | 8 | 2 |
| 6 | 7 | 16 | 7 |

| Orthodox N=106 | Catholics N=71 | Others N=42 | Total N=563 |
|---|---|---|---|
| 14 | 13 | 12 | 18 |
| 11 | 11 | 12 | 16 |
| 34 | 30 | 33 | 33 |
| 41 | 46 | 43 | 33 |

**Table 4.3. Religion and forms of government Lebanese university students prefer for Lebanon (%)**

| Preferred Form of Government | Sunnites N=78 | Shi'ites N=43 | Druzes N=15 | Maronites N=165 |
|---|---|---|---|---|
| Communism | 18 | 21 | 13 | 4 |
| Socialist democracy | 42 | 60 | 53 | 26 |
| Liberal democracy | 26 | 12 | 20 | 45 |
| Capitalistic democracy | 9 | 7 | 13 | 22 |
| Others | 5 | 0 | 0 | 3 |

**Table 4.4. Religion and degree of Lebanese university students' agreement with the statement "Ultimately, private property should be abolished and complete socialism introduced" (%)**

| Degree of Agreement | Sunnites N=87 | Shi'ites N=49 | Druzes N=20 | Maronites N=189 |
|---|---|---|---|---|
| Strongly agree | 20 | 43 | 20 | 9 |
| Agree | 23 | 24 | 20 | 14 |
| Disagree | 34 | 24 | 40 | 32 |
| Strongly disagree | 23 | 8 | 20 | 46 |

$X^2$ = 71.23; contingency coefficient = .3348; corrected con. coe. = .3749.

respondents (69 percent) disagreed with the statement, but religious differences continued to show. Only in the case of the Shi'ite students did the majority (67 percent) agree with the statement. Again, they were followed by the Sunnites (43 percent) and the Druzes (40 percent), and those who disagreed showed moderate rather than strong disagreement. The great majority of the Christian students disagreed with the statement, and on the whole they expressed strong rather than moderate disagreement. The Maronites registered the highest level of strong disagreement (46 percent), followed by Catholics (39 percent) and the Orthodox (37 percent). Comparisons across universities show that Christian students at LU expressed

| Orthodox N=69 | Catholics N=62 | Others N=20 | Total N=452 |
|---|---|---|---|
| 4 | 5 | 5 | 9 |
| 38 | 34 | 20 | 37 |
| 42 | 48 | 60 | 38 |
| 9 | 8 | 15 | 13 |
| 7 | 5 | 0 | 3 |

| Orthodox N=106 | Catholics N=72 | Others N=40 | Total N=563 |
|---|---|---|---|
| 12 | 8 | 5 | 14 |
| 16 | 13 | 18 | 17 |
| 35 | 40 | 33 | 34 |
| 37 | 39 | 45 | 35 |

more agreement with abolishing private property than Christian students at AUB and SJU: 33 percent of the Maronite students at LU in comparison to 11 percent at SJU approved of abolishing private ownership. Similarly, 52 percent of the Orthodox students at LU in comparison to 22 percent at SJU agreed with such abolishment. The same trend was found among Catholic students (39 percent at LU as compared to 15 percent at SJU). Among the Muslim students, only the Shi'ites showed significant variation between universities. While at LU 22 percent agreed and 56 percent strongly agreed with abolishing private property, 33 percent agreed and 8 percent strongly agreed at SJU.

*Religious Affiliation and Support of the Palestinian Cause*

The attitudes of Lebanese students toward the Palestinian resistance movement and their advocacy of either popular armed struggle or a peaceful solution to the Palestine problem are highly determined by their religious backgrounds.

As shown in Table 4.5, Muslim students expressed greater support than Christian students. About one-half of the Muslim students, in comparison to about one-fifth of the Christian students, expressed strong support. The Shi'ites from communities most influenced by the activities of the commandos were expected to show little support but actually expressed the strongest support in comparison with other religious groups.

Similarly, the Lebanese Muslim students in all three universities tended to prefer popular armed struggle as the best solution of the Palestine problem (see Table 4.6). The Lebanese Christian students, on the other hand, expressed strong preference for a peaceful solution through the United Nations.

*Religious Affiliation and Nationalistic Orientation*

It was pointed out in an earlier section that the Lebanese do not agree on the question of the national identity of Lebanon. While some conceive of Lebanon as an independent, separate, sovereign, and complete nation, others see the present arrangement as temporary and consider Lebanon as part of a Syrian nation or part of a more comprehensive Arab nation. The religious factor is at the base of such cleavages.

Where do Lebanese students stand on this matter? They were asked in the present study to indicate which of the following political loyalties best describes where they stand: Arab nationalism, Lebanese nationalism, Syrian nationalism, internationalism, or others. As shown in Table 4.7, the Lebanese Sunni and Shi'ite Muslims predominantly considered themselves Arab nationalists. Sixty-three percent of the former and 72 percent of the latter opted for Arab nationalism. Only 10 percent of the Lebanese Sunni students and 4 percent of the Shi'ite students preferred to identify with Lebanese nationalism. About one-third of Lebanese Druzes identified with Lebanese nationalism; 29 percent identified with Arab nationalism and 10 percent with Syrian nationalism.

The Lebanese Christian students largely opted for Lebanese nationalism. The Maronite students showed the strongest such inclination (62 percent), followed by the Catholics (57 percent), and the Orthodox (41 percent).[9] Among the Christian sects, the Orthodox showed the highest diffusion (41 percent opted for Lebanese nationalism, 25 percent for Syrian nationalism, 17 percent for internationalism, and 12 percent for Arab nationalism). An interesting result is that, while 63 percent of the Sunni students identified with Arab nationalism and only 10 percent with Lebanese nationalism, 62 percent of the Maronite students identified with Lebanese nationalism and only 10 percent with Arab nationalism. The stands of these two religious groups are exactly reversed on this issue.

Comparisons between universities also yield some interesting trends. The Sunni Muslims at LU showed greater identification with Arab nationalism (67 percent) and less identification with Lebanese nationalism (3 percent) than those at SJU, where 48 percent identified with Arab nationalism and 16 percent with Lebanese nationalism. In comparison, the Maronite students at LU showed less identification with Lebanese nationalism (52 percent) and more identification with Arab nationalism (19 percent) than those at SJU, where 71 percent identified with Lebanese nationalism and only 6 percent with Arab nationalism.

Other aspects of political behavior are highly influenced by the religious affiliation of students. The whole political perspective must have deep roots in the sectarian make-up of the Lebanese society. The question that needs to be raised at this point is whether religion as such is the determining force in Lebanon. In other words, in order to understand the above relationships we need to examine religious loyalty in the context of the socioeconomic conditions prevailing in the country. Before moving in that direction, it would be helpful to present some data on the relationship between religiosity and some of the above aspects of political behavior.

**Religiosity and Student Politics**

Apart from religious affiliation, degree of religiosity was measured in several ways, and in all instances was found to be related to diverse aspects of student politics. Students were asked to indicate to what degree (high, some, little) they felt that religious faith had been an influence in their lives and the lives of their parents, and whether or not they and their parents believed in God as a being responsible for the creation of the universe and to whom man is accountable after death. An attempt was also made to measure degree of alienation from religion by asking students to indicate to what extent they agreed with such statements as the following:

1. My religion gives me a lot of personal satisfaction.
2. I reject the basic teachings of my religion.
3. Religion is a barrier to advancement in my country.
4. Faith is a very poor substitute for reason. [10]

*Religiosity and Leftist-Rightist Tendencies*

In every instance and regardless of what measure was used, a negative relationship was found to exist between religiosity and leftist tendencies.

**Table 4.5. Religion and support of the Palestinian commandos among Lebanese university students (%)**

| Support for Commandos | Sunnites N=91 | Shi'ites N=51 | Druzes N=21 | Maronites N=197 |
|---|---|---|---|---|
| Strong support | 49 | 53 | 38 | 17 |
| Support | 44 | 45 | 48 | 62 |
| No support | 6 | 2 | 14 | 20 |

**Table 4.6. Religion and preferred solution of Palestine problem among Lebanese university students (%)**

| Preferred Solution | Sunnites N=86 | Shi'ites N=43 | Druzes N=17 | Maronites N=186 |
|---|---|---|---|---|
| Popular armed struggle | 35 | 37 | 41 | 17 |
| Classical war | 17 | 19 | 12 | 11 |
| Peaceful solution | 23 | 12 | 41 | 61 |
| Other solution | 24 | 33 | 6 | 12 |

**Table 4.7. Religion and national loyalty among Lebanese university students (%)**

| Type of National Loyalty | Sunnites N=91 | Shi'ites N=50 | Druzes N=21 | Maronites N=196 |
|---|---|---|---|---|
| Arab nationalism | 63 | 72 | 29 | 10 |
| Lebanese nationalism | 10 | 4 | 33 | 62 |
| Syrian nationalism | 4 | 4 | 10 | 10 |
| Internationalism | 16 | 18 | 19 | 16 |
| Other | 7 | 2 | 10 | 2 |

$X^2 = 279.22$; contingency coefficient = .5734; corrected con. coe. = .6230.

| Orthodox N=103 | Catholics N=74 | Others N=42 | Total N=579 |
|---|---|---|---|
| 27 | 16 | 5 | 27 |
| 49 | 55 | 38 | 52 |
| 24 | 28 | 58 | 21 |

| Orthodox N=96 | Catholics N=68 | Others N=39 | Total N=535 |
|---|---|---|---|
| 20 | 19 | 15 | 23 |
| 10 | 7 | 5 | 12 |
| 51 | 66 | 62 | 49 |
| 19 | 7 | 18 | 17 |

| Orthodox N=102 | Catholics N=72 | Others N=37 | Total N=569 |
|---|---|---|---|
| 12 | 11 | 3 | 24 |
| 41 | 57 | 35 | 41 |
| 25 | 7 | 51 | 14 |
| 17 | 18 | 11 | 16 |
| 5 | 7 | 0 | 4 |

As shown in Table 4.8A, the nonreligious students (i.e., those who said religion had little influence in their personal lives) were much more likely to consider themselves leftist than the religious students (i.e., those who said religion had great influence in their personal lives). Forty-five percent of the nonreligious students considered themselves leftists and 46 percent considered themselves reformists or rightists. By contrast, only 16 percent of the religious students considered themselves leftists and 69 percent considered themselves reformists and rightists. Similarly, those students who indicated that they did not believe in God as a being who is responsible for the creation of the universe and to whom man is accountable after death were more likely to consider themselves leftists than those who said they believed in such existence. While 57 percent of the nonbelievers considered themselves leftists and 37 percent reformists or rightists, only 20 percent of the believers considered themselves leftists and more than two-thirds of them (68 percent) said they were reformists or rightists.

The same trend is revealed in the data on the relationship between alienation from religion and leftist-rightist tendencies. Half the students who were alienated from religion (i.e., those who said they rejected the basic teaching of their religion) considered themselves leftists in comparison to one-fourth (24 percent) of the nonalienated.

At LU, of those who strongly agreed that they rejected the basic teachings of their religion, 79 percent considered themselves leftists, 18 percent reformists, and none rightists. Of those who strongly disagreed, on the other hand, only 17 percent considered themselves leftists. In other words, while only 5 percent of the revolutionary leftists strongly disagreed with the statement, 32 percent of the nonviolent leftists, 41 percent of the reformists, and 55 percent of the rightists did so. Likewise, more than two-thirds of those who strongly rejected the teachings of their religion strongly agreed that what is needed is revolution, not reform, in comparison to only 9 percent of those who strongly accepted the teachings of their religion.

The negative relationship between religiosity and leftist tendencies may be regarded as interactional. Those who are religiously marginal or up-rooted in a society such as Lebanon are more likely to become leftists than those who are well integrated in their religious communities. However, it could be argued that, in becoming exposed to leftist ideas, one may start to question one's religious heritage. For instance, those who become involved in a national liberation movement (as in the case of Palestinians) may gradually be exposed to leftist ideas, and the process of dereligionization may start to accelerate. Similarly, the deprived groups (such as the Shi'ites in Lebanon) who become involved in the struggle to alleviate their economic deprivation may develop class-consciousness and become less and less religious as a result of such involvement. Furthermore, as will be pointed out later, those whom the status quo favors are less likely to break with religion.

*Religiosity and Support for the Palestinian Commandos*

The data show that the less religious students are, the more likely they are to support the commandos and their popular armed struggle. Those students who felt religion had great influence in their lives were less likely to strongly support the commandos than those who felt it had little influence (22 percent versus 40 percent). Similarly, believers showed less strong support for the commandos and less preference for popular armed struggle as a solution to the Palestine problem than nonbelievers. As shown in Table 4.8B, 46 percent of the nonbelievers expressed strong support of the commandos, in comparison to 27 percent of the believers. These trends were revealed in all three universities under study. At SJU, where the overwhelming majority of students were Christian, 17 percent of the believers expressed strong support, in comparison to 44 percent of the nonbelievers. Likewise, 68 percent of the believers as compared to 45 percent of the nonbelievers preferred a peaceful solution to the Palestine problem as an alternative to popular armed struggle. Exactly twice as many nonbelievers as believers at SJU preferred popular armed struggle (30 percent versus 15 percent). At LU, where there has been a roughly balanced composition of religious groups, the differences between the religious and nonreligious groups proved even greater. The nonbelievers were much more likely to show support of the commandos and to prefer popular armed struggle than the believers. To illustrate, 45 percent of the nonbelievers in comparison to 19 percent of the believers said they preferred the commandos' popular armed struggle. On the other hand, 37 percent of the believers—as opposed to only 9 percent of the nonbelievers—preferred a peaceful solution.

Likewise, the findings confirmed the hypothesis that those alienated from religion were more likely to support the commandos and their armed struggle than those who were nonalienated. Thus, exactly twice as many alienated as nonalienated (50 percent versus 25 percent) strongly supported the commandos. Similarly, twice as many nonalienated as alienated (24 percent versus 12 percent) said they did not support the commandos. The data on students at LU show that out of those respondents who strongly rejected the basic teachings of their religion, 66 percent expressed strong support for the commandos, 33 percent preferred Yasser Arafat as a commando leader, 48 percent preferred George Habash, and 19 percent preferred Hawatmeh.[11] In contrast, out of those respondents who strongly accepted the basic teachings of their religion, 23 percent expressed strong

**Table 4.8. Religiosity and student politics (%)**

| Student Politics | Religious Influence | | Belief in God | |
|---|---|---|---|---|
| | Low | High | Yes | No |
| **A. Leftist-rightist tendencies** | | | | |
| Leftists | 45 | 16 | 20 | 57 |
| Reformists and rightists | 46 | 69 | 68 | 37 |
| Others | 9 | 15 | 12 | 6 |
| | [N=245] | [N=191] | [N=447] | [N=90] |
| **B. Support of commandos** | | | | |
| Strong support | 40 | 22 | 27 | 46 |
| Support | 40 | 55 | 53 | 41 |
| No support | 20 | 23 | 20 | 13 |
| | [N=247] | [N=188] | [N=445] | [N=94] |
| **C. Preferred form of government** | | | | |
| Communism | 21 | 2 | 2 | 38 |
| Socialism | 39 | 37 | 37 | 30 |
| Liberalism | 28 | 40 | 43 | 30 |
| Capitalism | 11 | 22 | 19 | 2 |
| | ]N=142][b] | [N=125][b] | [N=282][b] | [N=56][b] |

[a] Only at AUB and LU.
[b] Only at LU and SJU.
[c] Only at LU.

support for the commandos, 83 percent preferred Arafat, 5 percent preferred Habash, and 2 percent preferred Hawatmeh. The data further show that of those who strongly rejected the basic teachings of their religion, 44 percent preferred Fateh, 32 percent preferred the Popular Front for the Liberation of Palestine (PFLP), and 16 percent preferred the Democratic Front for the Liberation of Palestine (DFLP). In contrast, of those who strongly accepted these teachings 85 percent preferred Fateh, 6 percent PFLP, and 2 percent DFLP.

*Religiosity and Preferred Forms of Government*

The relationship between religiosity and the kinds of government students preferred for their country gives further insights into the problem. The

Alienation from Religion

| Alienated | Nonalienated |
| --- | --- |
| 50 | 24 |
| 40 | 58 |
| 11 | 18 |
| [N=130][a] | [N=278][a] |
| | |
| 50 | 25 |
| 38 | 51 |
| 12 | 24 |
| [N=119] | [N=199] |
| | |
| 35 | 2 |
| 49 | 50 |
| 13 | 29 |
| 3 | 19 |
| [N=60][c] | [N=140][c] |

differences between the religious and nonreligious students, between the believers and nonbelievers, or between the nonalienated and the alienated from religion were most significant in their preferences for communism and capitalism. Only about 2 percent of each of the religious, the believers, and the nonalienated preferred communism, in comparison to 21 percent of the nonreligious respondents, 38 percent of the nonbelievers, and 35 percent of the alienated. As for their preference for capitalism, the opposite trend emerged, the religious respondents being much more likely than the nonreligious respondents to prefer this form of government. As shown in Table 4.8C, 11 percent of those who said religion had little influence in their lives in comparison to 22 percent of those who said it had great influence, 2 percent of the nonbelievers in comparison to 19 percent of the believers, and 3 percent of the alienated in comparison to 19 percent of the nonalienated preferred capitalism. The religious respondents were also more inclined to prefer liberal democracy. In short, the religious respondents leaned toward liberal democracy and capitalism, and the nonreligious leaned toward socialism and communism.[12]

### Religion, Religiosity, and Socioeconomic Conditions

Why is it that religion and religiosity have great influence on the political views and behavior of the Lebanese students? Is it religion and religiosity per se that determine how Lebanese university students feel about their government, political change, the Palestinian problem, strikes and protests, other Arab countries, etc.?

The influence of social class on student politics will be dealt with in a later section. Yet a conclusive statement about the relationship between religion and student politics should take account of the general socioeconomic conditions prevailing in the society as a whole. As indicated by S. M. Lipset, "Churches composed of the more well-to-do, or the high-status ethnic strata, are often politically conservative."[13] The Lebanese Christians, regardless of their individual class situation, constitute a privileged group which occupies the more highly valued positions in the social, economic, and political structures of the Lebanese society. Consequently, the Lebanese Christian students of lower class origin may not feel relatively deprived because of their membership in a larger and more privileged group. They have relatively better prospects than their Muslim counterparts for upward social mobility and thus, regardless of their family social class origins, they are more likely to resist any kind of political and socioeconomic changes that might undermine the position of their community. Likewise, Lebanese Muslim students are more likely to be interested in political change, regardless of their family social backgrounds, because they belong to a less privileged segment of the society. The fact that Shi'ite students belong to the most deprived religious community in Lebanon explains why they showed the most radical tendencies.

At this point, the following notes should be made: First, when asked to subjectively rank the socioeconomic status of their families relative to their communities, students could have very well compared their families with those of their own religious groups. Second, as shown earlier, students in Lebanon come mostly from privileged families. Third, the fact that Sunni students were personally more privileged than other Muslim students and maybe as privileged as Christian students could explain why they tended to be less radical than Shi'ites but does not necessarily explain why they were more radical than Christians. This must be explained in the light of their community's position as a whole relative to Christian communities and not in the light of their personal family situations. This is why, as will be shown later, upper-class Muslims expressed more radical views than lower-class Christians. Fourth, the data also throw some light on the nature of the relationship between religiosity and student politics. The Maronite and Sunni students showed the highest degree of religiosity, while the Shi'ites showed the lowest degree, followed by the Orthodox students. More than half the Shi'ites said that religion had little influence in their lives in comparison to 46 percent of the Orthodox, 33 percent of the Druzes, 30 percent of the Sunnites, 29 percent of the Catholics, and finally 27 percent of the Maronites. Likewise the Sunnites and Maronites were the most likely to say they believed in the existence of God (71 percent and 70 percent respectively). These two religious groups, along with Catholics, also showed the least inclination toward alienation from their religions. In short, the Sunnites and Maronites showed the highest level of religiosity. They are also the two religious groups that have the greatest political power in Lebanon. In this sense, religiosity here could be conceived of as a mechanism for the perpetuation and promotion of political power. Fifth, another set of data indicate that students in the upper income bracket were twice as likely as those in the lower income bracket (41 percent versus 21 percent) not to reject the teachings of their religions. The link between religiosity and perpetuation of the status quo may be best supported by the positive relationship between religiosity and degree of agreement with the statement "The secret of happiness is to be contented with our lot and accept whatever befalls us, for it is not easy to change the status quo."[14] The greater the religiosity the greater the agreement with this statement. Thus, the data on students at LU show that 62 percent of those who strongly rejected the basic teachings of their religion said they strongly disagreed with the statement, in contrast to 34 percent of those who strongly accepted the teachings of their religion. Simply, members of privileged communities are more likely to subscribe to religiosity and contentment because such tendencies promote their class interests.

Since religion and religiosity per se are not necessarily determining factors and must be examined in a more general socioeconomic context, it may be suggested that the relationships between these variables and political views and behavior should be different in different societies. The Lebanese Christians have had a unique situation relative to other Arab Christians— they have had more privileged political and socioeconomic positions in the society. In fact, some of them feel that Lebanon is their own creation, designed to protect their interests and preserve their rights as a Christian community in a Muslim world. The West, and particularly France, helped in creating a nation for them, which led to the view of France as "the loving mother" who gave birth to Lebanon. Their strong ties with the West and almost complete openness to all its innovations have promoted a further alienation of Lebanon from other Arab countries. Muslims, on the other hand, were forced to split from their larger community, Syria in particular and the Arab world in general. They had little say in the creation of Lebanon; in fact, it was imposed on them and they were compelled to adjust to it. The system's most effective approach to curb their indignation and make them adjust to their new situation was to assign symbolic positions of power to their traditional leaders.

This was not the case for either the Christians or the Muslims in other Arab countries. Christians in other Arab countries do not occupy the privileged political and socioeconomic positions, and the Muslims have not been uprooted from their total community. In the case of Palestinians, both Christians and Muslims became the target of the Zionist threat which resulted in their uprootedness from their country and condemnation to a life of exile.

Considering these facts, it is expected that the differences in the political views and behavior among the Lebanese religious communities do not necessarily exist among communities in other Arab countries or at least that the differences fall into other patterns. Another set of data collected in 1970 at AUB on the occasion of student elections (reported in Table 4.9) confirms this expectation. As shown, while the Lebanese Muslim respondents at AUB were much more likely to consider themselves leftists than Lebanese Christian respondents (35 percent versus 12 percent), the situation was exactly reversed among the Jordanian-Palestinian Christian and Muslim respondents. The Jordanian-Palestinian Christian students were much more likely to consider themselves leftists than the Jordanian-Palestinian Muslims (69 percent versus 27 percent).

The same trends were exhibited in the areas of political alienation, leftist votes, and degree of admiration for Nasser. The Lebanese Christian students showed less political alienation (45 percent versus 70 percent), less admiration for Nasser (only 13 percent of them considered him as the most important Arab political leader, compared to 68 percent of the Lebanese Muslim students), and more inclination to vote rightist (53 percent versus only 5 percent) than their Muslim counterparts. Again, the opposite trends emerged among the Jordanian-Palestinians. The Christian students of the latter group showed more political alienation (71 percent versus 56 percent), a little more admiration for Nasser, and about the same voting patterns as their Muslim counterparts. In short, by ranking the above religious groups in order of their political radicalism, the following pattern emerged: the most radical were the Jordan-Palestinian Christian students, followed by the Lebanese Muslims, followed by the Jordanian-Palestinian Muslims, and finally, the Lebanese Christians.

The above data are only suggestive, because of the small sample and inability to separate "Jordanian" from "Palestinian." It is hoped that future

**Table 4.9. Religion by nationality and student politics at AUB (%)**

| Student Politics | Lebanese Students | | Jordanian and Palestinian Students | |
|---|---|---|---|---|
| | Christian | Muslim | Christian | Muslim |
| **A. Leftist-rightist tendencies** | | | | |
| Leftists | 12 | 35 | 69 | 27 |
| Reformists and rightists | 67 | 53 | 24 | 53 |
| Others | 21 | 12 | 7 | 20 |
| | [N=59] | [N=34] | [N=16] | [N=26] |
| **B. Political alienation** | | | | |
| Alienated | 45 | 70 | 71 | 56 |
| Nonalienated | 55 | 30 | 29 | 44 |
| | [N=55] | [N=33] | [N=14] | [N=27] |
| **C. Voting in student council elections (1970)** | | | | |
| Progressive | 15 | 52 | 63 | 79 |
| Rightist | 53 | 5 | 0 | 5 |
| Combination | 20 | 18 | 9 | 11 |
| Did not vote | 12 | 25 | 28 | 5 |
| | [N=62] | [N=39] | [N=14] | [N=19] |
| **D. Ranking Nasser** | | | | |
| As most important leader | 13 | 68 | 31 | 26 |
| As second or third most important leader | 13 | 9 | 20 | 30 |
| Not mentioned | 74 | 23 | 49 | 44 |
| | [N=60] | [N=34] | [N=16] | [N=28] |

surveys using the same research design but larger samples will be conducted to further check on the present finding.

## Conclusion

To conclude, religion was found to be a highly important differentiator or predictor of the political views and behavior of Lebanese university students. The Lebanese youth have not been able to liberate themselves from religious loyalties. They demonstrate strong alienation from religion, which does affect their political views, but political cleavages continue to be most significantly determined by their religious affiliations. However, this relationship between religion and student politics has to be examined in a general socioeconomic context. Religion per se is not necessarily the determining factor. It is clearly revealed that the socioeconomic and political status positions of the different religious communities are at the roots of their political orientations and perspectives.

# 5. Family and Student Politics

> We would expect that in non-Western societies also, members of the same family tend to hold similar political views. In fact, the relationships in non-Western, more traditional societies may well be even greater. As a rule family ties are stronger in traditional cultures, and there are not as many other agents of socialization. Only in these rapidly changing societies in which conflict between generations is intense are political orientations not likely to be tied to the family context.[1]

Traditionally a person in the Arab society is seen as a member of a family rather than as an independent individual. Each member shares with the rest of the family their responsibilities and rights, their joys and sorrows, and their pride and shame. The acts of any one member reflect on the family as a whole, and all members are affected by the consequences of such acts.

Furthermore, parents are usually overprotective and restrictive, and children grow up to feel secure only on familiar grounds. They avoid taking risks and trying new ways of doing things, for independence of mind, critical dissent, and adventure beyond the recognized limits are constantly and systematically discouraged by parents and other older members of the family.

While there is lack of individuality among Arabs, there is a great deal of individualism, selfishness, self-centeredness, and self-assertion. By *individuality* I mean to refer to a person's total uniqueness, peculiarity, and independence of mind. *Individualism*, on the other hand, is used here to refer to egoism, preoccupation with one's personal interests and concerns, and inclination to stress the "I" in opposition to the "we." In fact, the two phenomena are highly related. Individualism could be seen as a reaction to the constant attempts of the family and other institutions to crush individuality. In the face of all the attempts to transform persons into members and to suppress their individuality and independence, they develop the need to assert their egoes and proclaim themselves on all occasions. The "I," instead of being crushed, dominates the "we."

This chapter focuses on two basic aspects of the relationship between family life and student politics. First, it will attempt to show to what extent students are integrated into their families and how such an integration in the family influences student politics. Second, an attempt will be made to assess the importance of family as an agent of political socialization and to determine what variables influence this process.

## Integration into the Family and Student Politics

If family is the most important agency of socialization in traditional and even post-traditional societies, one would expect that, the greater the integration into family life, the greater the resistance to social and political transformation would be. The family in such societies promotes traditional value orientations, pressures its offspring to concern themselves with family problems and avoid politics, and provides the intimate personal relations that satisfy the economic and social psychological needs of its members and therefore serves as a shock absorber against all kinds of crises. In their studies of Latin American students, Arthur Liebman and his colleagues pointed out that the "value orientations associated with the family, such as ascription, particularism, affectivity, and diffuseness, are thought to be somewhat incompatible with leftist ideologies which emphasize achievement, universalism, and egalitarianism."[2] Their data indicated that conservative students were more likely to live with their parents or relatives and to be among the family traditionalists rather than among the family nontraditionalists. Thus, in Mexico and Colombia, the family traditionalists were twice as likely as the nontraditionalists to be rightists. In regard to traditionalism, the findings demonstrate that those "students who believed in marital faithfulness and opposed having women work outside the home . . . were also likely to evaluate Castro negatively and to be procapitalist . . . ; the data revealed that a conservative orientation in one sphere (i.e., family or politics) was supportive of a conservative orientation in the other."[3]

The study by Flacks on the American "liberated generation" or leftist activists demonstrated that these activists and their parents "tend to place greater stress on involvement in intellectual and aesthetic pursuits, humanitarian concerns, opportunity for self-expression, and tend to deemphasize or positively disvalue personal achievement, conventional morality and conventional religiosity."[4]

In the present study, degree of integration into the family was measured in two ways.

First, students were asked to indicate which of the following best described their current relations with their parents:

1. My parents and I are very close.
2. My parents and I are on good terms.
3. My parents and I are not close.
4. My parents and I do not get along.
5. Other (please specify).

Second, feelings of alienation from family were measured by asking students to indicate the extent to which they agreed, i.e., whether they strongly agreed, agreed, disagreed, or strongly disagreed, with each of the following statements:

1. I derive little satisfaction from my relationships with members of my family.
2. For reasons of my own, I do not feel that my family is of great value to me.
3. I would do anything for the sake of my family.
4. Doing my duties to my family gives me a great feeling of pleasure.

Using the above measures of integration into the family, an attempt will be made in the following sections to explore the nature of the relationship between such integration and student politics. Specifically, an attempt will be made to examine the influence of closeness to parents and alienation from family on several aspects of student political behavior and views: leftist-rightist orientations, support for the Palestinian resistance movement, social and political liberalism, and religiosity.

*Alienation from Family, Closeness to Parents, and Leftist-Rightist Orientation*

The basic hypothesis to be checked here is that the more students are alienated from family the more they show leftist tendencies. Yet it is recognized here that alienation may be an effect as well as a cause of political radicalization.

The extent to which alienation from family is positively related to leftist tendencies is shown in Table 5.1. The data presented in this table show a highly significant positive relationship no matter what leftist tendency is considered. The alienated students were more than three times as likely as the nonalienated students to consider themselves revolutionary leftists (69 percent of the alienated in opposition to 20 percent of the nonalienated). To put it the other way around, the nonalienated respondents were four times as likely as the alienated to consider themselves reformists and rightists.

**Table 5.1. Relationship between alienation from family and leftist-rightist orientations (% at LU)**

| | Alienation from Family | |
| --- | --- | --- |
| | Nonalienated | Alienated |
| **A. Leftist-rightist tendencies** | | |
| Leftists | 20 | 69 |
| Nonviolent leftists | 13 | 11 |
| Reformists and rightists | 55 | 14 |
| Others | 12 | 6 |
| | [N=178] (83%) | [N=36] (17%) |
| **B. Preferred form of government** | | |
| Communism | 5 | 42 |
| Socialist democracy | 50 | 44 |
| Liberal democracy | 26 | 8 |
| Capitalism | 15 | 3 |
| Others | 3 | 3 |
| | [N=175] (83%) | [N=36] (17%) |

$X^2 = 42.97$; contingency coefficient = .4113; corrected con. coe. = .5466.

| | Nonalienated | Alienated |
| --- | --- | --- |
| **C. Revolution, not reform** | | |
| Agree | 44 | 76 |
| Disagree | 56 | 24 |
| | [N=177] (83%) | [N=37] (17%) |
| **D. Abolishing private property** | | |
| Agree | 41 | 84 |
| Disagree | 59 | 16 |
| | [N=173] (82%) | [N=37] (18%) |

Total

_____

28
13
48
10
[N=214] (100%)


11
49
23
13
 3
[N=211] (100%)



50
50
[N=214] (100%)


49
51
[N=210] (100%)

_____

Table 5.1B reports the data (LU) showing a relationship between alienation from family and preferred form of government. Eighty-six percent of
the alienated, as compared to 55 percent of the nonalienated, preferred
communism and socialist democracy. The data also show that those alienated from the family were more than eight times as likely as the nonalienated to prefer communism. The latter group, on the other hand, were five
times as likely as the former to prefer capitalism.

The data presented in Table 5.1C show that the alienated at LU were
much more likely than the nonalienated (76 percent versus 44 percent) to
agree with the statement "What is needed is revolution, not reform."

Alienation from family is also positively related to approval of abolishing
private property and introducing complete socialism. Again, while the
great majority of those alienated from family (84 percent) approved, the
majority of the nonalienated (59 percent) disapproved.

*Alienation from Family and Attitude toward the Palestinian Resistance Movement*

How does alienation from family influence students' support for the Palestinian commandos, the kind of solution to Palestine problems they advocate, and what commando organization or leadership they prefer?

As shown in Table 5.2, the alienated were more likely than the nonalienated to express strong support for the commandos (51 percent versus 27
percent) and to advocate popular armed struggle as the best solution to
Palestine problem (45 percent versus 23 percent). Less than one-third (30
percent) preferred a peaceful solution and one-fourth (25 percent) proposed other solutions. The nonalienated, on the other hand, tended mostly
to prefer a peaceful solution (46 percent), but 23 percent preferred popular
armed struggle, and 31 percent preferred classical war or some kind of a
combination of both popular armed struggle and classical war.

Which commando organization was preferred by respondents and how
was that influenced by their alienation from family? As shown in Table
5.2C, the alienated showed greater support for PFLP than the nonalienated
(31 percent versus 16 percent). In comparison, the nonalienated showed
greater support for Fateh than the alienated (74 percent versus 44 percent).
In the case of commando leaderships, the alienated clearly preferred
Habash to Arafat. About half the alienated (48 percent) preferred Habash
and one-third preferred Arafat. In contrast, three quarters of the nonalienated preferred Arafat and only 18 percent preferred Habash.

*Alienation from Family and Social and Political Liberalism*

If family is the basic source of conventional values, one would expect a
positive relationship between alienation from family and liberalism. Here,

liberalism is operationally defined in terms of upholding freedom of expression for all political groups and for atheists, tolerating premarital sexual intercourse for girls, and calling for separation of religion from the state.

The data on students at LU (see Table 5.3) indicate that the alienated were much more likely (76 percent versus 23 percent) to strongly agree with the statement that every political movement should have the right to freely express itself regardless of its opinions and goals.

Again, those who were alienated from family were much more likely than the nonalienated to strongly agree with the freedom of atheists to express their opinions publicly against religions and prophets (65 percent versus 26 percent).

In the case of those aspects of liberalism that are more purely social, the data also show a positive relationship between alienation from family and tolerance of premarital sexual intercourse for girls. The majority of the alienated (62 percent) agreed, and the majority of the nonalienated (65 percent) disagreed.

The same trend is revealed by the data on the relationship between alienation from family and calling for separation of religion from the state (Table 5.3D). The data indicate a significant difference between the two groups: 95 percent of the alienated strongly agreed with separation of religion from the state, while only 46 percent of the nonalienated expressed such a degree of agreement.

In short, the data in all four instances show a positive relationship between alienation from family and political and social liberalism.

*Alienation from Family and Religiosity*

Loyalty to the family and loyalty to religion do not represent two stages in the development toward national or social class loyalty. On the contrary, these two traditional loyalties are strongly complementary, and both undermine the development of national and social class consciousness. This is evidenced by a variety of data in the present research. One instance of the complementarity of family and religious loyalty is shown in Table 5.4. The great majority of those alienated from family (86 percent) said that religion had little influence in their personal lives. In sharp contrast, less than one-fourth of the nonalienated (23 percent) said religion had little influence in their personal lives. The nonalienated were almost six times as likely as the alienated to say that religion had great influence in their personal lives.

The relationship between loyalty to family and loyalty to religion is shown to be even more significant when religiosity is measured in terms of whether or not students believed in the existence of God. The alienated

**Table 5.2. Relationship between alienation from family and support for the Palestinian resistance movement (%)**

| | Alienation from Family | |
| | Nonalienated | Alienated |
|---|---|---|
| **A. Support for commandos** | | |
| Strong support | 27 | 51 |
| Support | 53 | 35 |
| No support | 20 | 13 |
| | [N=354] (77%) | [N=104] (23%) |
| | | |
| **B. Preferred solution** | | |
| Popular armed struggle | 23 | 45 |
| Peaceful solution | 46 | 30 |
| Other solutions | 31 | 25 |
| | [N=344] (77%) | [N=101] (23%) |
| | | |
| **C. Preferred commando organization**[a] | | |
| Fateh | 74 | 44 |
| PFLP | 16 | 31 |
| Others | 10 | 26 |
| | [N=135] (81%) | [N=32] (19%) |
| | | |
| **D. Preferred commando leader**[a] | | |
| Arafat | 75 | 33 |
| Habash | 18 | 48 |
| Others | 8 | 19 |
| | [N=108] (80%) | [N=27] (20%) |

[a] Only at LU.

Total

_____

33
49
18
[N=458](100%)


28
42
30
[N=445] (100%)


68
19
13
[N=167] (100%)


67
24
 9
[N=135] (100%)

_____

**Table 5.3. Relationship between alienation from family and social and political liberalism (% at LU)**

| | Alienation from family |
| --- | --- |
| | Nonalienated |
| **A. Freedom of expression for all political groups** | |
| Strongly agree | 23 |
| Agree | 42 |
| Disagree | 35 |
| | [N=179] (83%) |
| **B. Freedom of expression for atheists** | |
| Strongly agree | 26 |
| Agree | 42 |
| Disagree | 33 |
| | [N=178] (83%) |
| **C. Premarital sexual intercourse for girls** | |
| Agree | 35 |
| Disagree | 34 |
| Strongly disagree | 31 |
| | [N=177] (83%) |
| **D. Separation of religion from the state** | |
| Strongly agree | 46 |
| Agree | 36 |
| Disagree | 18 |
| | [N=175] (83%) |

were fifteen times as likely as the nonalienated to say "no" (46 percent versus 3 percent). As shown, while three-quarters of the nonalienated said they believed in the existence of God, only a little more than one-fifth of the alienated (22 percent) said so.

This section has shown that integration into the family influences several aspects of students' political and social views and orientations. The data demonstrated a negative relationship between integration into the family and leftist orientations, support for the Palestinian resistance movement and its popular armed struggle as the best solution to the Palestine problem, and social and political liberalism. A highly significant positive rela-

| Alienated | Total |
| --- | --- |
| 76 | 32 |
| 22 | 39 |
| 3 | 29 |
| [N=37] (17%) | [N=216] (100%) |
| | |
| 65 | 33 |
| 22 | 38 |
| 13 | 30 |
| [N=37] (17%) | [N=215] (100%) |
| | |
| 62 | 40 |
| 27 | 33 |
| 11 | 27 |
| [N=37] (17%) | [N=214] (100%) |
| | |
| 95 | 54 |
| 0 | 30 |
| 5 | 16 |
| [N=37] (17%) | [N=212] (100%) |

tionship was found to exist between integration into the family and religiosity.

**Family and Political Socialization**

Several empirical investigations in Western societies show that the family
is highly important as an agency of political socialization. A review of these
investigations, such as that of Hyman, would show that there is a very
high intergenerational agreement in party identification, political attitudes,
and voting behavior.[5] For instance, in a survey taken in the United States,

**Table 5.4. Relationship between alienation from family and religiosity (% at LU)**

| | Alienation from family | |
| | Nonalienated | Alienated |
| --- | --- | --- |
| **A. Religious influence** | | |
| Little | 23 | 86 |
| Some | 42 | 8 |
| High | 34 | 6 |
| | [N=179] (83%) | [N=36] (17%) |

$X^2$ = 52.47; contingency coefficient = .4429; corrected con. coe. = .6065

| | | |
| --- | --- | --- |
| **B. Belief in God** | | |
| No | 3 | 46 |
| Uncertain | 22 | 32 |
| Yes | 75 | 22 |
| | [N=181] (83%) | [N=37] (17%) |

$X^2$ = 67.7937, contingency coefficient = .4870; corrected con. coe. = .7105

80 percent of the student respondents whose mother and father had the same party preference shared that preference.[6]

The study by Liebman, Walker, and Glazer on Latin American university students points out that the high correlation between party preferences of fathers and offspring suggests "that party choice is to an important degree an expression of family tradition . . . ; a majority of students, regardless of their ideology, support their father's party or one of similar ideological orientation. This is perhaps not surprising, but it is worth emphasizing to counteract the general belief in a sharp generational break between Latin American students and their parents. The persistence of the effect of family political socialization is well supported."[7] Similarly, the research findings of Flacks, Keniston, and others confirm the hypothesis of political consistency between parents and their children rather than the hypothesis of a generation gap.

The basic concern here is the extent to which students in Lebanon follow the political directions of their parents. It is this study's expectation that there is less intergenerational agreement on political matters in the Arab society than in Western societies. Rapid social change, the educational generation gap (i.e., the difference in levels of education of parents and their children), prevailing norms against parents' discussing politics with

Total

_____

34
37
29
[N=215] (100%)


11
23
66
[N=218] (100%)

_____


their children, lack of parents' (especially mothers') political involvement and concern, absence of a two-party system, and other factors will be explored in connection with this expected low intergeneration agreement.

The present study aims at checking the following basic hypotheses:

1. The degree of congruence between the political attitudes of individuals and those of their parents in the Arab society is lower than in Western societies.

2. The family in Arab countries is not as influential as the family in Western societies as an agency of political socialization because of differences in the rapidity of social change and the prevalence of an educational generation gap.

3. Rapid social change is likely to undermine family political socialization.

4. The greater the educational generation gap, the less likely that individuals will tend to identify politically with their parents.

These four hypotheses are directly related. Rapid social change in traditional societies is likely to result in a great educational gap between parents and offspring. In turn this educational gap renders parents less influential in transmitting their political ideas and attitudes to their offspring.

Since the educational gap between generations is much wider in Arab society than in Western societies, it is expected, in spite of strong family ties, that Arab respondents are more likely to be politically independent from their parents than Western respondents. Furthermore, because this chapter aims at showing the "educational generation gap" as an important intervening variable undermining the family political socialization process, comparisons will be made between students from three Arab societies (other than Lebanon) that are similar in every relevant respect except rapid social change. The three societies compared are Jordan, Bahrain, and Kuwait. All are traditional and essentially tribal in social structure. However, social change has proceeded at a much more rapid pace in Kuwait than in the others during the last decade and a half. Jordan and Bahrain began to experience social change earlier but at a comparatively slower pace. Because Kuwait has been experiencing such a sudden and rapid social change, the educational generation gap should be wider than in Jordan and Bahrain. Thus, it is predicted that intergenerational agreement on political matters and degree of political identification of children with their parents will be lower in Kuwait than in Jordan and Bahrain, and lower in Jordan and Bahrain than in Western countries.

To check on these expectations, three simple random samples of Jordanian, Bahraini, and Kuwaiti students at AUB were chosen and interviewed in the fall of 1969 and the fall of 1970. There were about 450 Jordanian students at AUB at that time. The great majority of their parents had secondary and university levels of education and belonged to the upper and upper-middle classes. A random sample representing these students was chosen by the Computer Center at AUB, resulting in a group of 40 respondents. As for Kuwaiti students, only about 75 such students were enrolled at AUB at that time. The majority of their parents had some secondary education or less. All were asked to participate in the survey, and the number of respondents came to 50. There were 54 Bahraini students at AUB and all were invited to participate, but only 28 responded. The majority (61 percent) of the parents of Bahraini students had university education.

The questionnaire and research design allowed for the testing of the following specific hypotheses:

1. Intergenerational agreement on political matters among both Jordanian and Bahraini students is lower than among similar respondents in Western societies. Among Arab respondents, the Lebanese will be the closest to the Western pattern.

2. Intergenerational agreement on political matters among Kuwaiti students is low in comparison to Jordanian, Bahraini, Lebanese, and Western societies.

3. Contrary to findings in Western societies, Lebanese, Jordanian, Bah-

raini, and Kuwaiti students are more likely to agree with their fathers than with their mothers.

4. Contrary to findings in Western societies, women in Arab societies are more likely to agree with their fathers than with their mothers.

5. Men in all samples are more independent from their parents than women.

6. The Bahraini and Jordanian students will show similar rates of intergenerational agreement because of similarities in rate of social change and educational generation gap in their two societies.

7. Upper-class students are more likely to be independent from their parents than middle-class students.

8. Jordanian, Bahraini, and Kuwaiti parents are more likely to agree with one another than parents in Western societies.

9. The higher the education of parents, the higher the intergenerational agreement.

The interview schedule used in this survey included items used to measure the political orientations of students as well as the following specific questions:

1. Would you rather discuss politics with your father, your mother, both parents, or neither?
2. Which one of your parents do you politically identify yourself with: your mother, father, both, or neither?
3. Which one of the following statements would you choose regarding your general attitude toward your government's politics?
   a. I support the majority of them.
   b. I support some, but not all.
   c. I support few of them, if any at all.
   d. I am indifferent to its policies.

   Which one of the above four would your father choose?
   Which one of the above four would your mother choose?

The above research design and items allow for comparisons to be made between groups of respondents occupying different positions on a continuum representing different degrees of educational generation gap.

*Findings and Explanations*

Because the family tends to monopolize the socialization of children in their early years, parents must be very effective in determining their attitudes, values, and behavior. As was pointed out in an earlier part of this chapter, empirical investigations in Western societies have provided ample evidence to support this contention. To illustrate, a study conducted in 1965 by the Survey Research Center of the University of Michigan on a national sample of American high school seniors shows that when both parents had the same party preference, 76 percent of these students agreed with them. Among those students whose parents were both Republican, 68 percent also preferred that party. Among those students whose parents were both Democratic, 85 percent identified with that party. In cases in which parents differed in their party preference, the father was by no means the decisive force in establishing a child's party identification. The results show that 39 percent of the students agreed with the mother, 37 percent with the father, and 24 percent with neither. When the mother was a Democrat and the father a Republican, 44 percent of students identified with the Democratic Party, 35 percent with the Republican Party, and 21 percent tended to be independent. When the mother was a Republican and the father a Democrat, 29 percent of the students identified with the Democratic Party, 33 percent with the Republican, and 38 percent tended to be independent.[8]

Similar studies conducted in the French, Swedish, and Norwegian societies report similar results, i.e., high intergenerational agreement on political party preferences. The frequency of agreement was found to be highest in the United States, followed by Sweden and Norway, then France.

These findings provide a sufficient basis to justify the conclusion by Richard E. Dawson and Kenneth Prewitt that "the family . . . tends to be a conserving rather than an initiating force. More than most other structures, it attempts to preserve and perpetuate traditional practices and modes of thought."[9]

In the light of the above findings, this study will now compare the data on the Jordanian, Bahraini, and Kuwaiti students. (Comparisons with Lebanese student respondents at LU and SJU will also be made whenever possible.)

The data presented in Tables 5.5 and 5.6 show that the Jordanian and Bahraini respondents are less likely to identify with their parents than Western respondents but more so than the Kuwaitis. This is reflected in the responses to the question of whether they politically identify with mother, father, both parents, or neither. Table 5.5 shows that political identification is not in accordance with Dawson and Prewitt's expectation that the tendency to hold similar political views may be even greater in traditional than in Western societies. As shown here, 29 percent of the Jordanian men reported that they identified politically with their fathers, 12 percent with their mothers, 12 percent with both parents, and 47 percent with neither. So far as Jordanian women are concerned, 24 percent reported that they

**Table 5.5. Students' political identification with parents (%)**

| Nationality | Sex | Political Identification with: | | | |
| --- | --- | --- | --- | --- | --- |
| | | Father | Mother | Both | Neither |
| **Jordanian students** | **Male** N=22 | 29 | 12 | 12 | 47 |
| | **Female** N=18 | 24 | 33 | 5 | 38 |
| **Bahraini students** | **Male** N=15 | 40 | 7 | 7 | 46 |
| | **Female** N=13 | 20 | 13.5 | 13.5 | 53 |
| **Kuwaiti students** | **Male** N=25 | 32 | 0 | 0 | 68 |
| | **Female** N=23 | 43 | 0 | 0 | 57 |

identified politically with their fathers, 33 percent with their mothers, 5 percent with both, and 38 percent with neither.

Table 5.5 shows also that the Bahraini men tended either to identify with their fathers or to deviate from both parents (40 percent identified with father and 46 percent deviated). The Bahraini women showed an even higher tendency to deviate than the Bahraini men.

The Bahraini men were more likely to identify with their fathers than the Jordanian men and the Bahraini women showed the highest deviations (53 percent) among the Jordanian and Bahraini respondents.

As expected, the Kuwaiti students showed the least tendency to identify politically with their parents. As shown, 32 percent of the men identified with their fathers and 68 percent deviated. The Kuwaiti women were more likely than the men to identify with the father; 43 percent identified with their fathers, and 57 percent deviated.

The data in Table 5.5 confirm the first three specific hypotheses, and the data on the Bahraini and Kuwaiti students confirm hypothesis 4 (i.e., women were found to agree with their fathers more than their mothers). But the data on the Jordanian students contradict this hypothesis because the women showed some tendency to identify with their mothers more than with their fathers.

Similarly, the data on the Jordanian and Kuwaiti students confirm hypothesis 5 (i.e., men were more likely to deviate than women), while the data on the Bahraini students fail to confirm it because the women in this sample showed more tendency to deviate than the men.

Table 5.6 shows the results based on a more specific question connected with definite political positions (i.e., being leftist, liberal, rightist, indifferent, etc.) which best described the respondents and their parents. Fourteen percent of the Jordanian men held the same political positions as their fathers, 5 percent as their mothers, 36 percent as both, and 45 percent as neither. Sixteen percent of the Jordanian women held the same political positions as their fathers, 16 percent as their mothers, 32 percent as both, and 36 percent deviated. The data on the Bahraini students is quite similar, except that none of the Bahraini women said she held the same political position as her mother. As stated by some of the women respondents, mothers did not show interest in politics. Thus, the women tended to hold the same political positions as their fathers (33 percent) or to deviate (67 percent).

In the case of Lebanese students, 59 percent at LU deviated and 34 percent had political positions identical with those of both their parents. At SJU, 51 percent deviated and 41 percent had political positions identical with those of both their parents.

Again, the Kuwaiti students showed the highest tendency to deviate: 72 percent of the men and 60 percent of the women did so. The percentages of deviation among Arab students (ranging between 36 percent and 72 percent) were found to be significantly higher than the percentage of deviation in the American sample, which was about 24 percent. The difference between Western and Arab respondents is not necessarily a true difference. Rather, it may be an artifact of differences in procedure of measurement.

The data based on the other specific questions connected with students' political loyalties, preferred forms of government, and support of their governments' policies show similar trends. To illustrate, Table 5.7 on intergenerational agreement on preferred forms of government shows similar patterns of tendencies to deviate from the political positions of parents. However, the Lebanese students in both LU and SJU tend to agree with parents on preferred form of government (64 percent at LU and 62 percent at SJU). The Lebanese students also show high intergenerational agreement on the question of nationalistic loyalties, i.e., whether they think of themselves as Arab nationalists, Lebanese nationalists, Syrian nationalists, or internationalists (67 percent at LU and 69 percent at SJU).

It might also be of some interest at this stage to refer to the significance of parents' agreement on political matters as a factor contributing to the influence of the family as an agency of political socialization. The majority of the Jordanian parents in our sample (65 percent) held the same political

**Table 5.6. Political positions of students relative to those of their parents (%)**

| Nationality | Sex | Political Position Identical to That of: | | | |
| | | Father | Mother | Both | Neither |
| --- | --- | --- | --- | --- | --- |
| **Jordanian students** | **Male** N=22 | 14 | 5 | 36 | 45 |
| | **Female** N=18 | 16 | 16 | 32 | 36 |
| **Bahraini students** | **Male** N=15 | 13 | 7 | 33 | 47 |
| | **Female** N=13 | 33 | 0 | 0 | 67 |
| **Kuwaiti students** | **Male** N=25 | 28 | 0 | 0 | 72 |
| | **Female** N=23 | 40 | 0 | 0 | 60 |
| **Lebanese students** **LU** N=190 | | 5 | 2 | 34 | 59 |
| **SJU** N=225 | | 6 | 2 | 41 | 51 |

positions. When both Jordanian parents held the same position, 63 percent of their children were found to agree with them. When parents differed, 39 percent agreed with their fathers and 15 percent with their mothers. Here, further comparisons between the American and Jordanian respondents could be made. In both sets of data, men tended to identify with their fathers and women with their mothers (though American women did so more than Jordanian women). Similarly, in both sets of data, men were more likely to deviate than women. On the whole, though, the Jordanian fathers had more influence than the Jordanian mothers. This was not the case among American respondents. As pointed out earlier, when one parent was a Republican and the other a Democrat, the American mother exerted greater influence on party loyalties of their offspring than the father.[10]

**Table 5.7. Bahraini and Lebanese students' preference of form of government relative to that of their parents (%)**

Prefer the Same Form of Government as:

| | Father | Mother | Both | Neither |
|---|---|---|---|---|
| **Bahraini** | | | | |
| **Male** | 27 | 0 | 33 | 40 |
| N=15 | | | | |
| **Female** | 16 | 0 | 46 | 38 |
| N=13 | | | | |
| | | | | |
| **Lebanese** | | | | |
| **LU** | 3 | 3 | 64 | 30 |
| N=181 | | | | |
| **SJU** | 5 | 3 | 62 | 30 |
| N=255 | | | | |

Another striking result is the complete absence of the Kuwaiti mother as a transmitter of political loyalties. The few Kuwaiti students who held the same political positions as their parents stated that they identified only with the father. Even among the women, none identified with the mother. Some Jordanian respondents commented on the margins of their questionnaires that their mothers agreed with whatever their fathers said. Others commented that their mothers were indifferent to politics. Still others commented that they were not sure of what political views their mothers held. Kuwaiti students commented that their mothers were completely passive politically.

This does not mean that the respondents were not close to their mothers. For instance, when Kuwaiti students were asked about the extent of their closeness to their parents, 40 percent said they were equally close to both parents, 37 percent said they were closer to their mothers, 14 percent to their fathers, and 9 percent to neither. What is interesting about these findings is that, even among those who said they were closer to their mothers, none showed any tendency to identify politically with them. Nevertheless, degree of closeness to parents must have some influence on deviation (see Table 5.8). Of those who said they were closer to their mothers, 27 percent held the same political positions as their fathers, and 73 percent deviated. In comparison, 43 percent of those who said they were closer to their fathers held the same political positions as the fathers did,

**Table 5.8. Relationship of closeness to parents to political positions of Kuwaiti students relative to those of their parents (%)**

| Closeness to Parents | Political Position Same as That of: | | |
| --- | --- | --- | --- |
| | Father | Mother | Neither |
| Closer to mother<br>N=18 | 27 | 0 | 73 |
| Equally close to both<br>N=19 | 32 | 0 | 68 |
| Closer to father<br>N=7 | 43 | 0 | 57 |
| Close to neither<br>N=4 | 0 | 0 | 100 |

and 57 percent deviated. Of those who said they were equally close to both parents, 32 percent held the same political positions as their fathers, and 68 percent deviated. Finally, all those who said they were close to neither parent deviated.

In short, the results show that intergenerational agreement on political matters is much lower among Kuwaiti students than among Bahraini, Lebanese, Jordanian, and American students. The general Kuwaiti trend is independence from parents rather than political identification. Furthermore, though there is an absence of political identification with the mother, there is not a corresponding predominance of identification with the father. The new generation of Kuwaiti students does not seem to be politically socialized in the family in spite of its strong ties and the relative lack of other agents of socialization.

Several questions need to be raised at this point: How do we explain the above findings? Why is it that Jordanian and Bahraini respondents are less likely to identify politically with their parents than Western respondents? Why is it that the majority of Kuwaiti students in our sample are politically independent from their parents? The importance of answering these questions becomes clear when we realize that family ties constitute the basic social structure and pattern of social organization in Jordan, Bahrain, Lebanon, and Kuwait.

Though the stress in explaining the above findings will be on the existing educational generation gap, a number of other variables and conditions will be identified as possible determinant forces.

During the last decade and a half the socioeconomic conditions in Kuwait have been changing very rapidly. The whole way of life in Kuwait has had to adapt to numerous challenges. The new generation of Kuwaitis, like the "people of the cave" in the Arab legend, awakened after centuries of deep sleep and suddenly found themselves face to face with all the technical and socioeconomic complexities of the twentieth century. All of a sudden, the old generation became something out of the distant past. A wide and deep gap separated the two generations. This gap is reflected very clearly in the differences in the levels of education of parents and their offspring. University education is now available to both sexes. In the case of our Kuwaiti respondents, the data showed that the great majority (88 percent) of their parents had some secondary education or less. This educational gap must have undermined the role of parents as agents of political socialization and thus prevented the offspring from identifying with them. The data presented in Table 5.9 support such a conclusion. As shown, the majority (67 percent) of the Kuwaiti students whose fathers had secondary education or higher tended to identify with them. Quite the opposite, the majority (73 percent) of the Kuwaiti students whose fathers had some secondary education or less tended to disagree with them. In other words, 33 percent of the former group in comparison to 73 percent of the latter tended to deviate from the political positions of their parents. The educational generation gap is narrower among the Bahraini, Lebanese, and Jordanian respondents than among the Kuwaitis. For instance, 39 percent of the parents of the Bahraini students had some university education. The data presented in Table 5.10 show that there is a negative relationship between educational gap and political identification with parents. Those whose parents have university education are less likely to deviate than those whose parents have secondary education or less.

Thus, the greater the educational generation gap, the lower the intergenerational agreement on political matters. This generalization might tell us why the Kuwaiti respondents who identified themselves as middle class tended to be more politically independent from their parents than those who identified themselves as upper class. The educational generation gap is greater among the middle and lower classes in Kuwait.

Finally, there are three other factors thought to undermine family political socialization among Arab students:

1. There is a low rate of membership in political parties relative to Western societies. Arab parents are much less likely to belong to political parties than their counterparts in the West. In all three universities in Lebanon, only 9 percent of the students said they belonged to political parties, and

**Table 5.9. Relationship between father's level of education and the political identification of Kuwaiti students (%)**

| Father's Level of Education | Political Identification with: | | |
| | Father | Mother | Neither |
| --- | --- | --- | --- |
| Secondary education or higher N=6 | 67 | 0 | 33 |
| Some secondary education or less N=44 | 27 | 0 | 73 |

**Table 5.10. Relationship between father's level of education and the political identification of Bahraini students (%)**

| Father's Level of Education | Political Identification with: | | | |
| | Father | Mother | Both | Neither |
| --- | --- | --- | --- | --- |
| University education N=17 | 36 | 10 | 18 | 36 |
| Secondary education or less N=11 | 18 | 5 | 12 | 65 |

only 3 percent said their fathers belonged to political parties. Furthermore, none of the Arab societies under study has a two-party system.

2. The prevailing norms in the Arab society discourage discussing politics with children. In response to the question as to whether they would discuss politics with their fathers, mothers, both parents, or neither, the great majority of Kuwaiti men (88 percent) and all the women said they would rather discuss politics with neither. This was not the case among the Jordanian and Bahraini respondents. Only 18 percent of the Jordanian men and 15 percent of the Jordanian women said they would rather discuss politics with neither parent. None, even among the women, preferred discussing politics with the mother. Similar responses were given by the Bahraini students, though they showed more tendency to discuss politics

with the father than with both parents. Similarly, the Lebanese students preferred to discuss politics with their fathers, but a significant segment (31 percent at LU and 28 percent at SJU) preferred not to discuss politics with their parents.

3. The mother plays a very passive political role in the Arab society. This should be an important factor undermining family political socialization.

## Conclusion

Despite the existence of several conditions in the Arab society that undermine the family as an agency of political socialization, Arab students in Lebanon were found to be highly integrated into their families. Such an integration influences a wide range of political views and behavior, including leftist-rightist orientations, attitudes towards the Palestinian resistance movement, and social and political liberalism. The family ties constitute the most basic network of social relations as well as the most basic source of value orientations.

# 6. Social Class and Student Politics

University students are privileged groups and aspire to elitist positions in society. Furthermore, higher education has been instrumental in the perpetuation of privileged positions and in vertical social mobility. Yet, as students, they "sit at the feet of the great masters of knowledge" and suffer from prolonged apprenticeship and subjection to predestined programs which they cannot influence except superficially.

The question that is of most relevance in the present context is the extent to which differences in social class backgrounds of students influence their political behavior and views. Specifically, where do Lebanese students from deprived classes stand relative to students from more privileged families? How does social class background influence leftist-rightist orientations, political activism, support for commandos, and nationalistic loyalties? What kind of relationships, if any, do students establish with the deprived classes? What are some of the social conditions that undermine social class consciousness?

## Theoretical Background

Class is the most central concept in the Marxist theory of change, for it is the proletariat that is historically determined to carry out the task of "the dissolution of the existing social order," and in carrying out this task "it does no more than disclose the secret of its own existence."[1] The proletariat, according to Marx, will be forced historically to take this course of action "in conformity with its own nature."[2] It is forced to take this course of action, not because of a metaphysical will, but because of "the reality of an inhuman situation . . . it is forced by the contradiction between its humanity and its situation, which is an open, clear and absolute negation of its humanity. Within the framework of alienation, therefore, the property owners are the conservative and the proletarians the destructive party. . . . It is for these reasons that the proletariat can and must emancipate itself.

But it can only emancipate itself by destroying its own conditions of existence. It can only destroy its own conditions of existence by destroying all the inhuman conditions of existence of present-day society."[3]

For Marx, the process of emancipation requires that the working class become conscious of its historic mission and role. It has to change from a "class-in-itself" to a "class-for-itself." In the first case, the working-class members do not have the proper understanding of their situation and long-term interests. In order for them to be transformed into a class-for-itself, they have to become aware of their common interests, unite, communicate, and organize themselves into a political party. Insofar as they do not develop social class consciousness and put themselves in hostile opposition to their exploiters, and as long as "the identity of their interests begets no community, no national bond and no political organization among them, they do not form a class."[4] Class struggle, thus, becomes also a political struggle for liberation.

The process of social class consciousness and organization into a political community could be undermined by several social conditions. In his analysis of the 1848 revolution, Marx singled out ethnic divisions as forces undermining the revolutionary solidarity. He also observed how ethnic loyalty inhibits working-class solidarity in England: "Every industrial and commercial center in England now possesses a working class divided into two hostile camps, English proletarians and Irish proletarians. The ordinary English worker hates the Irish worker as a competitor, who lowers his standard of living. In relation to the Irish worker he feels himself a member of the ruling nation and so turns himself into a tool of the aristocrats and capitalists of his country against Ireland, thus strengthening their domination over himself. He cherishes religious, social, and national prejudices against the Irish worker."[5]

Similarly, Engels regarded the ethnic heterogeneity of the American working class as one of the "very great and peculiar difficulties for a steady development of a worker's party."[6]

The ethnic, racial, tribal, national, linguistic, and religious cleavages in several societies all over Europe, America, Africa, and Asia have hampered working-class solidarity and contributed to the preservation of the status quo.

In spite of that, empirical research studies in several societies have demonstrated that working classes tend to identify with leftist and reform political groups, while the nonmanual classes tend to identify with conservative forces, especially in times of political crises. For instance, a study by John C. Leggett on working-class consciousness in the city of Detroit showed that black workers are more militant than white workers, that the combination of insecure economic status, economic deprivation, and union membership heightens class consciousness, that the unemployed are more class conscious than the employed, and that those of middle-class background are markedly less militant than those whose background is working class.[7]

**General Expectations**

How about students? Are students from a lower-class background more radical than those from an upper-class background? Should we expect different results in developed and underdeveloped societies?

Empirical data yield conflicting results on the question of the radicalism of students from deprived classes relative to those from privileged classes. The findings of research studies on students in the United States consistently show that leftist activists come predominantly from upper-middle-class backgrounds, while right-wing conservatives typically come from lower- and working-class homes.[8] These findings could be explained in terms of the following: First, these leftist activists come predominantly from economically privileged yet socially underprivileged ethnic groups in the American society, while the nonactivists and the right-wing conservatives come predominantly from white and Anglo-Saxon backgrounds. Second, "extreme right activists are generally found within status-threatened groups. It is precisely the lower-middle and working classes that are least secure and tend to feel threatened by the upward thrust of new minorities. Upper middle class status provides the social and economic security that is lacking in the lower middle and upper working class."[9] Third, students from lower status origins have been socialized to concentrate on higher education as an instrumental training leading to upward social mobility.

The student movement in France showed more concern with workers than other student movements have done and played a significant role in establishing some relation with labor unions, as in the Algerian Revolution and the May revolt of 1968. Daniel and Gabriel Cohn-Bendit began their book, *Obsolete Communism: The Left-Wing Alternative*, with a quotation from Marx that "a writer is a productive worker" and asserted that "the only chance of resuming the struggle is to put an end to the division between intellectuals, workers and peasants. Every revolution, every radical transformation of society, needs the conscious and creative participation of the working and peasant classes."[10]

In the Netherlands, "student activism originally took the form of a student union concerned with union issues." Thus, empirical findings show that "the lower the general social class status of a student's parents, the more likely he is to support the student union."[11]

The data on students in Third World societies show mostly a negative relationship between social class origins of students and their political activism and leftist orientations. In Latin America, studies by Frank Bonilla,

R. L. Scheman, D. Goldrich, D. Nasatir, R. E. Scott, Myron Glazer, Arthur Liebman, and others report data that reflect such a negative relationship.[12] Students of lower-class background were found to be more likely to revolt against the prevailing political order than those of more privileged classes. However, as noted by Nasatir, considering the importance of social class "as the single most important differentiator of political preference across societies . . . , the observed differences are not as large as might have been expected."[13]

To conclude, it may be generalized that in underdeveloped societies students from lower-class origins are more likely to adopt a leftist ideology than their middle- or upper-class colleagues. However, it should be emphasized that several social forces in underdeveloped and developing societies hamper the development of radical leftist movements among university students. This generalization will be explored in detail in the following section.

**Data on Social Class and Political Orientations among Lebanese Students**

Before exploring the relationships of class origins of students to their political behavior and views, it should be noted that social class was measured in terms of father's occupation, family yearly income, father's level of education, and subjective or personal ranking of one's family's social class relative to the community or society. All four indices were found to be positively correlated, and the highest correlation was found between father's occupation and father's education (.368). Scales based on several combinations of these indices were constructed and related to the different aspects of student politics. In reporting the data, the scale based on family yearly income and father's occupation will be used most often. It is to be noted also that the empirical nature of this study required measuring the social class origins of students in terms of the above indices rather than by their positions in the production structure.

*Social Class and Leftist Orientations*

The data on the relationship between social origins of students in all three universities and their leftist-rightist orientations are presented in Table 6.1. As shown in Table 6.1A, students of lower-class origins were to some extent more inclined than others to consider themselves leftist and less inclined to consider themselves rightist. Among Christian respondents, 27 percent, 21 percent, and 22 percent of respondents of lower-, middle-, and upper-class origins respectively considered themselves leftist, and among Muslim respondents, the ratios were 47 percent, 41 percent, and 35 percent respectively. Here, it should be noted that upper-class Muslim students were more likely to consider themselves leftist than lower-class Christian students. Among both groups, students of middle-class origins showed the highest inclination to consider themselves reformist.

When the father's level of education is used as an index of social class origin, comparable results emerge. Among Christian students, of those whose fathers were illiterate, 41 percent considered themselves leftist, in comparison to 22 percent of those whose fathers had elementary or secondary education and 23 percent of those whose fathers had university education. Among Muslim students, of those whose fathers were illiterate, 60 percent considered themselves leftist, in comparison to 41 percent of those whose fathers had elementary or secondary education and 32 percent of those whose fathers had university education.

Since a subjective index of social class may yield different results from those based on the above indices, students were asked to indicate to what social class they thought their families belonged relative to their own society or community. Among Christian respondents, 3 percent ranked their families as lower class, 15 percent as lower-middle, 56 percent as middle-middle, 22 percent as upper-middle, and 4 percent as upper class. Of those who ranked their families as lower and lower-middle class, 32 percent considered themselves leftist, 53 percent reformist, and 16 percent rightist. As for those who ranked their families as upper-middle and upper class, 18 percent considered themselves leftist, 45 percent reformist, 23 percent rightist, and 14 percent checked other alternatives. Among Muslim respondents, 3 percent ranked themselves as lower class, 21 percent as lower-middle class, 32 percent as middle-middle class, 37 percent as upper-middle class, and 7 percent as upper class. Of those who ranked their families as lower and lower-middle class, 42 percent considered themselves leftist, 40 percent reformist, 5 percent rightist, and 13 percent others. As to those who ranked their families as upper-middle or upper class, 34 percent considered themselves leftist, 43 percent reformist, 9 percent rightist, and 14 percent others.

The subjective index yields a much more significant trend at LU than at the other universities. There, of all those who ranked their families as lower and lower-middle class, 82 percent considered themselves leftist, 7 percent reformist, and none rightist. Of those who ranked their families as middle-middle class, 37 percent considered themselves leftist, 47 percent reformist, and 4 percent rightist. As to those who ranked their families as upper-middle and upper class, 27 percent ranked themselves as leftist, 51 percent as reformist, and 11 percent as rightist. This shows a very clear negative relationship between subjective social class and leftist orientation. The lower the social class students at LU identify with, the less they identify with the rightist ideology and the more they identify with the leftist ideology. At SJU and AUB the trend is not as significant.

**Table 6.1. Social class<sup>a</sup> and leftist-rightist orientations (%)**

| | Christian Lower Classes | Middle Classes | Upper Classes | Total |
|---|---|---|---|---|
| **A. Leftist-rightist orientation** | | | | |
| Leftists | 27 | 21 | 22 | 24 |
| Reformists | 45 | 58 | 46 | 50 |
| Rightists | 16 | 10 | 25 | 17 |
| Others | 12 | 10 | 7 | 10 |
| | [N=98] | [N=119] | [N=143] | [N=360] |
| **B. Preferred form of government** | | | | |
| Communism | 7 | 6 | 2 | 5 |
| Socialist democracy | 32 | 26 | 27 | 28 |
| Liberal democracy | 36 | 43 | 43 | 41 |
| Capitalism | 25 | 25 | 28 | 26 |
| | [N=96] | [N=120] | [N=143] | [N=359] |
| **C. Revolution, not reform** | | | | |
| Strongly agree | 17 | 14 | 12 | 14 |
| Agree | 13 | 9 | 11 | 11 |
| Disagree | 34 | 39 | 32 | 35 |
| Strongly disagree | 36 | 38 | 45 | 40 |
| | [N=93] | [N=116] | [N=140] | [N=349] |
| **D. Elimination of private property** | | | | |
| Strongly agree | 16 | 9 | 7 | 10 |
| Agree | 17 | 10 | 12 | 13 |
| Disagree | 34 | 39 | 32 | 35 |
| Strongly disagree | 33 | 41 | 49 | 42 |
| | [N=95] | [N=117] | [N=143] | [N=355] |

<sup>a</sup>Measured in terms of a scale based on family yearly income and father's occupation.

| Muslim Lower Classes | Middle Classes | Upper Classes | Total |
|---|---|---|---|
| 47 | 41 | 35 | 40 |
| 39 | 48 | 42 | 42 |
| 1 | 2 | 8 | 4 |
| 12 | 9 | 15 | 12 |
| [N=66] | [N=44] | [N=91] | [N=201] |
| | | | |
| 16 | 14 | 10 | 13 |
| 42 | 26 | 30 | 32 |
| 29 | 43 | 36 | 36 |
| 13 | 17 | 24 | 19 |
| [N=63] | [N=42] | [N=91] | [N=196] |
| | | | |
| 30 | 36 | 17 | 25 |
| 26 | 22 | 20 | 22 |
| 26 | 40 | 43 | 37 |
| 18 | 2 | 20 | 15 |
| [N=66] | [N=45] | [N=90] | [N=201] |
| | | | |
| 32 | 20 | 13 | 21 |
| 21 | 34 | 20 | 23 |
| 33 | 25 | 44 | 37 |
| 14 | 20 | 22 | 19 |
| [N=63] | [N=44] | [N=90] | [N=197] |

The leftist ideology is also measured in terms of preferred forms of government. Here again, the social class origins of students seem to have some influence on what form of government they prefer for their country. As shown in Table 6.1B, 39 percent of the Christian students from lower-class backgrounds preferred communism and socialist democracy, in comparison to 32 percent of those of middle-class origin and 29 percent of those of upper-class origin. In the case of Muslim students, 58 percent of the students of lower-class origin preferred communism and socialist democracy, in comparison to 40 percent each of those coming from middle and upper classes. Again, upper-class Muslim students were more likely than lower-class Christians to prefer communism.

When the subjective social class index is used, the data show significant positive relationships between social class and preference for capitalism among both Christian and Muslim students. Taking both groups together, 89 percent, 57 percent, and 43 percent of those who ranked their families as belonging to lower classes, middle-middle class, and upper classes respectively preferred communism and socialism.

A third aspect of the leftist ideology is the extent to which students agreed with the statement that what is needed in the political system is revolution, not reform. Using family yearly income and father's occupation as an index of social class background, the data in all three universities show a negative relationship between social class and degree of agreement with the statement (see Table 6.1C).

A fourth aspect is degree of agreement with the statement that in the last analysis private property should be eliminated. The data reported in Table 6.1D show a negative relationship between the social class origins of students and their agreement with elimination of private property, true of both Christian and Muslim students. Among the former group, about one-third of the students from lower-class families agreed with the statement, in comparison to less than one-fifth of those from middle or upper classes. Among the Muslim respondents, the data show that 32 percent, 20 percent, and 13 percent of those from lower, middle, and upper classes respectively strongly agreed with elimination of private property.

Using father's level of education as an index of social class, the same negative relationship emerges. The data show that 34 percent, 30 percent, 19 percent, and 11 percent of those Christian respondents whose fathers had no education, elementary, secondary, and university education respectively agreed with abolishing private property. Similarly, 59 percent, 49 percent, 40 percent, and 29 percent of the Muslim respondents in the same order agreed with the statement. At LU, the data show a highly significant negative relationship between subjective social class identification and agreement with elimination of private property. The great majority of all those who ranked their families as lower or lower-middle class (71 percent) agreed, in comparison to 48 percent of those who ranked their families as middle-middle class and 35 percent of those who ranked them as upper-middle or upper class.

To conclude, the relationship between social class origins of students and leftist orientation tended to be negative. In a few instances, however, this relationship was not consistent and in some cases it was not highly significant. Considering the importance of social class, the present findings indicate a lack of social class consciousness, especially when compared to religious affiliation, as upper-class Muslims were more inclined to the left than lower-class Christians.

*Social Class and Support for the Palestinian Commandos and for Popular Armed Struggle*

After the June War of 1967, the Palestinian resistance movement presented itself as a spearhead of revolutionary political and social change in the whole of Arab society and provided an alternative to the policies of existing governments and political parties for solving the Palestinian problem and for effecting change in the social fabric.

Several indices of social class will be used here in order to discover the extent to which it constitutes a significant independent variable determining the attitudes of university students in Lebanon toward the Palestinian commandos and popular armed struggle.

*1. Family yearly income.* The data presented in Table 6.2 show that family yearly income does not influence students' attitudes toward the commandos and their armed struggle. At AUB, those students whose parents earned £L 35,000 or more were a little more inclined than those whose parents earned £L 5,000 or less to support the commandos. Statistically, the relationship is not significant. Similarly, students whose families earned least showed the highest preference for the peaceful solution and the least for popular armed struggle. This trend at AUB was reversed at SJU, where those whose parents earned £L 5,000 or less were more inclined to express strong support for the commandos. In general, the relationship between income and support at SJU tended to be negative, for while 14 percent of those who belonged to the lower income bracket expressed nonsupport, about one-third (32 percent) of those who belonged to the upper income bracket did so. The same relationship, however, did not hold as strongly with regard to the preferred solution of the Palestine problem.

At LU, the relationship was not statistically significant, though there was some inclination among those whose parents made £L 35,000 or more to show much more nonsupport of the commandos (30 percent in comparison

**Table 6.2. Family yearly income, support for commandos, and preferred solution of Palestine problem (%)**

|  | Family Yearly Income (in Thousands of Lebanese Pounds) AUB | | | | |
|---|---|---|---|---|---|
|  | 5 or less | 5–10 | 10–20 | 20–35 | 35 or more |
| **A. Support for commandos** | | | | | |
| Strong support | 39 | 44 | 35 | 35 | 39 |
| Support | 30 | 32 | 43 | 44 | 42 |
| No support | 30 | 24 | 22 | 21 | 19 |
|  | [N=27] | [N=34] | [N=54] | [N=43] | [N=36] |
| **B. Best solution** | | | | | |
| Popular armed struggle | 25 | 31 | 42 | 28 | 42 |
| Peaceful solution | 65 | 31 | 32 | 35 | 33 |
| Other solutions | 10 | 37 | 26 | 37 | 25 |
|  | [N=20] | [N=35] | [N=53] | [N=43] | [N=36] |

**A. Support for commandos**
Strong support
Support
No support

**B. Best solution**
Popular armed struggle
Peaceful solution
Other solutions

| SJU<br>5 or<br>less | 5–10 | 10–20 | 20–35 | 35 or<br>more |
|---|---|---|---|---|
| 33 | 19 | 24 | 24 | 21 |
| 53 | 60 | 57 | 54 | 47 |
| 14 | 22 | 19 | 22 | 32 |
| [N=21] | [N=42] | [N=107] | [N=71] | [N=34] |
| 20 | 23 | 22 | 16 | 28 |
| 65 | 59 | 63 | 64 | 44 |
| 15 | 18 | 15 | 20 | 28 |
| [N=20] | [N=39] | [N=103] | [N=69] | [N=32] |

| LU<br>5 or<br>less | 5–10 | 10–20 | 20–35 | 35 or<br>more |
|---|---|---|---|---|
| 40 | 21 | 43 | 26 | 40 |
| 53 | 68 | 46 | 70 | 30 |
| 7 | 11 | 11 | 4 | 30 |
| [N=53] | [N=56] | [N=61] | [N=23] | [N=10] |
| 35 | 17 | 36 | 17 | 20 |
| 23 | 36 | 24 | 39 | 30 |
| 42 | 47 | 40 | 44 | 50 |
| [N=52] | [N=53] | [N=59] | [N=23] | [N=10] |

to 7 percent, 11 percent, 11 percent, and 4 percent of those of other income categories) and less preference for popular armed struggle than those whose parents earned £L 5,000 or less (20 percent versus 35 percent).

2. *Father's occupation.* The index of social class in terms of father's occupation yields almost the same results as that dealing with family yearly income. The data show no significant relationship between the father's occupation and attitudes toward the commandos and their armed struggle at either AUB or LU. This is not so at SJU, where, as expected, children of manual workers were more likely than others to support the commandos and their armed struggle and were the least inclined to prefer a peaceful solution.

3. *Social class identification.* The data presented in Table 6.3 show that the subjective index, i.e., social class identification, was more likely than the objective indices to reflect a negative relationship between social class and support for the commandos. Those who identified with the lower classes at both SJU and LU were more likely than others to support the commandos and their armed struggle and less likely to prefer a peaceful solution. At AUB the small number of respondents (only six) who identified with the lower class does not allow for comparison.

Before concluding this section, it should be noted that, when the attitudes of students toward the different Palestinian commando organizations were considered, some interesting findings emerged. Students at LU were asked specifically to indicate how they felt about Fateh, the Popular Front for the Liberation of Palestine (PFLP), the Democratic Front (DFLP), and others, as well as how they felt about the leadership of these organizations. The majority (52 percent) preferred Fateh, 15 percent preferred PFLP, 3 percent preferred DFLP, 6 percent preferred other organizations, and 24 percent did not respond. While 45 percent of those whose parents earned £L 5,000 or less supported Fateh and 21 percent supported PFLP, 70 percent of those whose parents earned £L 35,000 or more preferred Fateh and 10 percent preferred PFLP. When the subjective index of social class is used, 28 percent of those who ranked their families as belonging to the lower-middle class said they preferred Fateh and 32 percent preferred PFLP. In contrast, 57 percent of those who ranked their families as belonging to the upper-middle class preferred Fateh and 8 percent preferred PFLP. The same trends emerge in the case of their preferences for the different leaderships. For instance, of those who ranked their families as belonging to the upper-middle class, 47 percent preferred Arafat and only 6 percent preferred Habash. In contrast, of those who ranked their families as belonging to the lower-middle class, 20 percent preferred Arafat and 32 percent preferred Habash.

*Social Class and Nationalistic Loyalties*

Since the majority of the Muslims identify with Arab nationalism and the majority of Christians identify with Lebanese nationalism, it is to be expected that social class will have little influence in determining the nationalistic identity of students. The data reported in Table 6.4 demonstrate that lower-class Christian students were more likely to identify with Arab nationalism than middle-class or upper-class Christian students (17 percent versus 12 percent and 11 percent). It is also demonstrated that upper-class Christians were the most likely to identify with Lebanese nationalism (60 percent, in comparison to 51 percent of the lower class), but the difference is rather small. In the case of Muslim students, the data show no relationship, though those of upper-class origin showed a little more tendency to identify with Lebanese nationalism than those of lower-class origin, and the middle-class students showed the highest tendency (22 percent) to identify with internationalism.

The data at LU demonstrate a more significant relationship between social class and national identity (see Table 6.5). Sixty-one percent of those (of both religions) who identified with the lower classes preferred to identify with Arab nationalism, in comparison to 37 percent and 39 percent of those who identified with the middle and upper classes respectively. The data show also that about 30 percent of those who identified with the middle or upper classes preferred to identify with Lebanese nationalism, in comparison to only 7 percent of those who identified with the lower classes.

## Discussion

Social class origin of students was not found to be a very significant variable in predicting their political orientations, especially when compared with religion and family. Yet these variables could not be separated or studied outside the comprehensive context of the society as a whole. However, it remains true that students from deprived families were found to be immersed in their culture of deprivation and powerlessness.

Why is it that social class does not constitute the most significant single force that differentiates among the different political orientations of students?

The influence of vertical loyalties (and especially religious and family loyalties) in undermining social class consciousness was discussed in detail earlier. In this section, a number of other forces will be identified and briefly described. First, however, it should be noted that those students who came from deprived families and deprived religious communities—such as the poor Shi'ite students—showed the most significant inclination

**Table 6.3. Social class identification, support for commandos, and preferred solution of Palestine problem (%)**

|  | AUB Upper & Upper-Middle Classes | Middle Classes | Lower Classes |
|---|---|---|---|
| **A. Support for commandos** |  |  |  |
| Strong support | 38 | 46 | 50 |
| Support | 40 | 32 | 17 |
| No support | 22 | 22 | 33 |
|  | [N=162] | [N=37] | [N=6] |
| **B. Preferred solution** |  |  |  |
| Popular armed struggle | 33 | 36 | 33 |
| Peaceful solution | 36 | 39 | 33 |
| Other solutions | 31 | 25 | 33 |
|  | [N=159] | [N=36] | [N=6] |

**Table 6.4. Social class[a] and nationalistic loyalties (%)**

| Nationalistic Loyalties | Christian Lower Classes N=93 | Middle Classes N=114 | Upper Classes N=135 | Total N=342 |
|---|---|---|---|---|
| Arab nationalism | 17 | 12 | 11 | 13 |
| Lebanese nationalism | 51 | 58 | 60 | 57 |
| Syrian nationalism | 15 | 16 | 12 | 14 |
| Internationalism | 17 | 14 | 17 | 16 |

[a]As determined by family yearly income and father's occupation.

| SJU Upper & Upper-Middle Classes | Middle Classes | Lower Classes | LU Upper & Upper-Middle Classes | Middle Classes | Lower Classes |
|---|---|---|---|---|---|
| 20 | 21 | 33 | 29 | 33 | 52 |
| 48 | 59 | 45 | 55 | 59 | 37 |
| 32 | 21 | 22 | 16 | 8 | 11 |
| [N=25] | [N=188] | [N=73] | [N=55] | [N=129] | [N=27] |
| 22 | 18 | 31 | 22 | 27 | 41 |
| 61 | 63 | 53 | 37 | 30 | 11 |
| 17 | 19 | 16 | 41 | 43 | 48 |
| [N=23] | [N=179] | [N=73] | [N=51] | [N=124] | [N=27] |

| Muslim Lower Classes N=59 | Middle Classes N=41 | Upper Classes N=88 | Total N=188 |
|---|---|---|---|
| 71 | 59 | 72 | 69 |
| 12 | 15 | 16 | 15 |
| 2 | 5 | 3 | 3 |
| 15 | 22 | 9 | 13 |

**Table 6.5. Social class identification and nationalistic loyalties (% at LU)**

| Nationalistic Loyalties | Lower Classes N=28 | Middle Classes N=133 | Upper Classes N=51 | Total N=212 |
|---|---|---|---|---|
| Arab nationalism | 61 | 37 | 39 | 40 |
| Lebanese nationalism | 7 | 30 | 29 | 26 |
| Syrian nationalism | 0 | 8 | 14 | 9 |
| Internationalism | 25 | 18 | 12 | 17 |
| Other | 7 | 6 | 6 | 6 |

to adopt the leftist ideology. In contrast, those students who came from privileged families and privileged religious communities—such as the rich Maronite students—showed the most significant inclination to adopt the rightist ideology. However, the socioeconomic and political conditions of the religious community proved to be a more significant force than the socioeconomic and political conditions of individual families. Thus, the rich Muslims showed a greater tendency to adopt the leftist ideology than the poor Christians.

This finding suggests that forces undermining social class consciousness should be sought on the societal and community levels and not just in the individual's immediate environment. Some religious communities occupy the more highly valued socioeconomic and political positions in Lebanese society. Furthermore, the prevailing pattern of socialization in the society and its educational systems is confessional in essence and is directed to promote religious rather than social class consciousness. Thus, the deprived Lebanese Christians may not feel deprived, because of their membership in a privileged community and because of the kind of confessional socialization they have had since childhood. Consequently, regardless of their deprived social class origins, those students who identify with their privileged religious communities tend to resist any kind of drastic change that may undermine the position of their communities.

Besides religion and family, there are several other factors among Lebanese university students that may undermine their social class consciousness.

First, there is the anticipatory socialization of university students in regard to their prospects of obtaining elitist positions in the society. The chances of students at AUB and SJU for occupying such positions are much greater than those of students at LU. The two former universities have been training the future political elites, professionals, managers, administrators, and employees of foreign enterprises in the area. Students at LU have dim prospects of access to elitist positions, and they often complain about the threat of unemployment after graduation.

Second, university students constitute declassed or displaced groups in that they tend more than other groups to be uprooted from their communities and rarely return, especially if their communities are deprived in relation to the rest of the society. Students from southern or northern Lebanon and other deprived areas rarely return to these areas. They continue to live in Beirut or abroad and seek to improve their conditions.

Third, students in Lebanon have confined themselves to the university ghetto and have remained a strictly student movement that shows little concern with workers, peasants, and other deprived segments of the society. Students at LU have been almost solely occupied with reforming the university and promoting their interests. Some of the leaders of the student movement at AUB continue to be active on campus even after graduation instead of working in deprived communities. On the other hand, the AUB workers' union is pro-administration. The senior leaders, fully controlled by the university administration, preach workers' reconciliation to poverty. The *Bulletin*—a regular publication of the workers' union at AUB—stated in its editorial on August 9, 1972: "That man is poor, wretched, and degraded is possible, for that may be the verdict of fate . . . That man is unlucky and hit by disasters most often in his life is also the will of God."

Fourth, students of lower-class origins cannot afford to risk the threats of suspension, for they cannot continue their studies abroad as rich students usually do in such cases.

Fifth, the prosperity that reached some areas of Lebanon, on the one hand, and the political instability that prospered in some Arab countries, on the other, resulted in creating feelings of a relative lack of deprivation among some Lebanese. They persist in comparing themselves with other Arab countries that are worse off than Lebanon, and consequently feel satisfied and quite proud of their accomplishments. This mood is quite widespread among some Lebanese students and will change only when conditions change in other Arab countries and they start to compare themselves with countries or groups that are more fortunate. This process is illustrated by Marx with the story of a man who was happy with his small house until a palace was built next door. The worker's house suddenly became a hut in his eyes. The few students from lower-class families at AUB or SJU are in contact with students from wealthy families. Their feelings of deprivation are expected to be intensified, but in reality the deprivation effect is countered by the anticipatory-socialization effect.

Sixth, university students in Lebanon have been highly involved in verbal aggression or oral revolt. They are a part and an extension of an expressive society whose members reconcile themselves to their situations and experience catharsis by freely and spontaneously expressing their anger and aggression through verbal assault.

These factors, in addition to the vertical loyalties described in the previous two chapters, constitute the basic conditions undermining social class consciousness among students and in the society at large. Yet several other forces contribute to further alienation from the existing order, as will be seen in the next section of this work. At this stage it is sufficient to note the Tantalusian condition that prevails in Arab society. The Arabs find themselves impoverished and unable to face up to trying challenges that threaten their very existence, although they have all the wealth needed to transfer the society into a new era. The more acute their awareness of their problems and the more they become conscious of their situation, the greater the prospects for revolutionary change.

# 7. Some Correlates of Political Alienation and Radicalism

This chapter is an extension of the section on vertical and horizontal loyalties and student politics. The aim here is to further explore what social factors contribute to the making of leftist political radicalism and political alienation. Comparisons will be made between leftists, reformists, and rightists as well as between politically alienated and nonalienated students in order to reveal how differences between these groups consistently extend beyond political matters into other social spheres. A condition of such a generalized nature indicates a clear tendency toward the emergence of opposed perspectives on political and social change in the area.

In this context, political alienation and leftist radicalism are defined vis-à-vis the established order. While the alienated person is dissatisfied with and rejects the prevailing order, the leftist radical aims at actively transforming this order. Simply, the need to transcend the condition of alienation requires striving toward restructuring of the society. Consequently, alienation (when defined in terms of dissatisfaction and rejection of the prevailing order)[1] is conceived of as an intervening prerequisite for revolutionary change. The starting point is the prevailing social conditions which oppose human well-being and render one powerless, marginal to one's own activities and concerns, and nakedly exposed to all sorts of risks. The second stage in the process of alienation is to develop a new consciousness based on dissatisfaction with and rejection of one's conditions. This stage involves confrontation of a gap between the existing social reality and a desired order. Facing such a gap between reality and the dream of an ideal society generates pressure on one to act. The behavioral alternatives for an alienated person or group could be conceptualized on a retreat-compliance-involvement dimension. In other words, alienated persons or groups either retreat from, comply with, or act upon the system and/or society from which they are alienated, hoping to put an end to the disparity between the actual and desired orders. Hence, the present treatment of political alienation and leftist radicalism as highly interconnected phenomena. Leftist radicals are seen as persons or groups who resolve their alienation by revolting against the system. Their first task is the delegitimation of the legitimate. They conceive reasons for human misery, deprivation, inequality, exploitation, and domination as arising not from human nature but from the prevailing socioeconomic and political structures and cultural value orientations. Unlike the politically integrated rightists and liberals, the alienated leftists are dedicated to total transformation of the established order. The rightists' ongoing concern is preserving the existing system and "celebrating society as it is."[2] Any limitations they may see or admit are attributed to human nature and mismanagement rather than to the prevailing system and its socioeconomic and political structures. The liberals admit the existence of basic limitations and misgivings, but they believe that reform from within the system should be enough to overcome the existing problems. Their concern with reform is "a direct response to radical challenge or an anticipatory response to the prospect of it."[3] Their reform is an attempt to avoid the collapse of the established order and follows a "political strategy rather than social vision."[4] The liberals may even call for a white or constitutional revolution from above to avoid a violent revolution from below; it is reform from within the system to protect the system.[5]

In the light of the above distinctions, it may be generalized that the majority of students are liberal in orientation and the radical leftists represent only a significant minority. The data show that 11 percent of the students at SJU, 12 percent at AUB, and 28 percent at LU considered themselves leftists who "recommend the use of violence, if necessary." In comparison, 38 percent of students at AUB, 43 percent at LU, and 48 percent at SJU considered themselves reformists, moderates, or nonrevolutionaries. Finally, 5 percent at LU, 15 percent at AUB, and 19 percent at SJU considered themselves rightist in orientation. Yet, 22 percent at SJU, 29 percent at AUB, and 50 percent at LU said that what was needed was a revolution rather than reform.

In regard to the diffusion of feelings of alienation among students, the data reveal that the majority of students (ranging between 63 percent and 77 percent) in all three universities expressed dissatisfaction with the political conditions of the country, and about half (ranging between 43 percent and 58 percent) agreed that they totally rejected the basic goals for which their governments stood as well as the values on which these goals were based.

These feelings of alienation extended beyond the political system to the society as such. The percentages of students who stated that they felt at war with their society and rejected the basic values, goals, and trends dominant in it ranged between 36 percent and 75 percent. A specific question directed to students at LU required them to check one of four alternative statements measuring degree of integration into or alienation from the society. The data showed that about one-fifth (22 percent) of the students at LU were fully integrated, i.e., they felt satisfied with the society because it was not suffering from any basic weaknesses that required any special concern. Another one-fifth (21 percent) of the total student body felt dissatisfied, but preferred to accept reality and make peace with it as long as it seemed difficult to change (these are categorized here as the compliers). A third group (20 percent), the apathetic, indicated their dissatisfaction with the society, but they said they were indifferent and uninvolved in any activities directed at change. The last group (38 percent), the alienated activists, consisted of those who said they were dissatisfied and involved in several activities that might change society in the direction they preferred.

In the remaining sections of this chapter, attempts will be made to identify and describe some correlates of political alienation and leftist radicalism. The focus will be on two types of correlates that differentiate between the alienated and nonalienated as well as the leftists, liberals, and rightists: social variables and social orientations.

## Social Variables

### Sex

Female students were found to be less politically alienated than male students. The data from LU revealed that 42 percent of the women, in comparison to 67 percent of the men, agreed with the statement that they totally rejected the goals towards which their government worked as well as the values on which policies had been based. Furthermore, while the dominant tendency among men was to resolve their political alienation through active involvement (as shown in Table 7.1, 43 percent of the men said they were alienated activists in comparison to 22 percent of the women), the dominant tendency among women was to comply (i.e., 39 percent of the women said they were dissatisfied but preferred to accept reality in comparison to only 15 percent of the men). In fact, the statement intended to measure compliance was checked less often by men and more often by women than any of the other three alternatives.

Male students were also found to be more inclined to consider themselves leftist, to be more inclined to prefer communism and socialism, and to be more politically active. For instance, 33 percent of male students considered themselves leftists who believe in violence if necessary, 11 percent considered themselves nonviolent leftists, 39 percent reformists, and 4 percent rightists, in comparison to 8 percent, 18 percent, 57 percent, and 10 percent of the female students in the same order. On the other hand, 67 percent of the women in contrast to 43 percent of the men considered

**Table 7.1. Sex and type of integration–alienation from society (% at LU)**

| Integration–Alienation | Male N=164 | Female N=51 | Total N=215 |
|---|---|---|---|
| Integration | 21 | 25 | 22 |
| Compliance | 15 | 39 | 21 |
| Apathy | 21 | 14 | 20 |
| Active alienation | 43 | 22 | 38 |

$X^2$ = 16.84; contingency coefficient = .2697; corrected con. coe. = .3691

themselves liberals and rightists. Similarly, 31 percent of the women in comparison to 15 percent of the men said they were politically nonactive, and men were almost three times as likely as women to say they were very active (17 percent versus 6 percent).

A very interesting finding is revealed by the data on AUB. Student Council elections in 1970 showed no significant difference in the voting pattern between men and women, as is clearly demonstrated in Table 7.2.

However, when a control was made on the religious factor, significant differences between the two sexes emerged, as shown in Table 7.3. Among Christian students, men were much more likely than women to vote progressive (31 percent versus 3 percent). The opposite trend emerged among Muslim students, for women were more likely to vote progressive than men (69 percent versus 47 percent). One explanation of this finding may be that women are more likely to be integrated into their religious communities. Since political conservatism is the dominant trend among Lebanese Christians, female students are more likely than males to vote nonprogressive. Among Lebanese Muslims, on the other hand, female students are more likely than males to vote progressive because such a trend has been more dominant in their religious community.

*Nationality*

The Palestinian students showed the highest inclination toward political alienation and leftist radicalism. While 86 percent indicated that they were dissatisfied with the dominant political conditions, only 71 percent of other Arabs did so. The differences were great in the rejection of the prevailing political goals and values (87 percent of the Palestinian students as opposed to 58 percent of the Lebanese, 48 percent of the Jordanians, and 53 percent of other Arabs). A scale of alienation constructed on the bases of

**Table 7.2. Sex and voting in AUB Student Council elections of 1970 (% of Arab students only)**

| Voted for | Male N=99 | Female N=64 |
|---|---|---|
| Progressive list | 38 | 39 |
| Rightist list | 26 | 28 |
| Split list | 17 | 12 |
| Did not vote | 18 | 20 |

**Table 7.3. Sex and voting by religious affiliation in AUB Student Council elections of 1970 (% of Arab students only)**

| Voted for | Christian | | Muslim | |
|---|---|---|---|---|
| | Male N=54 | Female N=29 | Male N=45 | Female N=35 |
| Progressive list | 31 | 3 | 47 | 69 |
| Rightist list | 40 | 52 | 11 | 9 |
| Split list | 16 | 20 | 18 | 6 |
| Did not vote | 13 | 24 | 24 | 17 |

the above two items (dissatisfaction and rejection) showed that 67 percent of the Palestinian students were moderately alienated and 33 percent highly alienated in comparison to 37 percent and 34 percent of the Lebanese, 43 percent and 25 percent of the Jordanians, and 38 percent and 31 percent of other Arabs, respectively. A similar generalization can be made in respect to alienation from society. Thus, 94 percent of the Palestinian students said they rejected the prevailing social values, in contrast to 68 percent of the Lebanese, 63 percent of the Jordanians, and 70 percent of other Arabs.

*Religious Affiliation*

The data presented in Table 7.4 confirm the hypothesis that Lebanese Muslim students are more politically alienated than Lebanese Christian

**Table 7.4. Religion and political alienation among Lebanese university students[a] (%)**

| Degree of Alienation | Muslim Sunnites N=62 | Shi'ites N=38 | Druzes N=15 |
|---|---|---|---|
| Low | 21 | 13 | 14 |
| Medium | 42 | 21 | 40 |
| High | 37 | 66 | 47 |

[a] Scale of dissatisfaction with political conditions and rejection of government policies and goals; does not include students at SJU.

students. Among the former, the Shi'ites (the most deprived religious community) showed the highest degree of political alienation. About two-thirds of them were found to be highly alienated, and only 13 percent showed some integration into and satisfaction with the political system. The Lebanese Druze students came next, for about half of them (47 percent) were found to be highly alienated, and another 40 percent were found to be moderately alienated. Though the Lebanese Sunni Muslim students occupied the third position in terms of degree of political alienation, only about one-fifth were found to be relatively integrated. The rest showed a moderate (42 percent) or high (37 percent) degree of political alienation. Among the Christian student groups, Maronites (who occupy the most central positions in the political structure) were found to be the most highly integrated. As shown, 42 percent of them registered a low degree of political alienation, 35 percent a medium degree, and 24 percent a high degree. The Orthodox and the Catholics expressed moderate political alienation.

At LU, the Shi'ite students showed the least integration into the Lebanese society, as only 3 percent checked the statement "I am satisfied with my society, and I do not think it is suffering from any basic weaknesses." In comparison, 35 percent of the Maronites, about one-fourth of the Orthodox and the Catholics, 14 percent of the Sunnites, and 10 percent of the Druzes checked this statement. About 30 percent each of the Druzes and Sunnites felt dissatisfied, but preferred to accept reality as long as it seemed difficult to change it.

Political alienation was also found to be negatively related to religiosity, regardless of religious affiliation, and positively related to secularism. Those who were alienated from politics tended also to be alienated from

| | Christian Maronites N=75 | Orthodox N=56 | Catholics N=17 | Others N=28 | Total N=291 |
|---|---|---|---|---|---|
| | 42 | 33 | 24 | 39 | 29 |
| | 35 | 38 | 59 | 39 | 37 |
| | 24 | 30 | 18 | 21 | 34 |

religion. Sixty-seven percent of those who were alienated from society (in contrast to 17 percent of the nonalienated) were also alienated from religion. Another finding revealed that 49 percent of those who were dissatisfied with society in comparison to only 8 percent of the nonalienated said they rejected the teachings of their religions. Similarly, 52 percent of those who expressed dissatisfaction with the prevailing conditions (in contrast to 14 percent of those who expressed satisfaction) confessed that they were uncertain of or did not believe in the existence of God.

In regard to secularism, those who were alienated from politics were almost three times as likely as the nonalienated to strongly agree with separation of the state from religion and introduction of civil marriage (66 percent versus 23 percent).[6]

Thus, integration into the society and its political system was found to be highly correlated with integration into religion.

*Family*

If family is the most significant agency of socialization in traditional and transitional societies, one would expect that, the greater the integration into family, the greater the resistance would be to social and political transformation and alienation.

The data presented in Table 7.5 confirm the expected negative relationship between closeness to parents and political alienation. As shown, 27 percent, 33 percent, and 51 percent of the very close, close, and distant respondents respectively were found to be highly alienated from the existing political system. It is shown also that, while only 8 percent of the distant respondents were integrated into the political system (i.e., nonalien-

**Table 7.5. Relationship between closeness to parents and alienation from the political system and society (%)**

| Political Alienation[a] | Closeness to Parents | | | |
| | Very Close | Close | Distant | Total |
| --- | --- | --- | --- | --- |
| Little | 35 | 27 | 8 | 28 |
| Moderate | 38 | 40 | 41 | 39 |
| High | 27 | 33 | 51 | 33 |
| | [N=175] | [N=181] | [N=37] | [N=393] |
| | (45%) | (46%) | (9%) | (100%) |

[a]AUB and LU.

ated or slightly alienated), 27 percent of the close and 35 percent of the very close respondents were politically integrated.

A very interesting finding should be noted at this stage. The compliers, i.e., those who were dissatisfied but preferred to accept reality, were the least likely to say that their parents had been free with them and allowed them to make their own decisions. The data showed that 27 percent of the respondents who said their parents had been strict checked the statement indicating compliance, in comparison to 14 percent of those who said their parents had been free. The compliers were also the most likely to come from large families. Thirty percent of them said that the size of their immediate family was ten persons or more, in comparison to 12 percent of the alienated activists.[7]

*Social Class*

Alienation from the existing political system is expected to be related to the social class origins of students. The data presented in Table 7.6 confirm this expectation in the case of the Muslim students but not in the case of the Christians. Among the latter, the least alienated from politics were those from middle-class backgrounds, followed by those from lower classes, and finally those from upper classes. Among Muslim respondents, the higher the social class, the less the alienation from politics. Thus, while only 19 percent of those coming from lower-social-class families expressed little alienation, 30 percent from middle-class families and 43 percent from upper-class families did so. High political alienation is shown by 36 percent, 27 percent, and 20 percent of those from lower-, middle-, and upper-class origins respectively.

The data in Table 7.7 demonstrate that subjective social class identification is negatively related to political alienation among the Christian respondents. The few Christian students who ranked their families as belonging to the lower classes showed the greatest tendency (53 percent) to be highly alienated, in comparison to 21 percent of those who ranked their families as belonging to middle classes and 15 percent of those who ranked their families as belonging to upper classes. Among the Muslim students, those who ranked their families as belonging to middle classes expressed even more political alienation than those who ranked their families as belonging to lower classes, but both expressed much more political alienation than those who ranked their families as belonging to the upper classes.

The data collected at LU (reported in Table 7.8) contribute to further understanding of the nature of the relationship between social class and alienation. Here, regardless of how alienation is measured or whether it is political or social, the relationship is negative and highly significant. As shown in Table 7.8A, of the students who ranked their families as belonging to the lower class only 18 percent disagreed with the statement that they rejected the basic goals and policies of the government as well as the values on which these goals and policies are based. The majority (64 percent) expressed strong agreement with this statement. In contrast, 28 percent of those who ranked their families as belonging to the middle class strongly agreed with this statement. Finally, those who ranked their families as belonging to the upper class showed the lowest tendency (23 percent) to strongly agree with the statement. In short, 64 percent, 28 percent, and 23 percent of those respondents who identified with the lower, middle, and upper classes respectively expressed high political alienation.

Table 7.8B reports the data on behavioral alienation, measured in terms of preference for one of the four statements expressing degrees of dissatisfaction with the prevailing conditions and kinds of involvement in reforming the society. While only 7 percent of those who ranked their families as belonging to the lower classes selected the statement indicating integration into their society, 23 percent of those who ranked their families as middle class and 28 percent of those who ranked them as upper class selected this statement. The great majority of those who identified with the lower classes (72 percent) selected the statement indicating active alienation, in comparison to 32 percent and 31 percent of those who identified with the middle and upper classes.

In short, the data at LU showed a linear and significantly negative relationship between social class and political alienation. In the other two universities the findings were less significant among Muslim students (though in the same direction) and rather conflicting and inconsistent among Christian students.[8]

**Table 7.6. Social class[a] and political alienation (%)**

| Political Alienation (Rejection)[b] | Christian Lower Classes N=64 | Middle Classes N=53 | Upper Classes N=44 | Total N=161 |
|---|---|---|---|---|
| Little | 42 | 60 | 36 | 47 |
| Some | 34 | 26 | 32 | 31 |
| High | 24 | 13 | 32 | 22 |

[a]As determined by family yearly income and father's occupation.
[b]AUB and LU.

**Table 7.7. Social class identification and political alienation (%)**

| Political Alienation (Rejection)[a] | Christian Lower Classes N=17 | Middle Classes N=72 | Upper Classes N=80 | Total N=169 |
|---|---|---|---|---|
| Little | 35 | 53 | 45 | 47 |
| Some | 12 | 26 | 40 | 31 |
| High | 53 | 21 | 15 | 21 |

[a]AUB and LU.

## Social Orientations

Political radicalism and alienation are also highly related to a number of other specific social, political, and economical orientations. Such findings are indicative of the generalized nature of alienation and radicalism. To be more specific, political alienation and radicalism are parts of a more comprehensive socialist-democratic-secular ideology which aims at overcoming problems of exploitation and domination as well as at introducing new types of interpersonal, intergroup, and interinstitutional relations. This explains why this ideology calls for a new consciousness that liberates people from their illusions about their conditions. In the words of Marx, "the

| Muslim Lower Classes N=58 | Middle Classes N=33 | Upper Classes N=74 | Total N=165 |
|---|---|---|---|
| 19 | 30 | 43 | 32 |
| 45 | 42 | 37 | 41 |
| 36 | 27 | 20 | 27 |

| Muslim Lower Classes N=42 | Middle Classes N=50 | Upper Classes N=97 | Total N=189 |
|---|---|---|---|
| 26 | 18 | 43 | 33 |
| 43 | 42 | 34 | 38 |
| 31 | 40 | 23 | 29 |

call for men to abandon their illusions about their condition is a call for men to abandon a condition which requires illusion."[9]

In order to support this contention, the above list of social variables is extended to show how radicalism and/or alienation are highly related to several other social orientations:

*Social Liberalism*

A positive relationship was obtained between political alienation and social liberalism. The alienated were more likely to express agreement with religious, social, and political freedom (i.e., freedom to be critical of religions

**Table 7.8. Social class identification and political alienation (% at LU)**

|  | Lower Class | Middle Class | Upper Class | Total |
|---|---|---|---|---|
| **A. Political alienation (rejection)** | | | | |
| Little | 18 | 40 | 46 | 38 |
| Some | 18 | 32 | 31 | 30 |
| High | 64 | 28 | 23 | 32 |
|  | [N=28] | [N=131] | [N=52] | [N=211] |
| **B. Political alienation (behavioral types of responses to alienation)** | | | | |
| Integrated | 7 | 23 | 28 | 22 |
| Compliers | 7 | 23 | 24 | 21 |
| Apathetic | 14 | 23 | 17 | 20 |
| Alienated activists | 72 | 32 | 31 | 37 |
|  | [N=28] | [N=132] | [N=54] | [N=214] |

and the prophets, to have premarital sexual relations, and to grant free speech to all groups without exception). The higher the alienation the higher the liberalism on all these scores. Thus, 15 percent, 41 percent, 43 percent and 67 percent of the politically nonalienated, little alienated, moderately alienated, and highly alienated respectively were found to be highly liberal. Expressed differently, those who showed high political alienation were more than four times as likely as the nonalienated to believe strongly in these freedoms. At LU, the nonalienated were more than seven times as likely as the highly alienated to strongly disagree with the right of the atheists to express their opinions.

The data on students at LU demonstrated that the revolutionary leftists (i.e., those leftists who believed in violence if necessary) were the most likely to agree with the statement that premarital sexual intercourse should be tolerated for girls. The majority of them (63 percent) agreed, followed by the nonviolent leftists (33 percent), the reformists (29 percent), and finally the rightists (27 percent). In other words, the greater the political radicalism, the greater the tolerance of premarital sexual intercourse for girls. The data on SJU also revealed that the rightists were the most likely to disagree with the statement. About half of them (46 percent) disagreed, in comparison to 38 percent of the reformists, 19 percent of the nonviolent leftists, and only 6 percent of the revolutionary leftists.

The same trend was obtained in relating sexual liberalism to preferences

for forms of government in both LU and SJU (see Table 7.9). At the former
university, 76 percent of those who preferred communism agreed with the
above statement, in comparison to 37 percent of those who preferred
socialism (15 percent strongly agreed), 37 percent of those who preferred
liberal democracy (only 2 percent strongly agreed), and, finally, 29 percent
of those who preferred capitalism. At SJU, 100 percent of those who preferred communism agreed, compared with 63 percent of those who preferred socialism, 62 percent of those who preferred liberal democracy, and
46 percent of those who preferred capitalism.

The data also showed that the leftists were the most likely to agree that
"Atheists should have the freedom to express their opinions in public
against religions and the prophets." In all three universities, 45 percent of
the revolutionary leftists, 31 percent of the nonviolent leftists, 22 percent of
the liberals, and 23 percent of the rightists strongly agreed with such freedom. At SJU, 60 percent of those who preferred communism strongly
agreed with the statement, in comparison to 35 percent of those who preferred socialism, 30 percent of those who preferred liberal democracy, and
31 percent of those who preferred capitalism.

The data also revealed a positive relationship between secularism (i.e.,
agreement with separation of the state from religion and with civil marriage) and leftist orientation. For instance, 72 percent of the revolutionary
leftists, 57 percent of the nonviolent leftists, 46 percent of the reformists,
and 43 percent of the rightists strongly agreed.

The data at LU measuring the integration-alienation dimension showed
that 48 percent of the alienated activists strongly agreed with the right of
atheists to express their opinions, in comparison to 13 percent of the integrated respondents. Similarly, 23 percent of the former in comparison to
only 2 percent of the latter strongly agreed with premarital sexual intercourse for girls.

*Value Orientations*

A list of twenty-one values was presented to students at LU and they were
asked to check the five values they thought to be the most significant and
to rank them in order of importance. Freedom was checked most often,
with 20 percent ranking it as the most significant, 14 percent as second
most significant, 15 percent as third, and 13 percent as fourth and fifth.
Equality and justice were checked much less often. Only 10 percent ranked
equality as the most significant, and 59 percent did not mention it at all.
What is of concern here is the extent to which leftists, liberals, and rightists
selected different values. The data show that leftists were more likely to
select equality and revolution, while reformists tended to select friendship,
love, rebellion, honesty, openness, beauty, rationality, and responsibility.

**Table 7.9. Relationship between preferred form of government and agreement with premarital sexual intercourse for girls (%)**

| Premarital Intercourse for Girls | Preferred Form of Government | |
| --- | --- | --- |
| | Communism | Socialism |
| **A. Students at LU** | | |
| Strongly agree | 38 | 15 |
| Agree | 38 | 22 |
| Disagree | 8 | 41 |
| Strongly disagree | 13 | 19 |
| No response | 3 | 3 |
| | [N=24] | [N=103] |
| **B. Students at SJU** | | |
| Strongly agree | 67 | 19 |
| Agree | 33 | 44 |
| Disagree | 0 | 16 |
| Strongly disagree | 0 | 19 |
| No response | 0 | 2 |
| | [N=15] | [N=63] |

Rightists were the most likely to select success and freedom. For instance, 32 percent of the revolutionary leftists ranked equality as the first and second most significant value, in comparison to 22 percent of the nonviolent leftists, and 13 percent of the reformists and rightists.

Success or ambition was mentioned by 32 percent of those who preferred capitalism as the most significant value in comparison to only 12 percent of the socialists and communists. These achievement-oriented values were mentioned by 57 percent of non-party members and 35 percent of party members. The great majority of the rightists (91 percent) mentioned freedom among their top five values, in comparison to about 60 percent each of the leftists and liberals.

The reformists were twice as likely as the revolutionary leftists to mention affiliation-oriented values, such as friendship and love (61 percent versus 30 percent).

Another relevant question requested that students at LU indicate which of the following activities (one only) concerned them most and from which they derived the greatest intrinsic satisfaction: intellectual, political, artistic, religious, social, commercial, sports, others. The results showed that 36 percent checked intellectual activities, 22 percent social activities, 19 per-

| Liberal Democracy | Capitalism |
|---|---|
| 2 | 4 |
| 35 | 25 |
| 24 | 32 |
| 37 | 39 |
| 2 | 0 |
| [N=49] | [N=28] |
| | |
| 23 | 26 |
| 39 | 20 |
| 21 | 23 |
| 16 | 26 |
| 1 | 6 |
| [N=126] | [N=36] |

cent political, 7 percent sports, and 5 percent each artistic and religious activities.

The revolutionary leftists were most inclined to check political (43 percent) and intellectual (35 percent) activities; both the nonviolent leftists and liberals checked mostly intellectual (37 percent and 34 percent respectively) and social (37 percent and 28 percent) activities. The rightists checked mostly intellectual (27 percent), social (27 percent), sports (18 percent), and religious (18 percent) activities. Religious activity was checked by 18 percent of the rightists, 8 percent of the reformists, and none of the leftists.

*Nationalistic Loyalties*

The data in all three universities revealed that the Syrian nationalists expressed most dissatisfaction with the prevailing political conditions (84 percent), followed by the internationalists (79 percent), Arab nationalists (76 percent), and Lebanese nationalists (59 percent). A scale of political alienation (LU) based on three items (dissatisfaction, rejection, and seeing a gap between the actual and the desired) revealed also that 58 percent of the Syrian nationalists showed high alienation, in comparison to 38 percent

**Table 7.10. Relationship between nationalistic loyalties and political alienation (% at LU)**

|  | Arab Nationalists | Lebanese Nationalists | Syrian Nationalists |
|---|---|---|---|
| **A. Degree of alienation** | | | |
| None | 18 | 30 | 11 |
| Little | 20 | 42 | 11 |
| Moderate | 24 | 23 | 21 |
| High | 38 | 5 | 58 |
|  | [N=87] | [N=51] | [N=19] |

$X^2$ = 33.694; contingency coefficient = .3695; corrected con. coe. = .4283.

| | | | |
|---|---|---|---|
| **B. Integration-alienation** | | | |
| Integration | 11 | 50 | 5 |
| Compliance | 20 | 18 | 26 |
| Apathy | 21 | 16 | 16 |
| Active alienation | 48 | 16 | 53 |
|  | [N=87] | [N=56] | [N=19] |

$X^2$ = 45.37; contingency coefficient = .4206; corrected con. coe. = .4875.

of the Arab nationalists, 35 percent of the internationalists, and only 5 percent of the Lebanese nationalists. This latter set of data is presented in Table 7.10A.

The data in Table 7.10B show that the Lebanese nationalists showed the highest tendency to be integrated into society (50 percent), in comparison to 11 percent of Arab nationalists, 8 percent of internationalists, and 5 percent of Syrian nationalists.

The majority of students still think of themselves as nationalistic as well as leftist or rightist without considering the possibility of incompatibility between the two. The majority of Lebanese students at LU thought of themselves as Arab nationalists (38 percent), Lebanese nationalists (28 percent), or Syrian nationalists (9 percent). Eighteen percent said they were internationalists, and 5 percent either chose "other" or did not respond.

While the Arab and Syrian nationalists in this survey tended to consider themselves leftists, the Lebanese nationalists tended to consider themselves reformists and rightists. More specifically, 68 percent of the Syrian nationalists considered themselves revolutionary leftists, in comparison to 36 percent of the Arab nationalists and only 5 percent of the Lebanese na-

| Inter-<br>nationalists | Others |
|---|---|
| 16 | 31 |
| 30 | 15 |
| 19 | 31 |
| 35 | 23 |
| [N=37] | [N=13] |
| | |
| 8 | 31 |
| 19 | 31 |
| 29 | 15 |
| 44 | 23 |
| [N=36] | [N=13] |

tionalists. The majority of the Lebanese nationalists (47 percent) said they preferred liberal democracy or capitalism, as compared to 18 percent of the Arab nationalists and 16 percent of the Syrian nationalists. Over half of the Arab nationalists (57 percent) and Syrian nationalists (53 percent) agreed with elimination of private property, while the great majority of the Lebanese nationalists (79 percent) disagreed. Similarly, while the great majority of the Lebanese nationalists (86 percent) called for gradual and peaceful change, the majority of the Syrian nationalists (68 percent) and more than half of the Arab nationalists (53 percent) called for revolutionary change.

On nonpolitical matters such as premarital sexual intercourse for girls, the Arab nationalists showed the least inclination (32 percent) to agree with it, followed by Lebanese nationalists (46 percent); Syrian nationalists were the most likely (58 percent) to agree.

*Compliance and Resignation*

There is a negative relationship between attitudes of compliance or resignation and leftist tendencies. In other words, rightists and reformists are more likely than leftists to subscribe to the ideology of contentment and the culture of silence. This is measured simply in terms of agreement with the statement "The secret of happiness is not expecting too much out of life, and being content with what comes your way" and with willingness to accept reality when it seems very difficult to change. The data show that 61 percent of the revolutionary leftists strongly disagreed with the above statement, in comparison to 25 percent of the rightists and reformists. The subscribers to the ideology of contentment, compliance, and resignation were much less likely than the nonsubscribers to strongly support the Palestinian commandos (30 percent versus 50 percent at AUB, 17 percent versus 31 percent at SJU, and only 4 percent versus 53 percent at LU).

*Future-Orientation*

Another hypothesis confirmed here deals with future versus present orientations. The data demonstrate that those who are future-oriented are more likely to support the commandos than those who are present-oriented. This is measured in terms of strong agreement or disagreement with the statement "With things as they are today, one ought to think only about the present and not worry about the future." Those who strongly agreed with this statement were considered present-oriented; and those who strongly disagreed with it were considered future-oriented.

It is shown also that about half the future-oriented students in both AUB and LU expressed strong support for the commandos, in comparison to less than one-third of the present-oriented students at AUB (31 percent) and less than one-fifth of them at LU (17 percent). The future-oriented students were more likely to prefer the commandos' armed struggle, while the present-oriented were more likely to prefer peaceful solutions.

**Conclusion**

The above confirmed hypotheses and expectations are indicative both of the generalized nature of alienation and radicalism and of the emergence of two opposed ideologies among youths in Lebanon.

The state of being politically alienated and radically leftist is not an isolated phenomenon. On the contrary, alienation from politics is highly related to alienation from religion, family, and other social institutions, inasmuch as these are part of the established order. It is also part of a more comprehensive socialist-democratic-secular ideology. While the integrative-rightist ideology reflects great concern with maintaining the prevailing political and socioeconomic conditions which favor the few, the alienative-leftist ideology reflects a new consciousness of basic disparities and dysfunctions in the society. The rightest orientation requires defensive involvement in the preservation of the status quo, while the leftist requires offensive involvement to change the whole network of structures and value orientations in order to liberate humanity from domination, exploitation, and deprivation. People are not just exploited economically. All kinds of attempts have been made to deprive them of the right to grow freely, to control their destiny, and to participate in their own self-advancement. The role institutions have assumed is not to envision a more healthy future for humanity but to invent more sophisticated machines of manipulation, control, intimidation, dehumanization, and destruction. Alienation as rejection of this total legacy is a prelude to revolutionary change.

The present data on students in Lebanon reveal that a revolutionary-socialist-democratic-secular ideology is emerging in opposition to a conservative-capitalistic-elitist-religious ideology. This phenomenon will be further demonstrated in Part III, an in-depth historical case study of the student organizations and strikes in Lebanon. An attempt will be made to demonstrate that, despite the persistence of traditional loyalties, relationships between students and university administrations and between students and the government have begun to reveal a growing awareness of the need for radical change.

# Part III

# The Development of the Student Movement in Lebanon

# 8. Search for National Identity:

*Early Stages in the Development of the Student Movement*

Student activism in Lebanon can be traced back to the last quarter of the nineteenth century, when the number of college students in Lebanon was less than two hundred. It was a time of national struggle against Ottoman rule. Students and instructors joined secret societies and helped in fermenting Syrian and/or Arab nationalism in opposition to Ottoman despotic rule.

The aim of this chapter is to describe early student revolts and try to account for them within the framework of analysis developed earlier.

## The 1882 Student Revolt

The first recorded student uprising in the contemporary Arab world took place in 1882 at AUB (known then as the Syrian Protestant College) at a time of national upheaval.[1] It was triggered by a controversy over Professor E. R. Lewis's commencement address (July 19, 1882), which was construed by the college as endorsing Darwin's theory of evolution. According to the Board of Trustees' minutes of December 1, 1882, the board's president, W. Booth, expressed the opinion "that neither the Board of Managers, the Faculty, nor the Board of Trustees would be willing to have anything that favors what is called 'Darwinism' talked of or taught in the College."[2]

In response to the termination of Professor Lewis's services, all medical professors except George Post, all medical students (forty-five in number), and, as a gesture of support, students in the senior classes in arts and sciences, refrained from attending their classes. The medical students met and discussed their unity and continuity, after which each signed his name and pledged "by God and my honor to keep the promises which we have made in this meeting and to continue to the end with the mass."[3] In this meeting they protested the discontinuation of Professor Lewis's services and complained about (1) the nonrecognition of the college medical degrees in the Ottoman Empire and having to pass difficult examinations in

Constantinople (what added to the complexity was the information received by the college that year that examinations would not be accepted in Arabic but only in Turkish or French); (2) the nonteaching by the college of certain sciences which were required by the medical program of the Imperial School at Constantinople; (3) the oral examinations at the college, which caused anxiety among students. The next day (December 6) the students received a "final advice" that if they insisted on not attending classes they would expose themselves to due school punishment. In response to this threat the students wrote a lengthy protest in which they said: "The things which have lately taken place in the College have disturbed our minds. . . . We entered on condition that our examinations in Constantinople should take place in the language in which we study. . . . This agreement has also been broken in a very strange manner, the like of which has not been heard of, by the removal of one of you from the College, not withstanding that we need him. . . . We shall not be convinced by dilatory promises and future hopes."[4]

The next day, students received the following reply signed by President Daniel Bliss: "Your communication has been received. 1st. In regard to your examinations, we appointed a Committee . . . to devise a scheme. . . . In regard to Dr. Lewis's leaving the College, while we fully understand how your feelings are moved . . . yet we cannot see how this should lead you to absent yourselves from your classes."[5]

The students were not satisfied by this reply and called for a general meeting. They appointed a committee to draft a reply to the reply. The general assembly amended the draft and forwarded it to the administration: "After the proper salutation, we remind you that we have already written, asking about things which we find more important than our attendance . . . , and you answered one of them, and closed your eyes to the others. . . . We still await the reply, hoping that it will be unambiguous and speedy. . . . We found it necessary to write this, begging you to receive the assurance of our filial regard."[6]

The students again discussed unity and continuity and insisted that all students should attend the meetings regularly and whoever absented himself should pay a *majidi* (an Ottoman monetary unit) for every nonattendance. Every student in turn pledged continuity to the end. They warned that, if the administration intended to punish any one of them, they would all stand by him until the punishment was removed. They also decided to contact the missionaries in all parts of Syria and the "prominent elites in the country" (*zawat al-balad wa kibar a'ianiha*). They met with the governor of Mount Lebanon, Rustum Pasha (1873–1883), and the consuls of Britain, the United States, Italy, Prussia, France, and others. They also sent a petition to the Board of Managers[7] in which they presented their case and asked for support: ". . . We have resorted to you, honorable ones, . . . knowing you will not neglect the truth even when sought by despised ones like us, for truth is from God, and whoever loves God follows the truth."

On the back of this petition, students complained against Dr. George Post and President Bliss: "We find it necessary to reveal what caused us suffering and disturbance lately. . . . You know about the ill-temper of His Excellency [Janab] Dr. Post. . . . His ill treatment of students . . . does lots of damage to our decencies, makes our hearts heavy, and kills our emotions and desire to study. . . . And we have come to regard the President of our College with suspicion, after we used to show him fatherly respect, because he has been supporting His Excellency the physician."[8]

That evening the students waited anxiously to know the results of the deliberations of the Board of Managers. They discovered that it was voted not to read the complaint against Dr. Post. Jirji Zaydan commented on this decision as follows: "What led them to it was racial prejudice and disrespect for Arabs as they considered it too much for Arabs to complain against American professors."[9]

On December 18, the students read the following decision posted on the bulletin board in the basement: "Voted that whereas the Board of Managers have heard an improper petition which has been handed in to them . . . , that this petition be rejected and that the Board of Managers instruct the Faculty to suspend for one month those students whose names are attached to that petition, and that no student thus suspended be received back who does not in writing withdraw his name from that petition and give to the Faculty satisfactory guarantees that he will conform to all the rules of the institution."[10]

The students refused to withdraw their names from the petition and give any guarantees. Instead, they wrote a lengthy letter in which they said:

> Sirs, it never occurred to the knowledgeable persons [*augala*] of Syria nor to the students of the College that respected people like you who come from the country of freedom—America . . . would refuse to hear the demands of young people who did not show any signs of immaturity in anything they did, nor demanded but their rights. . . . Sirs, we thought that presenting demands to respected Americans like you and clarifying ourselves to pious people who come to our country claiming they are serving the truth and goodness were matters that would suffice to get what we demanded. . . . But we found out that in a single session . . . you jumped to the verdict . . . you did not hear, you did not examine, and you did not take your time as we did.[11]

*The Consequences of Rebellion*

This revolt had several repercussions. First, all the medical faculty except Dr. Post resigned. On December 18, Dr. Cornelius Van Dyck and his son Dr. William Van Dyck resigned, and they were followed by other members. They constituted themselves as a private medical school and instructed the suspended students outside the college.

Second, as a result of the uprising of 1882 the Board of Trustees decided to require instructors to sign a religious "declaration of principles,"[12] which embraced "the whole body of evangelical doctrine as contained in the inspired Word of God, and represented in the consensus of Protestant creeds, as opposed to the erroneous teachings of the Romish and Eastern Churches. We also declare our hearty sympathy with and pledge our active cooperation in advancing the chief aim of this institution which as a missionary agency is to train up young men in the knowledge of Christian truth."[13]

President Daniel Bliss, who continued to enforce signing this religious "declaration of principles" all during his presidency, is often quoted to have said: "This College is for all conditions and classes of men without regard to colour, nationality, race or religion. A man white, black or yellow; Christian, Jew, Mohammedan or heathen, may enter and enjoy all the advantages of this institution for three, four or eight years; and go out believing in one God, in many Gods, or in no God."[14]

In spite of the ideals expressed by President Bliss, the college attracted very few Muslims in its early history, especially during his presidency. The number of Muslims

> who entered and remained throughout the course was small until after the turn of the century. Even as late as 1894, when there was a total of 235 students enrolled, only five Moslems and two Jews were to be found in the preparatory department which had an enrollment of 136. This failure to draw non-Christians was caused in part by the consistent refusal of the Trustees to relax in any way the rules governing attendance at prayers, Bible classes, preaching services and the Sabbath School. . . . Both Moslem and Jewish students were rejected if they would not agree to take part in the compulsory religious exercises.[15]

Third, at the end of the academic year 1883–1884 the Board of Managers terminated the appointments of two of the most prominent Arab scholars, Yaqoub Sarruf and Faris Nimr, the editors of the famous magazine *al-Muqtataf*. Concerning their termination, a twentieth-century AUB presi-

dent, Bayard Dodge, has said "Although they were young men of out-
standing ability they were dropped for some mysterious reason, probably
because of being connected with one of the secret societies which were
beginning to ferment Arab nationalism."[16] Another twentieth-century
president, Stephen B. L. Penrose, mentions also that

> This mysterious action seems, in the light of recent studies, to
> have been based on well-founded suspicion that the two young
> men were playing too active a part in dangerous politics. There
> is now no question but that both were leaders in a secret Arab
> society which attempted to foment rebellion against the Turks,
> and which quite certainly was the effective beginning of the
> Arab Nationalist movement of the present day. . . . That no
> hard feelings were held is shown by the fact that both Sarruf and
> Nimr were given honorary Ph.D. degrees in 1890, the first hon-
> orary degrees awarded by the College.[17]

That there were hard feelings, however, is supported by other facts.

After their termination, Sarruf and Nimr published two fighting articles
in *al-Muqtataf*. The first article, published in the May issue of 1885 and
entitled "Learning and Universities," argues that the spread of knowledge
cannot be achieved by any university unless it

> rids itself of religious fanaticism and . . . gives religious freedom
> to its teachers and students. And we say that all our schools of
> higher education in Egypt and Syria express such a pride except
> the school which was foremost among them, for it has . . .
> turned away from its original purpose of spreading learning and
> sought to impose a particular creed on its pupils. . . .
> And there is another matter which has to be taken into ac-
> count in order for a university to spread knowledge, and that is
> its reliance on the language of the country in which it intends to
> spread knowledge. And we could have saved ourselves the
> trouble of mentioning this matter, for it is taken for granted,
> were it not for the fact that some foreigners who came to spread
> knowledge in the East abandoned the system of teaching
> through the medium of its language. They wanted to save them-
> selves the effort of studying and of writing books as well as to
> monopolize the teaching posts one generation after another so
> that once a master dies he is replaced by another master in pre-
> lude to the implementation of the word of the state whose word
> they wish to implement and whose flag they wish to spread.

The second article by Sarruf and Nimr was published in the July issue of 1885 under the title "al-Kulliyah fi Beirut" [The College in Beirut] and stated:

> . . . it seems that Syria is still in bad luck, for in no time young American teachers were tempted to achieve credit and to restrict the advantages of the College to themselves, their children and relatives after them. The first evidence of the change was their replacement of Arabic by English on the pretext of the availability of more books and studies in the latter. The truth of the matter . . . was to prevent replacing foreigners by natives in the College. . . . Those who remained in the College proclaimed that the College was American root and branch and that it will continue as such and indefinitely. Accordingly, they placed a limit beyond which native teachers could not advance in the academic hierarchy.

The few Arab scholars the college had (who were converts) were not promoted or involved in decision-making. The native scholars "had not enjoyed the same rank and salary as the Americans and they had not been members of the faculty group which served as local executive committee."[18] They served as tutors, instructors, and assistants. It took forty-three years to promote one Arab scholar to the rank of full professor, and that was Jabr Dumit, teacher of Arabic and head of the Arabic Department. Getting the rank, however, did not mean getting its privileges. As is pointed out by Dodge, "Even on the level of constitution professors of equal rank were not placed on equal basis regardless of nationality and sect until 1923."[19]

*Manipulative Tolerance*

In 1913 the college unveiled the statue of Dr. Cornelius Van Dyck on campus, and during the ceremony the acting president at that time, Dr. Harvey Porter, mentioned that, when the late Dr. Van Dyck resigned his post, a number of his students were upset and left the school to continue their studies outside and earned their degrees from the medical bureau in Constantinople. Porter announced on the occasion that the college had decided to add the names of those students to the list of the graduates of 1883, and they would be considered among the alumni of the medical school in the college. Thus after thirty years Van Dyck and his students regained their rights.

The same kind of manipulative tolerance was used in the case of Yaqoub Sarruf and Faris Nimr when their fame spread all over the Arab world as great scholars. They were granted honorary Ph.D. degrees in 1890. To further take advantage of their fame, the college had a big ceremony on the occasion of unveiling the bust of Sarruf on campus in 1937, about fifty-five years after his termination.

Repression has been practiced not only for religious and political reasons. Dr. Raif Abillama (M.D. 1915, of a Lebanese aristocratic family, professor of medicine at AUB, member of the Lebanese parliament and minister of education, assistant secretary-general of the Arab League, etc.) mentioned recently in an interview that he, along with two other students, had once established a university magazine, which they named *al-Fajr*:

> We used to write mainly campus and local news but once we overstepped our limits and criticized the College, especially the food we were offered. Full tuition and boarding fees was eight pounds Sterling in gold and we thought that on that we should be fed better. Howard Bliss was then President and he called us to his office and told us that we had to apologize for this in the paper itself or else we would be expelled from the College. . . . We felt it would be a blow to both our pride and prestige to apologize; naturally, we did not wish to be expelled. Finally it was Prof. Day, Dean of Arts and Sciences, who found the solution. *Al-Fajr* was discontinued.[20]

## The 1909 Rebellion

Another revolt began on January 8, 1909. Because of its sectarian overtones, it proved more dangerous than the 1882 revolt. On the above date, the Muslim students (128 out of 853 students in the college and its preparatory section) objected to the regulations requiring attendance at Bible classes and religious exercises, and absented themselves from chapel and Bible classes. Penrose mentions that the administration tried to avoid trouble—by a gentle but nonetheless firm statement which included the following:

> 1. The aim and purpose of the College is to develop character.
> . . .
> 2. The College believes that the highest type of character cannot be developed . . . without the aid of religion, and for that reason, we say to every student that he has no right to neglect his religious life. . . .
> 3. . . . It is self-evident that the College, as a Christian College, believes that the Christian religion can do more for character than any other form of religious faith . . .

4. This is a Christian College and was established with the money of Christian people. . . .[21]

The college used several pressure tactics. Some faculty members met with the students and expressed full appreciation for their feelings but tried to convince them to give up the strike. President Howard S. Bliss and Dr. D. S. Dodge called at once on U.S. President Theodore Roosevelt and the U.S. secretary of state. President Bliss also visited the Foreign Office in London and the American and British ambassadors in Constantinople. Finally, the following letter was sent to the parents of all the students, informing them that their sons would be required:

> (1) To disclaim everything that suggests the spirit of disloyalty or disobedience or conspiracy against the authority of the College.
> (2) To undertake in a special manner a strict observance of the regulations of the College.
> (3) To resume attendance at the regular Bible classes.
> . . . If there is any parent, however, who would prefer to withdraw his son from the College he can do so.[22]

The letter was signed by Howard S. Bliss, President, for the Faculty of the College.

All students except eight complied, and the college became more insistent that it was Christian; "no student was admitted who could not give satisfactory assurance that he fully understood the rules and regulations and intended to obey them. . . . The danger was safely passed."[23] In a special meeting of the Board of Trustees held on May 25, 1909, D. S. Dodge presented several reasons for not relaxing the maintenance of the above regulations. Among these reasons were the following:

> The College was not established merely for higher secular education, or the inculcation of morality. One of its chief objects is to teach the great truths of Scripture; to be a center of Christian light and influence; and to lead its students to understand and accept a pure Christianity, and go out to profess and commend it in every walk of life. . . .
> There is danger of interference by local authorities. . . .
> Our defense must be that we are entitled to regulate our own internal affairs as an American missionary enterprise . . . and possessing certain privileges under the protection of our own Government, and the official recognition of the Turkish Government.

> We desire to work in the closest harmony with all who are also endeavoring to enlighten, civilize, and Christianize the people of the Near East.[24]

## The Struggle for Independence

The present student movement began to emerge during the second quarter of this century when the struggle for independence started to take shape in the Middle East and the rest of the Third World countries. During this period, the Middle East witnessed several revolts against French, English, and Zionist colonization. Increasing national awareness brought about some organized political action. Thus Bayard Dodge (president of AUB at the time) mentions that the thirties were a period of political agitation, and "during this period of agitation, propaganda leaders did their best to stir up the youth. It was difficult to keep the University students from joining political societies, taking part in demonstrations, and making addresses in public places."[25] The university, as President Dodge confessed, tried to divert the attention of students from the pressing problem of independence of their country by keeping them happy with movies, sports, and other extracurricular activities.

In the thirties two national movements started to emerge among students of AUB. The first was the Arab nationalist movement, which looked to Constantine K. Zurayk and others for inspiration. The Arab nationalists organized themselves loosely around a university society, al-'Urwa al-Wuthqa, and published a magazine carrying the same title. The other movement was the Syrian Social Nationalist Party, founded at AUB in 1932 by a faculty member, Antun Saade; its first recruits were students from emerging middle-class families. In a short while, it became a highly organized party and spread into the big cities, towns, and distant villages in Lebanon, Syria, and Palestine.

Both movements concerned themselves with the question of national identity and struggle for independence. Both raised the question "Who are we?" but they reached different conclusions. One said, "We are Arabs," and called for unity of all Arab countries extending from the Atlantic Ocean to the Arab Gulf. The other said, "We are Syrians," and called mainly for the unity of Lebanon, present Syria, Palestine, and Jordan.

For almost three decades, the two movements dominated the political arena at AUB and competed for control of student societies and later the Student Council. They often clashed, especially after independence, but they were mostly engaged in arguments about the nature of nationalism and what constitutes a nation: one emphasized language and common historical experience, and the other geography and socioeconomic unity throughout history. There were a few communists who allied themselves with the Arab nationalists, but they were not fully accepted, as revealed by a special issue of *al-'Urwa al-Wuthqa* on Arab-Western relations:

> Those who recommend communism . . . are planting in the souls of the innocent among the people the seeds of fragmentation and hatred instead of faith and love. . . .
> The Marxian message is in full contradiction with the message we work for. . . . We teach people love and it calls for hatred. We plant the seeds of contentment and satisfaction in the heart of people and it plants the seeds of envy and revenge. We have learned from our fathers admiration for heroism and respect for heritage and high ideals. . . . The Arab nation which contributed a great deal to the elevation of the status of man will not be deceived by this artificial order offered to it by worshippers of materialism. . . .
> I do not think, God forbid it, that their teacher is more noble and humane than Muhammad and Jesus.[26]

The Arab nationalist movement has gradually developed to subscribe to the Marxist-Leninist doctrines and strategies in the struggle to liberate Palestine. As of 1975–1976, along with the Syrian nationalists and others, they constituted the Rejection Front, in opposition to Arab governments seeking settlement with Israel, and the Syrian nationalists fought on their side in the Lebanese civil war against the rightists.

In spite of fragmentation, now and then students showed some activism in the thirties and forties. Bayard Dodge mentions that "on May 3, 1941, Iraq engaged in hostilities against Great Britain [this is how wars of independence are described by Dodge] and propaganda agents instigated a large number of Iraqi students to march out from an assembly in West Hall and to parade down the main street of the town."[27] Previously, some student outbursts had taken place in response to Turkey's annexation of the Iskendaron region of Syria (1937) and the Palestinian revolt (1936–1939). The students also played some role in the struggle for Lebanese independence in 1943. "Between November 11th and 23rd, 1943, the city [Beirut] was in a state of siege. Eight hundred boarding students were interned on the campus. Several American military police were sent from Palestine to protect the campus gateways from violence. Classes were given up and an effort was made to keep the students happy with 'movies' and 'sports'."[28]

It is during this struggle that students at AUB felt the need for some kind of student representation. A Student Council, for the first time, was authorized. Its members were appointed in November 1943 by the administration, but it was soon dissolved, again by the administration. Students, led by members of the Student Council, staged demonstrations against the

French, and they were fired at by the Senegalese soldiers sent by France to keep order. Some were wounded, and arrest warrants were issued against others.

## The Struggle for Palestine

The impact of the Palestinian problem on the development of the student movement in Lebanon has been much stronger than any other single issue in the area.

The student struggle was greatly intensified during the academic year 1947–1948, which witnessed the Arab-Zionist war, the establishment of the state of Israel, and the uprooting of the Palestinians from their country. The tragic events of 1947–1948 hit almost all Palestinian Arabs, regardless of their religious, regional, or social class backgrounds. The Palestinian students, who constituted the second largest national group after the Lebanese at AUB (between 15 and 20 percent in the forties) were personally hit (in addition to the national experience).

The impact of the 1947–1948 event was so great that it marked a new stage in the history of Arab society. As put by Zurayk, "the intensified sense of the tragedy aroused a feeling of revolt, not only against the external powers and interests which caused the tragedy, but also against the regimes, leaderships, organizations and systems of government and of life which made it possible. This feeling was a reflection of the general spread of discontent among the Arab peoples which produced a succession of coups d'état and gave new life and vigor to ideologies and parties calling for radical change."[29] While the 1947–1948 tragedy aroused a feeling of revolt, the 1967 tragedy aroused a mood for revolution.

The direct impact of the first tragedy on the student movement in Lebanon was its contribution to the following developments:

First, students became more involved in ideological political parties. Some joined already existing political parties, such as the Syrian Social Nationalist Party and the Ba'ath Party. Others started new movements, which spread all over the Arab countries and continued to gain new vigor and appeal to the masses.

Second, students became increasingly disenchanted with the West and began to realize that colonization had continued to plague their countries in spite of independence.

Students staged several violent demonstrations: in 1951 against the French for their measures against Morocco; in 1954 against the Baghdad Pact; in 1956 against the Tripartite invasion of Egypt; and in the late fifties in support of the Algerian Revolution.

Third, the Palestinian students took over the leadership and have constituted the core of the student movement since then. Furthermore, the present leadership of the Palestinian resistance movement emerged from the ranks of the Palestinian student activists. The Popular Front for the Liberation of Palestine (PFLP) is a radical transformation of the Arab Nationalist Movement which was founded at AUB by George Habash and other student activists. A number of other prominent leaders and members of PFLP such as Wadi' Haddad, Hani al-Hindi, Tayseer Qub'a, Leila Khalid, Ghassan Kanafani, and Bassam Abou Sherif were politically active as students. Similarly, Fateh was initially formed in the early fifties by three Palestinian students: Yasser Arafat, Hani al-Hassan, and Khalil al-Wazir.

Fourth, the university consistently resorted to repressive measures after student strikes and demonstrations. During the academic year 1950–1951, the president of the university, Dr. Stephen F. L. Penrose, informed the student council that three students, Mansour Armali (a fourth-year medical student), Abdul Alim Saadi (a second-year medical student), and Albert Kharrat (a freshman student), had been notified that they were suspended from readmission to the university until further notice because of violation of AUB's statement of policy. Soon after that, three other students, Fuad Shabi, Camille Majdalemi, and Farrouk Ta'i, were suspended for distributing pamphlets attacking the United States, France, Britain, and AUB. When the president of the Student Council, Afif Talhouk, asked the president of the university "if there were any grounds for reconsideration or pardon for at least Saadi and Armali, the president expressed his deep regret that he was forced to interrupt or perhaps destroy the career of two prospective doctors."[30]

In the summer of 1951, two students, Farid Saba and Shafiq El-Hout, were expelled for their political activities. In October–November of the same year, seven more students were expelled from the university for leading a demonstration on October 22 against British policy in the Middle East. At the end of January 1952 the Student Council was suspended indefinitely following student protests, and all AUB students were henceforth required to sign a pledge not to take action interfering with the academic functions of the university. Students remained without student government for seventeen years.

Similarly, on January 25, 1954, the university administration ordered the student organization al-'Urwa al-Wuthqa, to disband and dismissed seventeen students for their connection with political demonstrations. Immediately about two hundred students went on a sit-down strike. Security forces surrounded the striking students and made several arrests.

On November 1, 1960, a group of AUB students participated in a rally and demonstration commemorating the anniversary of the start of the Algerian Revolution. In reaction, the university suspended five students for one semester and eight others for two semesters, and one student, Mohammad Kawash, was expelled from the university. Kawash was arrested with nine other students by the Lebanese Security Forces; he received insults and brutal blows and had to be hospitalized. The arrested students found out that the Security Forces had obtained their information from the University Office of Student Affairs.

These repressive measures were mainly directed against Arab nationalists, whose core leadership in the university was Palestinian. This meant, especially to students, that the university was antagonistic to national aspirations. The gap between the students and the administration widened in times of national crises, for the more students showed concern with the political problems of the area, the more the university resorted to repressive measures.

## Conclusion

In short, the early stages in the development of the student movement in Lebanon may be characterized by the following features. First, in spite of continuity and organization into working movements, student activism has been intermittent, depending on national crises. In between, it has remained somewhat dormant, and most of its activities have continued to take place in reaction to major events in the area. Second, much of student activism has been in terms of clashes within its ranks and between groups subscribing to different national identities. Third, whenever students have become active in response to national crises, the university administration has resorted to several measures of repression or to diverting their attention to other kinds of activities, encouraging counter groups, and suspending student leaders.

Yet, through their struggle, students began to discover that the liberation of their country depended on basic transformation in their attitudes, value orientations, views, and conceptions, as well as in the very fabric of Arab society and its political and social systems. They became more internationally oriented, more alienated from the prevailing political systems and leaderships, more concerned about social liberation, more convinced that they should put an end to dependency, and more aware of class struggle in the Arab society. They began to identify with the deprived and oppressed within as well as outside their society. As will be shown in the next chapter, a shift toward a socialist revolutionary ideology and class analysis has been in the making within the context of the Palestinian struggle.

# 9. Confrontation or Negation:

*Recent Developments in the Student Movement*

The student movement in Lebanon has continued to be partly a movement against itself. Students have continued to be divided along lines and issues connected with the search for national identity. In addition, the last two decades have witnessed the emergence of some regrouping and splintering as a result of the development of a higher order of consciousness connected with economical, social, and political transformation.

Thus, after almost one hundred years of student activism, the student movement has continued to exhibit such general characteristic features as the following:

First, there is no enduring cooperation of students across universities and colleges in Lebanon, although they are all located in Beirut. There is no general union, and students of each university have their own organizations, concerns, activities, and unique points of departure.

Second, student politics reflect the existing sectarian and authoritarian tendencies in Lebanese society. In spite of their alienation, students continue to be divided along lines and issues similar to those at the bases of cleavages in the society itself. This is most visibly reflected in the current civil war, for students have joined the ranks of the opposed fighting groups on the right and the left.

Third, student leaders have continued to resort to the elitists and those in positions of power in the country to help them in their fight against university officials. In 1882 the student strikers resorted to the elitists in Beirut (*zawat al-balad wa kibar a'ianiha*). After almost one hundred years of experience, student leaders threatened university officials, in leaflets distributed on campus in 1974, that they would contact the "Lebanese government to see to it that this University . . . becomes subject to the supervision of the Lebanese government." Instead of supervising the university, Lebanese authorities stormed it in 1974 to remove the student strikers and take them to prison or outside the country.

Fourth, students are characterized by what one of them (an activist) called a boy-scout mentality in their confrontation with those in positions of authority. When faced with polite and congenial officials, they find themselves unable to maintain the ideological aggression which they express very forcefully in student gatherings and strikes. Instead, they show respect and express readiness to compromise away their issues. Hence, they can be easily outsmarted and outmaneuvered by their opponents. When they reach "the point where the next logical step is violent action," the student leaders lose their nerve. Their strikes had been "kind of a game, but violence is serious." Therefore, "they would be treated like players and the game would be soon over. Moderate tactics presuppose moderate adversaries, genuinely willing to compromise, and not very far apart in their demands. . . . Negotiation presupposes a very high level of understanding and cooperation, and unless it takes place between equals, it is always a mask to hide defeat."[1]

This chapter will describe the major student strikes and demonstrations as well as the contending student organizations and their programs since the June War of 1967. The basic aim is to identify the major repeated patterns of behavior in student strikes and to show how vertical cleavages and factionalism may undermine student unity and convert the process of confrontation into one of self-negation.

## Student Organizations

There have been leftist, liberal, and rightist student organizations in universities operating in Lebanon, but an alliance of several student groups who think of themselves as progressive has been in control of the student movement.

### Leftist Organizations

In many ways the June War of 1967 initiated a new stage in the development of the student movement. New alliances and groups of leftist students emerged, including Palestinian resistance student organizations (Fateh, PFLP, DFLP, and others), the Union of Democratic Youth (members of the Lebanese Communist Party), Progressive Socialists, Committees for Student Action, the Organization of Lebanese Socialists, The Syrian Social Nationalists, Nasserite Forces, the Organization of Communist Action, and others.

The alliance of progressive groups has been constantly threatened by conflicts and even splits. Charges and countercharges have been exchanged, and in certain instances, the charges and countercharges have resulted in violent encounters. On the whole, however, there has been great pressure on progressive groups to cooperate, since they are constantly threatened by the rightists and some liberal groups.

Though divided, the progressive groups have been able to dominate student politics in Lebanon, especially at AUB, LU, and BAU. They have (1) contributed to the spread of leftist ideas, national and social class consciousness, and student participation in running universities; (2) supported and participated in the Palestinian struggle, which they conceive of as an inseparable part of the Arab revolution and the world liberation front; (3) raised the battle cry against imperialists and their agents and institutions, pointing out that national education should replace the classical imperialist curricula; (4) worked toward reforming LU and calling attention to the educational crisis in Lebanon; (5) exposed the nondemocratic practices of the universities, governments, and other agencies; (6) called attention to ongoing processes of exploitation and domination in the society; (7) struggled for democratization of education, creating new applied colleges at LU, introducing a system of national scholarship grants, securing health insurance for students, and guaranteeing student participation in running LU; (8) expressed an urgent need for cooperating with socialist and leftist movements all over the world and supporting the just struggle of the peoples of the Third World.

*Liberal Organizations*

Founders and members of liberal organizations belong marginally to the prevailing system and are most often socialized into moderation and rationality. They develop a consciousness that the system is threatened by both the leftists and the rightists. Thus, their starting point is to disaffiliate themselves from both wings and from existing political parties. Two such student movements appeared in Lebanon in the late sixties and early seventies: the Wa'i Movement (LU) and As-Sana' (AUB).

*The Wa'i Movement.* This movement was founded by a number of Christian students from marginal Lebanese villages who had been seeking higher education in Beirut. Though critical of existing parties, they considered themselves Lebanese nationalists, but of a new caliber and outlook. They provided an example par excellence of loyal opposition. Though Lebanese in orientation, the movement tended to support Palestinian causes. Though its founders come from traditionally conservative and Christian communities, they called for secularism, democratization of schools, rejection of the right-wing parties prevailing in Christian communities, renewal of the existing institutions and laws, civil marriage, progressive taxation, and unionization of the student movement. They rejected imperialism and borrowed some leftist concepts in describing the Lebanese socioeconomic and political structures.

The movement started in 1969 as a coalition of several groups and was seen by the leftists as an attempt to create a rightist front. Soon, however, it became clear that there were two wings. One was a group of nonpartisan liberals headed by Antoine Douaihi, Isam Khalifeh, and Paul Shawoul, who called for transcending fragmentation and unionization of the student movement. The other wing was mostly rightist and belonged to al-Kata'ib, the National Bloc, and the Free Nationalists, a party led by Ex-President of the Lebanese Republic Camille Sham'oun. The first group was the dynamic force behind the movement, as was shown by the movement's first working program, which carried the seeds of the ideas and views of Douaihi, Khalifeh, and Shawoul. It referred to the Wa'i Movement as a democratic syndicated union whose aim was to work toward blasting the underdeveloped educational system in Lebanon and putting an end to the cultural uprootedness of the Lebanese. In addition to proposing solutions for educational and administrative reform on all levels, it called for showing concern with basic issues, "the most urgent of which is the Palestinian problem and support of armed struggle of Palestinians within the framework of the Lebanese interest." A distinction was also made in the early stages between a syndicate and a political party, with the intention of asserting that the movement should be independent from political parties and concern itself with student issues.

This liberal wing, calling itself the Wa'i Movement–Front of Lebanese Youth, held a conference in September 1971 in which four reports were presented: an educational report, an internal report, a socioeconomic report, and a political report.

The educational report pledged commitment to democratization of education. Among its basic postulates was the following: Any scientific solution for educational problems must be an integral part of a comprehensive educational and economical plan, which could not be possible in a political system based on monopolization and governed by confessional and feudal lords.

The internal report was critical of the existing political parties and labor unions and recommended independence from them.

The socioeconomic report used official statistics to demonstrate inequalities in distribution of national wealth and how such districts as South Lebanon, Akkar, and Hermel suffer from poverty and underdevelopment. It concluded that feudal and primitive productive relations coexist with more modern exploitive relations.

The political report examined the Lebanese political situation in the context of Arab and world politics. On the world level, the report observed a process of new regroupings on the basis of industrial and technological development rather than on purely abstract ideologies (specifically, the growing gap between the Soviet Union and China and the narrowing of the gaps between each of them and the United States). On the other hand, the gap and imbalance between the developed and undeveloped societies are growing increasingly more intense. The solution, according to this report, lies in commitment to the practice of organized democratic pressure through unionization of all sectors of the society, toward moving "the people from the feudal and confessional position to the national, secular, and political position."[2]

As a result of increasing radicalization, due to gradual awareness of the difficulties of introducing reforms from within the existing system, the Wa'i Movement split again in 1975 when one of the founders, Isam Khalifeh, allied himself with the leftist Democratic Forces. As of February 1975, there were three groups: the Wa'i Movement University Forces (rightists), the Lebanese Wa'i Movement (liberal and led by Douaihi and Shawoul), and the Wa'i Movement–Front of Lebanese Youth (more leftist and led by Khalifeh.)

*As-Sana'.* This liberal movement emerged at AUB in 1971 and defined itself as a unionized student movement working toward uniting students and liberating them from isolation and partisanship in order to play a pioneering and effective role in the development of their society. As-Sana' has posed itself as a believer in openness to all currents of thought and respect for different political philosophies and ideas but has asserted that student politics should be independent from the existing political parties which try to control the student body. The students, according to As-Sana', should be the prime movers in society, but, in order to play such a role, they have first to solve their own problems. This is why, As-Sana' says, the priority should be given to student issues and student unity, a priority which requires self-restraint and resorting to dialogue, rationality, persuasion, and never to violence. The distinguishing characteristic of As-Sana' as a liberal group is its psychologizing of revolution. It asserts in one of its leaflets that students' foremost battle should be a battle with the self: "The revolution which we should be preaching . . . is a revolution against the self before being a revolution against the Administration, traditionalism, imperialism, and cultural colonization."

Again, this liberal group was increasingly radicalized through confrontation with the social and political systems which resisted change and gradually forced some members to re-examine the assumption that such systems could be reformed from within.

Once radical ideas start to infiltrate a liberal organization, the group is likely to split, for the great majority of those who are attracted to such organizations are loyal to the system and cannot afford to go beyond loyal opposition. This is exactly what happened in the cases of As-Sana' and the Wa'i Movement. For As-Sana' the split was fatal—the movement collapsed into nonexistence.

*Right-Wing Organizations*

Rightists have organized themselves most effectively at AUB and SJU, and to some extent at LU. The rightist wing at AUB is represented by the Lebanese League, founded during the sectarian violent events of 1958 by conservative Christian students and faculty members with the blessing of the university administration. On the occasion of Lebanese Independence Day[3] in 1970, the League released a communiqué in a press conference in which it asserted its dedication "to a noble national idea which it seeks to safeguard and to propagate. This idea can be summarized in two points: First, Lebanon is a natural nation standing on its own and worthy of continuity. . . . Second, the Lebanese nation assumes, in this part of the world, a humanitarian mission, namely, the call for freedom and the advocation of free social systems. . . . The League stands committed to Lebanon as an entity and as a regime."[4]

In this communiqué, the League responds to several accusations leveled by critics, including religious fanaticism and isolationism. Their answer to the accusation of fanaticism is, "We are a Lebanese national institution which does not undertake statistical surveys to know the religious composition of its membership and because such queries and the answers to them constitute fanaticism par excellence." To the accusation of isolationism, the communiqué responds: "If one's love to his nation is tantamount to isolation, we proudly state: 'We are isolationists in our determination to safeguard Lebanese values. . . . We have, however, our own interest in what lies outside Lebanon. We consider, for instance, that Lebanon has a humanitarian mission in the Arab World. The idea of freedom on which the Lebanese regime is founded can be exported. . . . It is important for us, as Lebanese, to propagate the Lebanese view of freedom in various parts of the Arab World.' "

What is the League's view of freedom? No attempt has been made to define its content. Some indications, however, are reflected in a number of its proclamations and actions. In effect, these indications may be summarized as follows: (1) The League has refrained from involvement in ideological discussions. In the communiqué mentioned above, there is reference to attempts being made "to involve it [the League] in ideological discussion which we preferred to avoid because they cannot be of intellectual benefit to us or to others." In the same press conference, the president of the League made the following remark: "But, as for me, I would not like to engage in fruitless arguments with those who do not believe in what I believe."[5] (2) The Lebanese League has been involved in several clashes at AUB. Some of these clashes were explained by the League president as "due to attacks by the latter [critics] on our Lebanese values . . . but we stopped them short in the past and we will continue to do so. . . . The people who criticize the League are those who do not believe in our Lebanese values or in the Lebanese government."[6] (3) The League has served as a counter group in student strikes, demonstrations, and occupations of buildings. A statement signed by the president of the League, Nabil Bakhazi, on May 19, 1970, said: ". . . it is ironic that some complain of lack of freedom at AUB, while we all know that we complain of its excess."[7]

The League's battle cry to preserve law and order against student protests and strikes is repeated quite often. On the occasion of the visit by Chase Manhattan Bank President David Rockefeller to Beirut on March 10, 1971, some ten thousand demonstrators marched to the airport protesting against his visit. Violent clashes erupted between student demonstrators and security forces, and scores of students were injured and others arrested in the clash. On March 12, the Lebanese League issued a statement signed by its president, Walid Hajjar, which said: "We, as Lebanese citizens who believe in order, cannot condemn the security forces for confronting a demonstration that resulted in blocking the way to the airport, an action which goes beyond the limit of applying legitimate pressure on the government and causes damage to Lebanon's interest, and consequently, the interests of the Lebanese."[8]

The League has supported the army on several occasions because of "its defense of Lebanon, which will continue to survive disasters for *Lebanon was created to stay*." This slip of the tongue (for such a phrase is often used to describe Israel) was made in a statement issued by the Lebanese League on the occasion of its decision to consider Thursday, May 14, 1970, "Army Day at AUB." On the occasion it saluted the army for its continual defense of the "everlasting Lebanon" and "put itself at its disposal" for "the preservation of quietness and order, and for continuity in everyday work." In its publication, *al-Rabita*, in the spring of 1971, it glorified the role of the army in the following terms: "Its message is more than a duty, . . . it is the sacred honor which is more precious than life. Its institution excels as a factory of death for a better life. We strike with a hand of iron those who try to meddle with the sacred institutions of the country; . . . military service is priesthood."

This extreme rightist tendency is explained by a League member in the first issue of *al-Rabita*: The fact that "few Christians are surrounded by many Muslims . . . called for fear and isolation in order to preserve their existence. And quite often fear leads to extremism . . . ; no matter how understanding the Lebanese Nationalists may be of the Pan-Arab cause, they will never accept to join their ranks as long as there is the slightest threat to the fate of the Christians."[9] The feeling of threat is clearly conveyed in a piece of literary writing by a League member, in which Lebanon is presented as a threatened child: "My country is an anxious child climbing time by weak robes. . . . My country is a child falling . . . and when the child of my country falls, time will fall with it. . . . Oh, my country, I thought you were a castle . . ., a small flower that no wind could reach . . ."[10] This fear serves also to mask the fact that the Lebanese Christians occupy the most privileged social, political, and economical positions in Lebanon. The present data show that members and supporters of the League are more likely to come from rich families and aspire to elitist positions than are other students. For instance, the supporters of the League were more likely than the supporters of the revolutionary leftists to come from families that earned a yearly income of £L 20,000 or more (63 percent versus 34 percent), and to rank their families as belonging to upper and upper-middle classes (67 percent versus 36 percent). Their right-wing politics best preserves their interests and privileges.

**Student Strikes and Demonstrations**

In the aftermath of the June War of 1967, student strikes have been an ongoing phenomenon in Lebanon. Almost the same pattern evolves each time, and violent encounters between police and students (especially at LU) or between student groups (mostly at AUB) have been familiar sights. Because strikes differ in the different universities, they will be described separately. At AUB, strikes are usually directed against the university administration, and clashes take place between students themselves. At LU, on the other hand, strikes are directed against the government, and clashes occur between students and security forces.

In this section, an attempt will be made to briefly describe the major strikes and demonstrations on the different university campuses with the intention of identifying the major repeated behavioral patterns, themes, and factors that seem to determine the course of events. Further evidence of student vertical cleavages and factionalism will also be provided. These encounters could be seen as indicators of the approaching storm of the civil war.[11]

*The December 28 Uprising*

The Israeli attack on Beirut International Airport, December 18, 1968, shocked concerned Lebanese and dispelled a number of myths. The general mood was one of indignation and outrage at the army and the government for showing no resistance whatsoever. The army had to do something about its image. Being unable to entertain the idea of confronting Israeli attacks, it moved to deal with the source of embarrassment, namely, the Palestinian commandos.

The outrage against the army and government was manifested in the student strike following the attack and in statements issued by professors, political parties, and others. The strike was initiated immediately after the Israeli attack by students at BAU (students at other universities were on vacation), to be followed by AUB students on January 4, and LU and SJU students on January 6. Representatives of all these universities met and decided on a general strike until the government realized the following demands:

   *1.* Immediate investigation and exposure of all people responsible, whether civilian or military, for nonresistance to the Israeli attack on Beirut International Airport, followed by a public trial.

   2. General mobilization of the Lebanese people and fortification of the Lebanese front villages.

   *3.* Emphasis on the legitimacy of the commandos' action in Lebanon and abstention from interfering with it.

Similar demands were adopted by a number of professors at AUB and LU and by the Union of Lebanese Writers. Thirty-two Lebanese professors at AUB addressed a letter to the Lebanese parliament in which they stated:

> The Israeli aggression on Lebanese land has brought to light a great gap between how this country should be and how it actually is. . . . This gap openly condemns civilian and noncivilian officials as well as those in power in the Lebanese system. . . . The undersigned Lebanese professors . . . who are calling for comprehensive self-criticism of all our conditions . . . wish to demand the following: (1) . . . formation of a trustworthy commission of investigation; (2) punishing severely the responsible without cover-up of the senior ones among them as usual; (3) establishment of obligatory military service, training the people in military and civil defense, and fortification of frontier villages and establishments all over Lebanon; (4) combatting espionage activities and foreign interference; (5) imposing taxes on the privileged classes . . . ; (6) supporting the Palestinian revolution by all available means; (7) complete and sincere cooperation with all other Arab countries in defending the Arab character of Palestine.

Three of the professors who signed this statement have since become ministers in the Lebanese cabinet.

A group of fifty-three professors at the Science College of LU issued a statement which pointed out that the aggression on December 28 revealed that:

> (1) the state has no power to enforce laws; (2) confessionalism has undermined our unity; (3) the conception of public interest was emptied of any content . . . ; (4) spread of educational confusion and cultural fragmentation under the pretext of freedom of teaching . . . ; (5) distortion of moral values . . . to the extent that democratic freedoms become the freedom of the powerful to exploit the weak, and free economy becomes free monopolization and control . . . ; (6) the defense of Lebanon in a clownish way without dependence on the people.
>
> It is time to open a new page. It is required that the country adopt a new legitimacy based . . . on (1) elimination of confessionalism; (2) spread of public secular education and making it compulsory at least on the elementary level; (3) adoption of unified civil laws in the area of personal status; (4) participation of all citizens in serving the flag . . . ; (5) adopting a just and effective ascending system of taxation; (6) securing democratic freedoms; (7) use of individual qualifications in recruiting civil servants.
>
> With regard to the current situation resulting from repeated Israeli aggressions on Lebanon and other Arab countries, we demand . . . fortification of frontier villages; legitimization of commando action; and training of the people in armed resistance.

Several slogans were devised in this strike. Some of them were honest expressions of deep feelings, and others were meant for public consumption or for relief of tension. A sample of these slogans includes the following, without any attempt at categorization: "Government: Why don't you start a tent factory for future use?" "They have Kibbutz and we have the Caves de Rois [a night club]." "At last, we will die united." "We want to return to Lebanon, too." "Any reform starts by *REFUSAL*. Support this *REFUSAL*." "Stop building movies. Start building shelters." "Visit our South before it's too late." "Boys, cut your hair before they cut your heads." "Wanted: a Che Guevara to start a revolution for the Lebanese."

*A new gap.* The immediate result of public indignation and student strikes was the resignation of the Lebanese cabinet. The battle, however, was not over and continued to linger under the ashes of events. It was pointed out earlier that the Lebanese government and the army were unable to entertain the idea of confronting Israeli attacks. Instead they preached the idea of strength through weakness and secretly moved to deal with the source of embarrassment, namely, the Palestinian commandos. Gradually, a gap began to form between the Lebanese government and the Palestinian resistance movement. This was accompanied by the diminishing of support for the Palestinian commandos in some Christian communities. Wall inscriptions appeared in Ashrafiyah and other neighborhoods saying, "No to the Resistance." In fact, violent clashes occurred between the Lebanese army and commandos in 1969, and the tension was reflected on university campuses. On October 29, 1969, AUB became the scene of fierce fighting between the supporters of the commandos and members of the Lebanese League. These clashes may be regarded as early signs of the approaching civil war.

*Yearly Strikes at Lebanese University*

Students at LU have been increasingly radicalized, and the gap between them and the government has been extended. They have constantly pressed for educational reform, both of their own university and of the total educational system in Lebanon. As a result of encounters with government officials, they have come to realize that the government has no vision or plans for reform and lacks sensitivity to major needs and problems on all levels. Consequently, a greater number of students have become aware that educational reform is inseparable from comprehensive and basic change of the socioeconomic and political structures prevailing in the society.

*Typical strikes at LU.* A general review of the major strikes at LU since 1970 would adequately acquaint us with the student movement there and the nature of its confrontations with the authorities as well as the dynamics of its involvement in the process of reform. The early part of January 1970 witnessed a new development when, in a forty-day strike, a group of students occupied the School of Education to protest the arrest of a few students. They took over the offices, evacuated the employees, started to form committees for security, supplies, foreign relations, auto-management, etc., and raised slogans such as "Students are on night guard while officials are asleep." Three days later (January 9, 1970), some students occupied the College of Law and Politics while the others were proceeding with their march. On January 13, students from LU, SJU, and BAU launched a demonstration and clashed with the security forces on their way to the parliament, where about thee thousand students started a sit-in and chanted "Basita . . . Basita, Tis'a Wts' in Tijlita" (No problem, no problem, just ninety-nine phonies), referring to the ninety-nine deputies of the Lebanese parliament, and "Al-Majlis Badou Tandhif, yalla yā Baladieh" (The parliament needs cleaning; rush up, municipality). The strike, occupation, and demonstrations continued until their demands were orally met by the officials.

*Resuming the strike in 1971 and 1972.* The strike erupted again in March–April of 1971. Students occupied buildings, held conferences and rallies, demonstrated, and converged on the Parliament Square, supported by students from other universities and secondary schools. Similar activities were staged in Tripoli, Sidon, Zahlah, Nabatiyyah, Ba'albek, and other towns. The students occupied several major streets and squares, chanting slogans against the government's failure to meet their demands, which included:

1. Creating new applied colleges, i.e., engineering, medical, and agricultural schools.

2. Introducing a system of national scholarships, grants, and other forms of student aid.

3. Securing health insurance for students.

4. Revising the curricula and systems of examinations.

5. Securing jobs for the increasing number of graduating students.

6. Democratizing education.

7. Eliminating the two years of internship for students of law and reducing the fee to join the Lebanese Lawyers Syndicate.

8. Strengthening national education and putting an end to dependence on foreign schools and universities.

9. Allocating the money necessary to construct new buildings and execute new projects.

10. Recruiting qualified faculty.

11. Planning to make Lebanese University the center of education in Lebanon.

12. Student participation in running the university.

In 1972, again in March and April, a more violent and decisive strike took place. The strike was slow at the beginning and continued to stagger until March 28, when students invaded the building of the Ministry of Education with the intention of staging a sit-in. Suddenly, fierce clashes ensued between the student invaders and the security forces—twenty students were wounded and thirteen others arrested.

What the students hoped to accomplish came to be true: Student groups and unions in all other universities and colleges met and issued a strong statement condemning "the cruel repression to which students were exposed" and strongly supporting "their fair demands." They accused the government of evasiveness, proclaimed a general one-day strike in their universities and colleges, and promised to participate in the symbolic demonstration the next day.

On March 29, an impressively quiet and large demonstration did take place. The President of the Republic expressed his regret that students "resorted to the streets" and warned against "elements that seek to create confusion by exploiting the university students to serve their interests."

The students tried again to invade the building of the Ministry of Education and stage a sit-in, disregarding the warnings of the minister that all necessary measures would be used to prevent the occupation.

At this point, the students changed their strategy and decided to stage a sit-in and "hunger strike till death" on the street pavement outside the building.

About 60 students participated in the hunger strike and about 150 in the sit-in. The number began to increase when some of those on strike collapsed and had to be carried to hospitals. On April 18, more than 5,000 students from all universities and thirty-five other institutions participated in a demonstration in support of their fellow students at LU. They blocked streets, and the most violent confrontation to date occurred on April 20, when students tried to invade the main gate of the ministry. Several students and security men were wounded and dozens of demonstrators arrested. The reactions outside the student body were ones of shock among certain segments and serious concern among others. The representatives of twenty unions and eight political parties held a conference, concluded that the demands of students "constitute the minimum requirements for strengthening the Lebanese University," and threatened to organize a national strike.

The minister of education and the prime minister announced on April 21 and 22 their full agreement and adoption of the demands. The prime minister stated: "We will establish the schools of medicine and engineering and the applied schools and will work on developing the University at maximum speed. I believe this is binding. . . . I hope, after this clarification, that our sons the students will not resort to disruption and confusion . . . for they are our sons and we are as concerned with their needs and even more concerned, and we do not like to see them waste their time in the street."[12]

On April 26, students moved from the streets into classes after rejecting paternalistic attitudes and warning against "impotent promises."

*1973 strikes: O Freedom.* The students at LU had to resort to interrupted strikes before March–April of 1973. In addition to their permanent crisis within the university, they had to be concerned with problems of democratic freedoms of public school teachers and peasants in South Lebanon. On January 24, 1973, two peasants were shot and killed and several others were wounded by security forces during a peaceful protest in Nabatiyyah. Previously, two workers had been shot to death by security forces in a similar strike in Shiah, a suburb of Beirut (which also witnessed the first incidents of the current civil war). The next day strikes were proclaimed by students in all universities and a number of secondary schools. A student speaker pointed out that "the number of those who were killed by the bullets of the system is greater than that of the martyrs of Israeli aggression against Lebanon." Another student noted that "the authorities that run away in times of Israeli aggression shoot to kill the people in the South." The system was also accused of protecting monopoly and exploitation.

A few days later (January 13) fighting between students and security forces erupted around the Ministry of Education. It was reported that twenty-five students were wounded and eighty-two others arrested. The students resorted then to flying strikes, in which they scattered into small groups that would disperse and suddenly appear in commercial areas and crowded streets and start chanting, "O freedom, we are your men; we want to prevent your assassination" (Ya hurriyyi Nihna Rjalik, badna nimn' ightialik). By the time security forces reached the area they had dispersed and appeared somewhere else. This tactic resulted in indiscriminate attacks on bystanders and the arrest of about one hundred persons.

Meanwhile, two activities had been contributing to further intensification of the situation. One was the sit-in by 309 public school teachers dismissed from work because of their participation in a teachers' strike. The other was the preparation by university students for their First National Conference for Education, which was to be held on April 16–18 of that year. The preparation resulted in issuance of the most comprehensive and accurate assessment by students of the educational situation so far. The document included the following:

> First: The National Conference for Education held at the UNESCO on April 16–18, 1973, sees the following:
>
> 1. The state continues to look at education through a traditional perspective which does not take account of contemporaneous developments in Lebanon and the world, and consequently lacks in comprehensive educational policy.
>
> 2. The absence of a comprehensive educational policy has led to the intensification of the crisis which threatens the human bases of the country and preserves discrimination in all its forms and prevents equal opportunities among citizens. . . .
>
> Second: in the light of the above, the First National Conference for Education proclaims the following:
>
> 1. Lebanon is in need of a new conception of education which delivers it from myths and complexes. . . .
>
> 2. Such an education should be an integral part of a comprehensive national plan for economical and social changes. . . .

3. Planning is basic for real democracy. . . .

4. Real democracy is social in essence. . . .

5. It is not possible to achieve real democracy except through actual application of the principle of participation on all levels. . . . The school or college should be managed by the representatives of four groups: administrators, teachers, students, and parents.

6. . . . Democratization of education (i.e., free education for all . . .).

7. . . . Diversification of education. . . .

8. . . . The Lebanese University should be the axis and the base of education. . . .

Third, the First National Conference for Education . . . recommends the following:

1. Assertion on guaranteeing . . . democracy in thought and practice and warning the authorities against their continued disrespect for the most elementary democratic rights of citizens, and especially their violent and repressive measures against unionized action. . . .

2. Unification of the university student movement by way of developing forms of coordination and cooperation between student unions . . . in preparation for the creation of a National Union of Students in Lebanon. . . .[13]

The students called for a general national demonstration on March 29, 1973, in support of the return of the dismissed public school teachers, and of the demands stated in the above document. The government refused to grant the permission for such a general march and threatened to prevent it, but the students insisted on proceeding with it as scheduled. And so they did, as more than ten thousand students showed up for the march. The government, surprised by the turnout, withdrew its refusal to allow the march and instructed the security forces to retreat from the scene. Thus, confrontation was temporarily avoided.

On April 5, about ten thousand students marched toward the parliament. The clash was inevitable, and shots were soon heard all around, resulting in general confusion. Tanks, jeeps, and ambulances moved fast, and reinforcements were received by both sides. Tires were burnt in an effort to block streets all over the city. Again, several students and security men were wounded and had to be hospitalized, and eighty-one were arrested.

The strike continued until it was temporarily interrupted by a great tragedy. Three Palestinian leaders (Kamal Nasser, Yusuf Najjar, and Kamal Adwan) were assassinated in their homes in Beirut by Israeli agents without any interference from the Lebanese army. The shock engulfed Lebanon and the Arab world and every other issue became irrelevant for a while.

*The May Strike of 1971 at AUB*

On May 10, 1971, the students at AUB were provided with an issue they had been looking for in their campaign for Student Council elections to be held on May 27. The Student Affairs Committee (appointed by the president and composed then of Professor Salem, Provost Thabet, and Dean of Students Najemy[14]) retreated with fifteen student representatives to a one-day symposium at one of Lebanon's most expensive and luxurious hotels (al-Bustan in Beit Merry). It is reported that the question of the university's financial difficulties was raised at a lavish meal after which cigars were offered to students. After the elaborate introduction, it was revealed to the student representatives that the university had not been able to meet its expenses and that the administration had decided to raise tuition fees by 10 percent beginning the next academic year, 1971–1972.

Two days later, the Student Council issued a statement protesting the 10 percent increase and declaring:

> an open strike starting tomorrow, Thursday, May 13, 1971, until the President of this University comes out with a clear cut statement in which he:
> 1. Declares the cancellation of the 10 percent increase in tuition fees.
> 2. Announces his readiness to negotiate with the Student Council the possibility of reasonable decreases in the current tuition fees.
> 3. Declares his acceptance of the Student Council demands to investigate the books of the University at the Comptroller's Office to see whether there are reasonable grounds for decrease in current tuition fees.

All student groups (including the rightists) responded and started the open strike by abstaining from classes. They crowded into a general assembly meeting in which Student Council President Maher Masri (a charismatic student leader affiliated with Fateh student organization) revealed that the increase was to be extended in subsequent years, making the overall increase in tuition fees by 1975–1976 almost 50 percent. Professor Salem then explained the administration's position, pointing out that there had been no increase in tuition fees since 1962–1963 and that student tuition fees accounted for only about 15 percent of AUB's total operating revenue for that academic year. He pointed out that the remaining 85 percent was covered through grants from U.S. institutions and foundations but failed to mention that AUB had received about $11 million from the U.S. government during fiscal year 1970 (more than two-thirds of the university's total budget) and $6.3 million during fiscal year 1971.[15] The second day of the strike witnessed further escalation, as students staged a sit-in and closed the doors of College Hall, making it impossible for administrators (including the president, the four vice-presidents, and the provost) to enter or to leave the building. As the strike entered its third day and continued to gain increasing momentum, Student Council President Masri held a press conference to reveal that Director of Operations John E. Gill (a former full colonel in the U.S. Army) tried to call security troops onto the campus, that the administration expenses had rocketed by 95 percent, and that in the last year along $60,000 had been allocated to repair the president's house.

The students reacted strongly. One of them pointed out that AUB is "organized along the lines of a patrilocal social structure. Indeed everything in our society works along this principle where authority flows in one direction from top to bottom. . . . Moreover, it is my hope that the Student Council be very cautious not to fall into the mistake of also acting along the principle of patrilocal authority, and impose its decisions on the student body . . . ; it is very important that in revolting, we do not do so along the principles and values of our rotten social system."[16] Some students showed concern also with the consequences of increasing tuition fees in terms of blocking the way of those who are economically at a disadvantage, a policy which will make AUB an increasingly "exclusive club of a select class."[17]

There were a few students who expressed disagreement with the strike. One student candidly said, "I am against the strike, [because] I am graduating in June, and I don't want the semester to be either cancelled or extended because I want to go back home." Another student was against the strike because "AUB is a private institution that is free to charge as much as it likes. If somebody finds it too dear, he can go somewhere else."[18]

The strike took a serious turn on May 19, when the university president decided to refuse to cancel the intended 10 percent increase after the forty-eight-hour period of deliberation which he asked for before responding to the student demands.

The students besieged College Hall and the president's house, where thirty-two members of the University Senate were locked inside and had no way to leave for twenty-two hours. Finally the ministers of education and defense (former AUB professors) mediated and succeeded in getting the approval of the Student Council to lift the siege so that the Senate could consider a set of proposals.

The response was received within three hours, and an urgent general assembly session was convened at 11 P.M. to consider the following proposal from President Kirkwood:

1. No student currently registered in the University will be compelled to withdraw as a result of the tuition increase, i.e., as a result of financial hardship.
2. That the Senate accept the principle of adding the 10 percent tuition increase for 1971–1972 to the budgeted University Scholarship Funds for 1970–1971, for scholarship and financial aid for needy students, and that this be continued for 1972–1973.
3. Representation on University Scholarship Committee and faculty Scholarship Committee shall have a majority of students.
. . .
4. There will be no tuition increase for the academic year 1972–1973.
5. . . . a joint committee from the faculty and students will be established to look into the ways and means of raising funds for the University.

Masri tried to explain to the general assembly that the new resolution was a victory for the students, but he would leave it up to the student body at large to accept or reject it in the same democratic spirit that had prevailed so far. Masri was challenged openly for the first time by another Student Council member, Tony Shuwayri, who has represented the far left. What Masri considered to be a victory was considered a failure by Shuwayri.

The latter view dominated. Disturbed by the challenge and the overwhelmingly antagonistic response, Masri tendered his resignation and left the assembly. This incident revealed the inaccuracy of the claim that only a few students are responsible for disturbances. The mass of the student body proved more radical than its leadership. Masri and his group (Fateh Student Organization) realized they had made a mistake in judgment as they witnessed a surge of student power in the general assembly and in the Speakers' Corner debate the next day against accepting the resolution. The popularity of Masri helped him to correct his misinterpretation of the student mood and resume his role before a new leadership could emerge. The Student Council met and decided to sponsor a referendum on Monday, May 24, over the new proposals made by President Kirkwood. On May 24, Masri urged a packed, cheering assembly to vote "no" in the referendum and asserted that the Student Council continued to stand by its three original demands. The faculty-supervised referendum resulted in an overwhelming rejection of the president's proposal. Seventy-four percent of the total body of full-time and part-time students participated in the referendum. Eighty-five percent voted against the proposal, 14 percent voted for it, and one percent cast blank ballots.

Immediately, the students began occupying university halls. The immediate move of the university president was to withdraw his proposal and declare that the academic program for the year 1970–1971 was suspended; that, "if conditions permit, examinations for all graduating students will be given beginning June 14"; and that "degrees can be given only upon completion of those conditions required by the University." Vice-President George Hakim met with the public prosecutor to discuss the question of student occupation of university buildings. The seven hundred graduating students began to show alarm and exert pressure on the Student Council to find a solution to their problem. Meanwhile, the faculty of Arts and Sciences provided a way to end the strike with honor. They met on May 31 and passed the following motion, as proposed by Dr. Constantine K. Zurayk: "We express the faith that a university is a locus of rational discussion. We regret that students have occupied University buildings and appeal to them to vacate them. We believe that a university is for students, and we as a Faculty will do all that we possibly can for them. We realize that all points at issue (tuition increase, student participation, examination, etc.) need lengthy, rational discussion, and we will do everything to bring about a fair solution to these issues."

A general student assembly meeting convened, and Masri announced that, in reply to requests by the faculty of Arts and Sciences, the evacuation of the buildings would start on June 4 in order to allow for negotiations over student demands and to permit senior students to graduate.

The faculty never did anything "to bring about a fair solution to these issues." On July 26, President Kirkwood issued a statement to all members of the AUB community in which he announced that the Senate had voted the following: "The University dissolves the present Student Council and suspends its constitution. . . ." The decision had been kept a secret for almost two months, but the most surprising fact to students was that those who drafted the faculty motion saying that "a university is a locus of rational discussion" and implying that all points at issue were negotiable were Senate members who had already known about the decision to deprive students of representation. The credibility gap widened and deepened, and the tiny bridges of confidence burned to ashes.

To further widen the gap, the university president suspended twenty-two students, warned twenty-nine, and served conduct probation on twenty-two others. The decision was announced on August 19, 1971, without benefit of due process and without allowing these students to defend themselves.

On July 28, the Student Council issued a statement in which it made the following threat:

> The Student Council has already started contacts with the Lebanese government to see to it that this University, its overall policy, its budget, and its specific practices become subject to the supervision of the Lebanese government. . . .
> The Student Council has already compiled some important data, based on facts and figures relevant to the operations of this university, which shall be used in its contacts and negotiations with Lebanese authorities, concerning the future status of this University.
> *Demand Life—Support the Strike*

The University resumed its academic program October 11, 1971, when the provost announced to a local paper that "the crisis is over. We are able to confront the students without cancelling the 10 percent increase. The students registered and paid the increase. . . . Since when does the suspension of 22 students constitute a crisis in an educational institution."[19] On October 25, the students announced an open strike until all those suspended were admitted to the university. Nicely Hall was occupied, and rumors spread that the occupiers had planted bombs, with the intention of exploding themselves and the hall if attacked. Student Council President Masri spoke to a large gathering of students, accusing the administration of forcing its workers to use violence against the striking students. He added that the strikers were ready to negotiate only if the suspended students were admitted. "The strikers," he concluded, "would leave the hall only for prison or hospital." The administration resorted to liberal professors, as it had during the May–June strike. Professor Walid Khalidi (a well-known Palestinian scholar) was asked to mediate and persuade the striking students to leave the building. His meeting lasted for more than ten hours to no avail.

The determination of the striking students and the interference of influential politicians including the President of the Lebanese Republic resulted in an agreement by the university administration on October 28 to readmit the suspended students for the second semester.

*Student Council versus General Union.* The alliance of the progressive groups did not last beyond the May–June strikes. Soon the more leftist group split, accusing the Fateh students of monopolistic and compromising attitudes. The Fateh group continued their struggle to reinstate the Student Council, while the more leftist group invited the students to struggle toward the formation of a General Union independent from the university administration. The Fateh organization was able to reinstate the Student Council in February 1972, and the University Senate issued a new Student Council constitution, which stated that the "actions of the Council and its committees shall in all instances abide by the spirit and letter of the standing rules and regulation of the University"; "the Council shall in all its actions be responsible before the University"; and "the Dean of Students shall be an ex-officio member of the Student Council without the voting privilege." As to the responsibilities of the Student Council, it was supposed: "to promote and coordinate social, recreational and cultural activities of students at the University"; "to coordinate all activities of the student societies on campus"; and "to assume full responsibility for specific programs such as: 1. The New Students Program; 2. The Spring Festival; 3. Fund Collecting on Campus; 4. Blood Donation Programs; 5. Spectators Control at Athletic Events; 6. The Speakers' Corner. The Student Council was also intended "to cooperate with the Office of Student Affairs in matters relating to student conduct and behavior on campus" and "to be concerned about symptoms of disorder."

The reactions to this constitution varied widely and reflected the existing trends in the university. The more leftist groups, including basically the Committees for the Defense of Democratic Rights and the Popular Front for the Liberation of Palestine, categorically rejected the document and insisted on the formation of a General Union of students independent from the university administration.

The gap between the Student Council and the General Union group continued to widen, and each separately conducted its own activities. Charges and countercharges were exchanged in papers and Speakers' Corner. The situation has worsened with time and resulted in violent encounters between the two groups. Members of the General Union were rounded up and beaten on campus after one of the sessions of the Speakers' Corner. The Student Council tried to prevent any group from staging activities on campus without its approval.

A sense of disappointment with the Student Council and its politics has since prevailed among students. When I surveyed the Arts and Sciences student attitudes toward the Student Council in June 1972, the data showed that 51 percent felt the Student Council of the academic year 1971–1972 was a failure, 34 percent felt it was relatively successful, and only 5 percent felt it was quite a success. When asked to indicate their preference for forms of student participation, 43 percent said they preferred a General Union independent from the administration, 28 percent said they preferred the Student Council, 19 percent preferred departmental societies, and 4 percent stood for other forms.

Though divided, the progressive groups at AUB have continued to dominate student politics when the university is in session.

*The 10 Percent Strike Revisited in 1974*

The strike of May 1971 was repeated at AUB in March 1974. In the midst of student strikes, demonstrations, and police-student clashes in support of student demands at LU, the AUB president announced on March 12 that the Board of Trustees had decided to increase tuition fees by another 10 percent as of the coming fall. The decision was expected by the Student Council, and warnings had already been forwarded to the university officials and the Board of Trustees. Before the official announcement was made, Student Council President Muhammad Matar specified the following student demands in a general conference held at the end of February and attended by student representatives in universities and secondary schools:

> 1. The cancellation of the 10 percent increase in tuition fees, due to its drastic consequences: the transformation of AUB into a selective elitist University.
> 2. Student participation in the Admission, Scholarship, and Curriculum Committees as well as the Senate.
> 3. The increase in scholarships. . . .
> 4. National supervision over all institutions of learning.

In response to the official announcement of the increase in tuition fees, the Student Council called for a general assembly on March 14. During this general assembly, attended by 1,500 students, it was commented that "the price of one Phantom equals ten times the university deficit." A general strike was declared, and the president of AUB forwarded on March 16 the following letter to the faculty and students:

> This letter is by far the most important I have written to you. I urge you to read it fully and carefully.
> Two major issues stand before the University at the present time:
> Can the University survive financially?
> Can the University survive academically?
> Throughout its history the AUB has been able to meet the expenses of its operation each year. This had become increasingly difficult. . . . In the hope that substantial amounts, in the near future, may be available to the University from the Middle East, the University will attempt to meet its expenses meanwhile by funds secured from selling some of its endowment assets and some of its land. . . .

The strike was escalated on March 19 and 20 by the occupation of a number of university buildings. Students entered the office of the dean of Arts and Sciences and demanded immediate evacuation of the dean and his staff.

The university used several tactics to undermine student unity and gain public support:

First, it was announced that the university had decided to sell land to meet financial obligations. To counter this claim, students exposed the fact that the university had been engaged in the purchase of land and identified the purchased lots as reported in the *Government Official Bulletin*. The university admitted that it had "been engaged in the purchase of small plots of land . . . to regularize AUB boundaries."[20]

Second, the university suggested that its survival was in question, as clearly evidenced by the above letter of the president. The suggestion was meant to arouse the anxiety of faculty and other employees, anxiety often rechanneled against students, who would be seen as the only force threatening the survival of the university. This tactic has often been accompanied by another tactic, that of demonstrating the economic relevance of the university by publishing statistics about the number of families depending on it for their livelihood.

Third, the university threatened that classes would be suspended and that students would not receive credit for the semester.

Fourth, a number of faculty members requested students to evacuate the buildings and suspend the strike in exchange for a pledge by the faculty to cooperate with students in their negotiation for participation on committees and to "work with the Student Council and the student body in mutual confidence to establish the best relations among all university groups." The Student Council refused the guarantee "because the power of decision is not in their [faculty's] hands . . . and because in 1971 a similar guarantee was not respected, leading to the dissolution of the Council and the expulsion of 22 students."

Fifth, the university resorted to the Alumni Association for support. In cooperation with the Ministries of Education and Information, the Alumni Association formed an Educational Reform Committee that promised to start a special fund to help needy students at AUB. The reform committee was composed of Abdalla al-Mashnoug (whose son was a high official of the Ministry of Information), Khalil Taki-edeen (an ex-diplomat and the brother of the minister of interior affairs at the time), Rushdi Maloof (a journalist and brother of the president of the Alumni Association), and Shafi Wazzan (a deputy in the Lebanese parliament). The committee aimed at "putting out the fire at AUB" and was able to convince the rightist students that their proposal to start a special fund constituted a face-saving solution of the problem. Once they accomplished their aim of splitting the students, they never convened again.

Sixth, university officials sought government support through different channels and received a pledge to protect the university. On March 26, the minister of education, Edmond Rizk (a member of the Phalangist Party), held a press conference in support of AUB.

This was followed by an open letter to the President of the Republic by about two hundred women who claimed to be mothers of students (some of them were not even married; others were on the university staff or married to university staff members). In this letter, they stated: "We the mothers of students at AUB acknowledge the contributions of the University to Lebanon and the Middle East in general. . . . Consequently, we find it imperative that the Lebanese Government and its people take the necessary measures to put an end to this crisis. . . . The University has been confronted by a small minority of students who imposed a terrorist climate. . . . We request that you enforce the law against all those who disturb order."[21]

In response to this letter, an invitation was advertised in the papers requesting the women who had signed the open letter to meet with the minister of education.[22] In this meeting, the minister pointed out that, "if security forces interfere, students would accuse the police of violating the sacredness of the campus. When parents wish to return their children to schools, we can interfere."[23] As will be shown later, the security forces raided the campus the next day.

Seventh, the university officials used the Union of AUB Workers against the strike by manipulating students' insecurity that the university might be closed down. The president of the Union of AUB workers, John Saba, sent a telegram on March 22 to the President of the Republic saying that the continuation of student strikes at AUB endangered the livelihood of three thousand Lebanese families and requesting his personal intervention.

Eighth, conservative faculty members played a significant role in splitting students, organizing rightist students, pressuring the government to interfere, supplying the administration with information against students and colleagues, etc. One such faculty member forwarded an open letter to the Student Council saying: "During my school days . . . I was always among the needy students along with my three brothers at AUB. . . . I remember very clearly that the University used to generously grant us financial assistance. . . . Frankly, during the eight years I spent at AUB, I never heard that a student was suspended from the University for not being able to pay his fees. But some were suspended because they failed to pass because they did not study hard. . . . Quiet dialogue without strikes is the soundest way."[24]

This same faculty member mentioned in my presence that during the strike he had called on the president of the university and said, "There are many faculty members, and not only students, who are disloyal to the

University . . . ; I can provide you with at least two hundred names of faculty members who are disloyal and who do not deserve to be at AUB either academically or morally."

In spite of the above tactics, the strike dragged on for forty-one days. On April 24 at 2 A.M., the security forces (about five hundred in number) raided the AUB campus. Armored cars knocked down the campus gates and arrested sixty-one students (forty-five of them Lebanese), including the president of the Student Council. Students reacted violently to the storming of the university. They blocked highways by burning tires, demonstrated, and clashed with security forces.

The president of the university declared the suspension of the Student Council, and on July 23, 1974, he declared the suspension of 103 students for "participating in events that led to the disruption of the academic program."[25] Another 150 students received warnings.

## Conclusion

The student movement in Lebanon has been fragmented across and within the different universities. All attempts to form an effective general national union of students or to coordinate their activities have failed.

A general critical overview of student strikes clearly reveals specific patterns of behavior that repeat themselves:

1. Student strikes occur in times of national crises. In Lebanon, student strikes have occurred most often in times of fermentation of national movements, national struggle for independence, and national calamities. In between, students have led a quiet life and sought self-promotion through conformity and pleasure.

2. Student strikes occur in response to (a) undemocratic moves by university administrators (such as forcing Professor Lewis to resign in 1882, forcing students to attend Bible classes, increasing tuition fees without involving faculty and students in the decision, suspending students without allowing for due process), (b) rigid enforcement of obsolete rules, (c) failure of the system to respond to challenges and make overdue reforms, and (d) connection of the university with outside centers of power.

3. The first move by the AUB administration in times of strikes is to seek and insure the support of the President of the Lebanese Republic and its prime minister, the American and other foreign embassies in Beirut, the Alumni Association, and those who have authority over students, such as their parents.

4. Students are gradually radicalized as a result of disappointing encounters with the system. They become more conscious of the dynamic forces operating in the system and the society, and of their position in the social structure.

5. Immediately after student strikes, the university system becomes more rather than less restrictive and repressive. Following the described strikes at AUB, students were selectively suspended and Student Councils dissolved, a few faculty members were terminated, rigid rules were introduced (such as the requirement to sign a religious declaration of principles after the 1882 strike and the requirement to sign a political noninvolvement pledge in the fifties).

6. Decisions are made in isolation and within closed systems. No attempts are made to justify these decisions or to explain why certain verdicts were made and what rules were violated. The accused are not informed of the charges against them or given the opportunity to defend themselves or appeal. In short, no due process is followed.

7. In times of strikes, the administrators resort to liberal professors who have retained some influence and respect among student activists to serve as mediators. In the 1882 revolt, Yaqoub Sarruf, Faris Nimr, and John Wortabet were asked to mediate; and in present times the university administration has called upon Professors Zurayk, Khalidi, and others. The liberal mediators try to convince students to give up their strikes in return for unfulfilled promises. The mediators have not been fair to themselves, for they must realize they could not influence administrators to honor their promises.

8. The university puts a premium on faculty loyalty. In fact, greater emphasis is placed on loyalty to the university than on competence in recruiting, promoting, and retaining faculty members. Thus, the university has depended (especially in times of difficulties) on achievement-oriented families and individuals for support and perpetuation of tradition.

9. In addition to dependency on conservatives with the right connections, on liberal professors in times of crises, and on loyal faculty members, the university administration resorts to several tactics to undermine student activism: (*a*) creating extracurricular activities and societies as alternatives to student government and political activities; (*b*) creating and/or encouraging counter groups such as the Lebanese League; (*c*) emphasizing the economic relevance of the university and the fact that thousands of families depend on it for their livelihoods; (*d*) crying wolf in time of crises by spreading rumors that the university will be forced to close down; (*e*) making threats geared to divide the student movement and to intimidate critics.

10. Real motives are usually revealed in times of crises. The religious motives and objectives of the college were revealed in their most concrete forms during the revolts of 1882 and 1909: "This is a Christian College and was established with the money of Christian people. . . . One of its chief objects is to teach the great truths of Scripture . . . [and] to enlighten,

civilize, and Christianize the people of the Near East."[26] After the May–June 1971 strike, Charles Malik said, "The actual controlling truth is that the AUB is a private, free, independent . . . institution . . . and conducts its life on the basis of free, independent and private laws and regulations of its own."[27]

11. Insofar as the administration is concerned, the strikes reveal that the religious sensitivity has been replaced by a political one. The taboo was Darwin in 1882, and now it is Marx. The consequences in both cases are the same: intimidation, manipulation, suspension, termination.

The strikes have also revealed certain basic limitations in the behavior and views of the student movement:

1. There is a lack of cooperation of students across universities and colleges in Lebanon and consequent failure to establish a general union.

2. Student politics reflect the existing authoritarian tendencies in the society. This is vividly exhibited in the behavior of the student leaders.

3. Students have continued to resort to the elitists in seeking help against university officials.

4. A gap exists between oral and behavioral revolution. When faced with those in positions of power, students are inclined to show congeniality as well as express readiness to compromise their issues. They constantly threaten to use violence, but when they reach the point where the next logical step is violent action in consistency with their threat, they often lose their nerve and find themselves unable to force the other party even into compromise. In response to this gap one student wondered whether student activists were boy scouts or revolutionaries.

5. The student leadership has been fighting its own battle to improve its position in the power structure.

6. Student activists are usually members of political movements functioning in the society, but they rarely establish contact with the deprived segments and groups even in their communities of origin. They tend to focus only on university-related issues, except in times of national crises.

The liberators, then, need to liberate themselves and transcend the loyalties and legacies they have inherited. Real liberation is possible only through continuous involvement guided by a new social vision which aims at placing people in the center of their own activities, ending exploitation and domination, and redefining democracy.

In spite of the above limitations, students have been gradually radicalized. They have become increasingly aware that the dominant systems, structures, and cultural orientations in Lebanon and the rest of the Arab society are essentially opposed to change. Gradually, students have found themselves involved in an ongoing confrontation between forces for change and forces for maintaining the dominant order. Though some of them joined the ranks of the latter, the majority have sided with forces for change. This is most visibly demonstrated in the current Lebanese civil war in which many students, including a number who were subjects of this study, have been killed.

# Epilogue
# The Lebanese Civil War:

*Its Social Origins and Prospects*

This final chapter is neither a conclusion nor a summary of the basic topics of the book. It is rather an extension of the theses described earlier into the risky grounds of the current civil war, with the purpose of exploring its social origins and prospects.

It is most difficult to discuss the Lebanese civil war in an objective and relaxed manner while the war continues to rage on. The prevailing emotional mood and the tragedies that mercilessly and constantly bombard concerned minds undermine precise assessment. Yet the concerned observers of the situation can little afford evasiveness, for the issue needs to be faced and explained in a rational way. Furthermore, and this should be a more significant reason for this endeavor, the findings and conclusions of this book allow for rational speculation on the nature of the forces that brought about the civil war. In fact, this study is a witness of a war in the making at least since 1967. Detailed data and documents on the forces, events, and attitudes making for polarization were collected and analyzed immediately before the fighting began. In this sense, the book may be considered a study in anticipation.

According to the framework of analysis employed in this study, the current civil war in Lebanon is a culmination of a confrontation that has been building up between the forces for change and forces for maintaining the established order against all odds and, quite often, in opposition to the professed principles of the society and government.

In perusing the scholarly literature on Lebanese society for an explanation of the conflict, we find at least two opposing points of view.

One has stemmed from a strong conviction that "the Lebanese genius" devised a unique system of government that accommodated an unusual number of religious communities into one unified and harmonious pluralistic entity. This viewpoint was most clearly articulated in a book, edited by L. Binder, entitled *Politics in Lebanon* (1966), a collection of papers read in a special symposium held in 1963 at the University of Chicago. Here we are told by the famous American sociologist Edward Shils, who as far as I can tell never set foot in the country, that Lebanon is "a happy phenomenon unique in the Third World, a prosperous liberal country. It has a parliamentary body freely elected in the competition of a plurality of independent political parties."[1] This view is a poor restating of an older idea by Michel Shiha, one of the architects of the Lebanese sectarian political system, that "Living in Lebanon is a bliss which will continue unless the ideologists and reformers become strong enough to put an end to it."[2] In the 1975 Middle East Studies Association convention the famous scholar Albert Hourani confessed with dismay that the analysis of the Lebanese situation in the Chicago symposium had proved overoptimistic. He pointed out that the current civil war was a great surprise to him.

A 1973 book by the Lebanese scholar Elie Salem expressed at least as much optimism about the prospects of development and stability in the country. Salem asserted that the "society has developed successful institutions to ensure continuing modernization with a minimum of social and political strain and without resort to a radical ideology. The diversity of beliefs and attitudes in Lebanese society has furthered rather than hindered modernization. The slow gains accomplished . . . are the result of stable political institutions and of a formula for government based on conciliation and consensus."[3]

Salem further predicted that the possibility of a popular revolution "involving radical changes in the governing formula is . . . remote. Those most readily available for violence . . . are largely under the control of the Za'im class, which has no interest in changing the rules of the game," and thus, "if a revolutionary attack against the existing political balance is unlikely to succeed, and if radical changes within the formula are also unlikely, then the conclusion is clear . . .—future modernization involving the public must occur within the prevailing political structure. This prospect becomes the most probable possibility . . . and is likely to continue."[4]

Some subscribers to this point of view have claimed that the Lebanese political system was able to produce political integration and unity through diversity during the last half-century. Consequently the civil war is not regarded as a culmination of increasing polarization but as a sudden coincidence of external and internal challenges which undermined the existing political integration and unity.[5] Such a conceptualization comes close to saying that the civil war occurred in spite of the system, not because of it, and springs from a ruling-class ideology. Similar assertions have been made by Ex-Presidents Suleiman Franjieh and Camille Sham'oun in two messages which they forwarded to the convention of Lebanese immigrants held in Ecuador in June 1976. Franjieh's message asserts that "Lebanon . . . was able to build a prosperous and developed society as a result of its affiliation with the Free World, its democratic system, and the talents of its children. . . . This Lebanon . . . is now exposed to a fierce plot carried out by the Palestinians and the destructive left." Similarly, Sham'oun says in his message, "I assure you that there is no civil war in Lebanon nor class struggle on its holy land. . . . Lebanon is facing a most fierce plot against its existence and civilization. . . . Our war is with the strangers [*al-ghourabā'* —a term used by the rightists to refer to the Palestinians]. . . . The war is not sectarian."[6]

An opposite point of view, to which I subscribe, has described the Lebanese political system as a unique, unstable form of nongovernment that has reflected as well as sustained the existing social cleavages at the base of recurrent civil wars in the country. The American political scientist Michael C. Hudson published a book on Lebanon in 1968 carrying the prophetic title *The Precarious Republic*. During the same year, I published a paper in Arabic (published later in English in the *Middle East Journal*) which ends with the following prediction: "Unity and assimilation into a unified national order remain as a prospect only. As long as the above conditions continue to be unchallenged in a systematic and rational way, Lebanon will remain a mosaic society with dim prospects for stability and national unity and, thus, threatened at its very roots."[7]

In a 1972 paper on the religious factor and voting behavior in Lebanese elections, I pointed out that the influence of religion on elections has been increasing rather than decreasing, that the established order promotes sectarianism, and that, consequently, a process of polarization between the Christian and Muslim communities has been taking place—a situation which will render the political system less able to solve the accumulating problems from within the system.[8]

These points are mentioned here in detail in support of the claim that the current civil war is a culmination of an ongoing confrontation that has been gathering momentum and polarizing the society into two opposed camps.[9] Attempts to characterize it as mere religious warfare or as an isolationist versus nationalist conflict or as pure class struggle suffer from oversimplification and fail to explain certain inconsistencies.

Characterization of the war as purely religious in nature ignores these phenomena:

First, the Phalangist (rightist Christian) camp has received visible support from a number of Muslim leaders, factions, and countries.

Second, a significant segment of the Lebanese Christians have sided and fought with the nationalist-leftist camp.

Third, the rightist camp has attacked a number of Lebanese Christian communities, groups, and individuals.

Granted, each of the opposing camps has a disproportionate number of members sharing a common religion, with Lebanese Christians forming the ranks of rightist-isolationists and Muslims tending to be leftist-nationalists, but the above phenomena (among others) indicate that the real conflict goes beyond religious boundaries. Explanation must be sought in a comprehensive socioeconomic and political context. The research presented in this study has demonstrated that the prevailing attitudes and beliefs among the Lebanese Christians are highly entrenched in their occupation of the privileged central positions in the social, political, and economic structures of the Lebanese society.

But again, to characterize the conflict solely in isolationist-versus-nationalist or purely economic terms is to ignore a significant set of facts:

First, some Arab nationalists have subscribed to points of view and proposed solutions that have satisfied the Lebanese isolationists rather than their fellow nationalists. The Syrian government has departed from Syria's traditional role as "a fortress of Arab nationalism" and "the heart of pan-Arabism" and supported the isolationists, who never trusted Syria. This development (which surprised many observers and strategists) demands a redefinition of the concept of Arab nationalism to take account of class analysis and international alliances.

Second, some poor Christians have been fighting on the rightist side. This certainly can be interpreted as an instance of false social class consciousness. It can even be argued that these poor Christians are most alienated from their own true cause because they defend a system that is against their well-being. Yet this fact is consistent with my empirical data on youth, which showed that upper-class Muslim university students were more likely to think of themselves as leftists than their lower-class Christian counterparts.

Third, leftist forces condemned some Muslim groups for indiscriminate attacks on Christian communities and for killing even leftist elements.

Fourth, some Muslim supporters of the right-wing parties have similarly renounced these parties for their indiscriminate attacks on Muslims.

In the light of the above arguments and according to the findings of the present study, then, the complexity and intricacy of the Lebanese situation cannot be explained in terms of a single causal factor. It is more accurately characterized as a complex and intricate fusion of the sectarian loyalties, isolationist-versus-nationalist tendencies, and deprived-versus-privileged struggle. The civil war, it must be asserted, cannot be explained exclusively in terms of just one of the above three conditions. These conditions should not be separated even for the purpose of abstract analysis, for they intimately overlap, coincide, and interconnect to the extent that each becomes strongly transformed in its very essence.

With this kind of analysis in mind, we may now proceed to identify and describe the specific causes of the current civil war. In order to do so, we need to distinguish between *causal forces*, which lie at the root of the problem and are directly connected with it, and *contributing forces* that facilitate the process or trigger the set of events already in the making and awaiting the proper time and place. The contributing factors have merely allowed for events to take their historical course of action. The causal forces must have been inherent in the social and political structures.

## Causal Forces

A historical overview of the Lebanese civil wars and uprisings since independence reveals that several highly interconnected conditions have shaped the Lebanese political destiny and made for the current civil war. Among these conditions, five need to be highlighted as causal forces in their very nature: the prevailing social mosaic structure, the social class structure, the weak central government, the inability of the political system to transform itself, and the widespread condition of social unrest and anomie.

### The Prevailing Social Mosaic Structure

Chapter 3 of this book attempted to describe the social mosaic structure in detail. Here, the reader will note that the sources of the recurrent civil wars are connected with the following features of the complex religious diversity of the Lebanese society, described fully in earlier chapters.

1. Lack of consensus on fundamental issues and particularly on the national identity of Lebanon.

2. Lack of extensive, deep, and open dialogue between the Lebanese religious communities.

3. Loyalty of the Lebanese to their sectarian, kinship, and local communities rather than to the country as a whole.

4. Increasing legitimization of the sectarian system and nonseparation of religion from the state, which has prevented the adoption of secularism and civil marriage.

5. Absence of a unified educational system, a situation which allows for socialization of the young into their traditional sectarian communities and promotion of religious identity.

These features render Lebanon a fragmented mosaic society that continues to be dominated by conflicting loyalties and value orientations. They also allow for external interference in Lebanese affairs (a condition that has constantly undermined Lebanon's sovereignty). Furthermore, these features have created an ideal situation for the traditional leaders to remain in power in alliance with the religious institutions that preach loyalty to the established order.

*The Lebanese Social Class Structure*

The social class structure in Lebanon, as indicated earlier in the book, is pyramidal in that the great majority of the Lebanese are poor, a small proportion are middle class, and very few are ultra-rich. The government-sponsored study conducted by a French research team (IRFED) revealed that 4 percent of the Lebanese received about one-third of the total national income in 1960. Since then, constant reference has been made to "the 4 percent class" ruling Lebanon and monopolizing its wealth. In spite of the great wealth that has been pouring into Lebanon, rendering it the finance center of the area, prosperity has continued to be confined to some areas and groups, and the gap between the rich and the poor has continued to widen and deepen. Mount Lebanon and some neighborhoods in Beirut have been growing prosperous at a much more rapid pace than the South, the North, and the Beqa'.

Two poverty belts inhabited predominantly by Muslims emerged in Lebanon and bear evidence of the disproportion of wealth and rewards. One belt includes the poor areas of the South, the Beqa', and the North which have surrounded the prosperous Mount Lebanon. The disparities are many, including the availability of schools, roads, hospitals, and other facilities. The other belt has surrounded Beirut, for its suburbs were converted into overcrowded, poverty-stricken slum areas. A large number of young families have been moving from villages into these neighborhoods. Recently, this village-city migration increased immensely and at a rapid rate because of Israeli raids on the South. Such areas as Ghbeiri, Shiah, and an-Naba became overcrowded; quite often one single room would be inhabited by ten persons, and swarms of children filled the narrow, dirty streets.

The problem was intensified by a general lack of employment and the existence of cheap labor in factories owned by rich Christians. Furthermore, these uprooted Lebanese communities found themselves close to or intermingling with the Palestinian refugees and other disinherited and destitute groups. The disinherited found themselves sharing the same destiny. The socioeconomic disparities coincided with sectarian affiliations. The fact that the bulk of the destitute were Muslims contributed to further aggravation of religious differences and polarization of the two communities. Further aggravation was caused by increasing inflation which hit the lower classes.

*Weak Central Government*

While other societies complain of "big government," the Lebanese complain of lack of government. The political system governing Lebanon has been based on the traditional mosaic social diversity and dominated by traditional leaders (*z'aims*). Kinship, religious, and local loyalties resulted in the weakening of any form of central government and in the emergence of several states and centers of power within the state long before the Palestinians moved to Lebanon. The lack of a strong central government in Lebanon has contributed to the emergence of private militias, to helplessness in enforcing laws, to the constant interference of all sorts of external forces in Lebanese internal affairs, and to the difficulty of imposing solutions even when solutions are reached. In the eruption of the present civil war, the central government was totally helpless, and some members of the cabinet were simultaneously playing conflicting roles: the role of maintaining law and order and that of leading their private militias in the ongoing war.

*The Inability of the Political System to Transform Itself*

The Lebanese political system emerged out of the above mosaic social structure and was conceived of and arranged according to a sectarian quota system which allocated the parliamentary, cabinet, and administrative posts to the various religious communities in accordance with an arbitrary population ratio based on the 1932 census by the French mandate. This sectarian formula rendered the Lebanese political system highly rigid and static because it did not take into account the fact that religious ratios change. It has been constantly feared that any basic reforms would certainly upset the balance. Hence, the tendency of the ruling class to resist political reform. The Lebanese government has failed to adopt a policy on immigration, naturalization, and citizenship rights. While some groups were granted citizenship (such as Armenians), others were deprived of it (such as Kurds).

The most significant phenomenon, however, is that Lebanon has continued to be ruled by traditional leaders. The Lebanese aristocracy has maintained itself in power, and political positions have been inherited like family names. Some children could not wait for the death of the father. Hence, the phenomenon of voting both father and son into parliament (as in the cases of Pierre Jumayel and his son Amin). Some liberal professionals and newly prosperous businessmen were able to reach the parliament and cabinet, but only under the wing of the traditional *z'aims* and quite often by buying their nominations on the *z'aims'* slates. Once in power the liberal technocrats and businessmen could maintain their positions only by adhering to the policies of these traditional leaders.

Statistically speaking, one may note some turnover of deputies from one election to another. Because an increasing number of professionals and businessmen have been voted into the parliament, generalizations have been made that aristocratic and feudal families have ceased to rule Lebanon.[10] If we explore the situation beyond mere statistical numbers and examine the decision-making process more thoroughly, we will find that the Lebanese traditional notables have continued to rule the country. Lately, these notables have tended to refuse to hold formal positions and have preferred the informal role of running the show from behind the screen.

Some liberal technocrats were appointed to the cabinet in the early 1970s (Ghassan Tueini, Elias Saba, Emile Bitar, Henry Eddeh, and others), and they tried to introduce such reforms as imposing higher taxes on luxury items, reducing the soaring prices of medical drugs, enforcing laws governing taxation, improving public schools, and reforming educational curricula. All these attempts at change failed, and all these ministers were compelled to resign; in one instance, a minister (Henry Eddeh) was expelled from office.

After the successive resignations of these officials, I wrote an article in 1971 in which I raised a number of questions connected with the nature of relationships between the established order and the failure of liberals to introduce simple and overdue reform. Among these questions, the following are noteworthy here: Is there a relationship between the series of resignations and the prevailing free system? Is it possible for the free system to prevent monopolization? Does this system conflict with reform? Does monopolization occur as a result of this kind of system or in spite of it?

In response to these questions and others, I pointed out then that the Lebanese political system had been characterized by three features insofar as its ability to introduce change is concerned.

1. The system robs the majority of people of their freedom and power. With time, people are rendered powerless vis-à-vis the system, for all material power has become centralized in the hands of a few greedy monopolizers.

2. The system resists change because it realizes that reform will encourage the people to demand further and more radical reform.

3. The present system links the society to the international net or centers of monopolization. Hence, the alliance between the Lebanese monopolizers and world exporters-importers who cooperated in the present Lebanese crisis.

In this article I expressed amazement at the fact that Lebanese merchants proclaimed a general strike when their privileges were threatened, while the people remained silent in the face of concrete attempts to undermine their rights to education and medicine.

The inability of the system to transform itself is also reflected in three interrelated phenomena: First, there has been a great disparity between popular support for nationalistic and progressive parties and their representation in parliament and cabinet. The immensity of this disparity has been demonstrated in the current civil war. Second, the political system has proved nonresponsive to public opinion and to demands for reform. A research survey conducted by Iliya Harik and myself in two voting districts of Beirut in 1972 showed that the majority of the Muslim (86 percent) and Christian (61 percent) respondents favored ending Maronite monopoly over the office of President of the Republic and that they believed it should be accessible to all Lebanese alike, regardless of their religious affiliation. The system proved unable to accommodate liberal demands, let alone the radical ones. The dependence of Franjieh's regime on traditional leaders such as Kamil al-Asaad precluded any serious consideration of the urgent demands of the Shi'ites' liberal leader Imām Mousa Assadr and his Movement of the Deprived. The regime also vehemently rejected the liberal demands of the nationalist movement as voiced by Kamal Junblat: secularization of the political system, reform of the electoral laws, amendment of the constitution, lifting of restrictions on naturalization, and reorganization of the army. Third, the office of premier, reserved for Sunni Muslims, has been gradually undermined by the President of the Republic, particularly during Franjieh's regime. In short, the current civil war is an eruption of repressed silence. The system has proved closed, rigid, and static in a dynamic society. Simply, it does not possess the ability to transform itself and solve challenging problems. On the contrary, it has been able only to generate new problems. Its genius has been channeled totally in the direction of manipulating religious loyalties for the sole purpose of maintaining its power and promoting its interests.

## Condition of Social Unrest and Anomie

During the last quarter-century Lebanon has witnessed sudden prosperity, fascination with status symbols, the emergence of high hopes for achievement, and a great rat race for procuring the biggest share of the fortune in the shortest time possible, by legitimate or illegitimate means. The intensity of the dream of success undermined the capacity for mutual respect, consideration, and conformity to norms regulating cooperation and cohesiveness. This situation was aggravated by inequities in opportunity and a scarcity of legitimate means. A great gap existed between unlimited ambitions and limited opportunities. Hence the condition of anomie, whereby illegitimate means became justifiable as long as they could lead to success. Even ardent conservatives (such as Jumayel and Malik) at one and the same time condemned the "immorality of the Lebanese" and took pride in the free and competitive system of Lebanon and the ambitions of its people, without perceiving the interconnection between these two conditions.

Another paradox that could be clearly observed on the Lebanese scene was the great gap between friendliness in face-to-face relations with acquaintances (such as politeness and insistence that others pass before one) and aggressiveness in passing relations with unknown others (as in driving cars and waiting in line).

This social unrest and its consequent aggressiveness exhibited themselves in building construction. Within a few years Beirut was converted into an ugly, overcrowded cement forest, without the benefit of any city planning or public parks. Another source of aggressiveness is apparent prosperity. In an interesting editorial of *an-Nahar*, Ghassan Tueini described Lebanon as "the donkey of prosperity,"[11] referring to the fact that Lebanon became the finance center for the Middle East only to channel money to be invested elsewhere instead of developing the country. In effect, prosperity meant increasing the wealth of the rich and the poverty of the poor. Above all, it meant that the poor became more aware of their deprivation.

The violence shown in the current civil war has surprised many observers. Comments have been made that the easy-going, spoiled, neatly dressed, fun-oriented Lebanese youths were not expected to show that much toughness, cruelty, and hatred. Such comments demonstrate lack of insight into the dynamics of social unrest and its potential for violence.

## Contributing Forces

What forces were responsible for breaking the long repressed silence of the Lebanese? What conditions triggered the successive events of the civil war in 1975 and not earlier or later? The causal forces described above have been shown to stem from the very structure of the society and the political system based on it; the addition of a set of circumstantial factors acted as a contributing force in triggering the war in April 1975 and in sustaining it. These circumstances included the presence of the Palestinian resistance movement in Lebanon and the search for a peaceful solution to the Arab-Israeli conflict.

### Presence of the Palestinian Resistance Movement in Lebanon

The existing gap between the Lebanese religious-political communities widened, deepened, and polarized as a result of the presence of the Palestinian resistance movement in Lebanon. The movement served as a catalyst element by spontaneously diffusing radical ideas, encouraging the leftists to press for fulfillment of overdue demands, inviting radical elements from other Arab countries and the world into Lebanon, training and arming dissidents, threatening Western interests in the area, upsetting the delicate balance of power within Lebanon, etc., and this alarmed the rightist political parties that flourished in the Christian communities. They began to further solidify their ranks and strengthen their militias. This process was accompanied by objections that the Palestinians were forming a state within the state, stopping Lebanese in certain areas and asking them to produce their identity cards, and interfering in the internal affairs of Lebanon. An increasing reference to the Palestinians as foreigners or strangers (*ghourabā'*) began to circulate, and inscriptions saying "No to the Resistance," "No to Syria," and "No to the coward strangers [*al-ghourabā' al-joubnā*]" appeared on walls in Christian quarters and on banners across streets along with signs of the cross and initials of emerging armed organizations. Exactly opposed inscriptions saying "Yes to the Resistance" and "Yes to Syria" appeared in Muslim and leftist-dominated Christian quarters.

The Israeli raids further complicated the situation. They threatened the Lebanese economy; drove thousands of peasants from southern Lebanon into the cities, where they lived with other destitute groups and became a receptive audience for leftist political appeals; and embarrassed the Lebanese army, which realizing it could not face Israel, sought to remove the source of embarrassment, namely, to contain the Palestinian resistance movement. Though the army failed in this endeavor, it succeeded in generating further animosity toward the Palestinian cause in the ranks of the rightists. The failure of the military is due to the image it has developed of itself as a guardian of the privileged and the status quo, not of the country, by serving as a security force in labor and peasant strikes. After the killing of a nationalist leader in one of these strikes in Sidon immediately preceding the outbreak of the civil war, Christian elementary and secondary school students were excused from classes to demonstrate in support of the army. Nuns and military officers led some of these demonstrations and delivered fiery speeches which reinforced the image of the army as partisan to the conflict, siding with the rightists. The net effect of the Israeli raids (which initially aimed at driving a wedge between the Lebanese and the Palestinians) was further polarization among the Lebanese themselves into leftist and rightist camps. The Palestinian cause merged with the cause of the deprived Lebanese.

Meanwhile, the Palestinian resistance movement, fearing the repetition of the 1970 massacre in Jordan, where it isolated itself from the Jordanian nationalists, sought to strengthen its alliance with the leftist-nationalist groups in Lebanon. Since then, an attack on one has meant an attack on the other, and defending the other means defending oneself. This alliance (strengthened by similarities in interests and ideology) reinforced in turn the beliefs of the rightists that the Palestinians constitute a force disruptive of the existing internal balance. Hence, their insistence on bringing the Palestinian camp under government control.

Even though the Palestinians have been the target of attack and wanted initially to stay out of the fighting and focus on Israel, they have often been forced into the battle. After all, it was the massacre of a busload of twenty-seven Palestinians and other leftists in Ain ar-Rummani on April 13, 1975, that triggered the civil war. Throughout the first year of the war, the Palestine Liberation Organization (PLO), and particularly its leader, Arafat, continued to call for a peaceful solution and constantly warned that the PLO might not be able to pursue a "policy of moderation" any longer. The capture of Dbayeh, Jisr al-Basha, and Tel az-Zaater camps by Lebanese rightists with the help of the Syrians has increasingly pushed the PLO into the fight and suggested the existence of a plan on the part of the rightists to partition the country and/or make it "a graveyard for Palestinians."

Since the Palestinians have been the target, as will be further elaborated in the following section, it is incorrect to say that the PLO made a mistake in joining the fight on the side of the leftists. One may even argue the opposite, namely, that the Lebanese leftists rushed to the rescue of the Palestinians. The fact of the matter, however, is that the Lebanese leftist cause and the Palestinian cause merged into one, and both faced a common destiny.

*Search for a Peaceful Solution to the Arab-Israeli Conflict*

The civil war in Lebanon has to be regarded also against the background of the ongoing diplomatic attempt to settle the Middle East question which has prompted several Arab governments, the West, and Israel to follow a policy of containing the Palestinian resistance movement. The rightists, who were anxiously concerned with the settlement plan, received arms and training from Jordan, Iran, Israel, and Western countries, the backing of Saudi Arabia and Egypt, and finally the military support of the Syrian regime.

Israel was particularly interested in stopping the PLO's drive for international recognition as the sole legitimate representative of the Palestinian people. It preferred to keep the West Bank or, if need be, to link it with Jordan or deliver it to more moderate elements, rather than allow the PLO to control it. The Israeli officials also saw several other benefits in the Lebanese civil war besides that of eliminating the Palestinian resistance movement. The war further distracted Syria, divided the Arab governments, ended Israel's isolation, and postponed the question of withdrawing from occupied Arab lands. The Israeli government took advantage of the situation in Lebanon to strengthen its grip over the occupied lands and to launch a campaign against the Palestinian guerrillas. The Western press reported Israel's missions in Lebanon, its role in supplying guns and ammunition to the rightists, and its "open-fence" policy with southern Lebanon. In short, Israel wanted to prolong the war and prevent a leftist victory which might make Lebanon into a socialist state and a confrontation power threatening Israeli security.

The most intriguing development in the war has been the Syrian military intervention in Lebanon on the side of the rightists—intriguing both because of Syria's traditional role as a fortress of pan-Arab nationalism and as a reference group for the Lebanese Muslim community and because of the animosity of the Christian rightists to Syria, with its deep-rooted heritage of championing the Palestinian cause. Yet the Syrian regime did intervene to stop leftist victory. Syrian troops removed leftist forces from the Beqa' and some other areas in the South and North; broke the siege of a number of rightist communities; helped the rightists to capture leftist strongholds, including Tel az-Zaater, which became the symbol of the Palestinians' plight and their will to resist; clashed with the Palestinian commandos who represented Arab dignity, embodied Palestine's hopes for liberation since 1967, and constituted a spearhead for revolutionary change in the entire area; overlooked Israeli armament of the rightists; and sealed off Lebanese ports to cut off supply lines of the leftists.

The Syrian role in the Lebanese civil war should be examined in the context of the ongoing search for a peaceful solution in the area. Once a regime defines its goals, its behavior will be determined not by emotions and traditions as much as by these goals and existing realities. This is particularly true in case of pragmatic leadership. Specifically, Syrian intervention on the side of the rightists may be explained in the following terms:

1. The logic of the plan for a peaceful solution required that President Hafiz Assad of Syria follow steps similar to those of President Anwar Sadat of Egypt in improving his country's relationship with the United States in return for pressuring Israel into an overall settlement. The plans to regain the Golan Heights resulted in driving a wedge between the Syrian regime and the Palestinian resistance movement, exactly as the plans to regain Sinai resulted in driving a wedge between Egypt and Syria. Like Sadat, Assad had to get along with Henry Kissinger, open the country to Western investment, improve relations with the United States, allow businessmen who had fled the country to come back, permit importation of luxury consumer goods, suppress radical elements, prove his moderation, strengthen ties with conservative and reactionary governments, and contain the Palestinian resistance movement, which could obstruct peaceful settlement. Simply, the Syrian regime opted for a military solution against the Palestinians for the purpose of securing a peaceful solution with Israel. This explains why the United States saw Syria as "playing a constructive role" and why Israel overlooked the presence of the Syrian army in Lebanon. Slowly, Syria, like Egypt and other Arab countries, is being cemented to the West.

2. Being primarily concerned with the safety and stability of his regime, Assad feared the emergence of a radical state in a country he wished to keep within Syria's sphere of influence. In case of a leftist victory, other radical Arabs would be likely to make further inroads in Lebanon and interfere more directly with Syria's internal problems. It is further speculated by some that the Syrian regime has its own design for incorporating Lebanon or parts of it into some sort of Syrian confederacy.

3. The Syrian regime feared that leftist victory could provoke a confrontation with Israel. In fact, Syria's concern about the balance of power within Lebanon is part of its concern about the balance of the entire region. Simply, Syria does not wish to have uncontrolled war on its frontiers.

A number of other reasons for Syrian intervention have been reported in the press and in private discussion, including speculative guessing about "Assad being a minority man" who "could not be happy about the prospect of another minority regime—the Maronites of Lebanon—being violently overthrown."[12] The source of that speculation refers also to the existence of a "business arrangement" between Assad's brother and Frangieh's son as a possible reason for Syria's siding with the rightists. Such a speculative, personally oriented explanation should be dismissed without much reservation, along with similar attempts to attribute the Syrian attacks on the leftists to Assad's anger because of the collapse of his solution. (To begin with, the Syrian regime wanted to impose a solution rather than to mediate or play the role of an impartial arbiter. The terms of this solution were in fact totally opposed to the leftist program for a secular democratic system and completely in harmony with the rightists' desire to retain the antiquated sectarian political system.)

With all the above causal and contributing forces in mind, the prospects for a satisfactory solution appear very dim indeed. The military victory of the Syrian regime at the time of final revision of this chapter at the end of November 1976 has been legitimized and financed by a number of Arab governments. The Lebanese rightists continue to sound as noncompromising as ever and seem to be bent on maintaining Lebanon as a national home for the Maronites in a region of the world afflicted with medieval loyalties.

Arabs are faced with two alternative designs for themselves. One design aims at the further dismantling of Arab society by the establishment of small states as national homes for different ethnic and religious communities in the area. It is important to point out that the prevailing conditions in Arab countries provide the needed climate for the implementation of this design. These prevailing conditions are not merely political; much more basic is the dominance in the Arab countries of traditional loyalties and value orientations. The alternative design aims at the establishment of a unified secular-democratic-socialist Arab society which requires the development of a higher order of national and social class consciousness.

At a time when the nationalist and progressive movement has reached its lowest ebb, the Arab world stretches across continents like a huge stranded octopus, drained of its water of life and indignation. Traditional and authoritarian governments have silenced the Arab people. In the immediate future, there will be more pressure on the various factions to negotiate a solution. In the long run, however, a popular movement will have to re-emerge in a different shape and with a new outlook. Meanwhile the confrontation will continue, in one form or another, for it has been in the making over a long period.

According to the findings of this study, youth in Lebanon, though repressed, have managed to play a significant role in bringing about basic change by crystallizing issues and breaking the well-enforced silence. It is my conviction that a fair and durable solution to the civil war should aim at restructuring the society and its institutions. Those kinds of solutions that are based on maintaining the old sectarian formula and economic disparities will only prolong the Lebanese agony. The ultimate solution must lie in a qualitative transformation of the Lebanese society into the direction of a secular-socialist-democratic system.

# Appendix
# University Students in Lebanon:

*A Survey Questionnaire*

*Note:* The survey was self-administered by students at the American University of Beirut (AUB), Saint Joseph University (SJU), and Lebanese University (LU) in 1970–1971. See the introduction to Part II for information on the number of respondents and the sampling techniques used. This appendix includes all questions used in the English version of the questionnaire. There were some additional questions, not reproduced here, in the Arabic version.

In these critical times for our society, the focus of attention has been increasingly directed to the role of university students. However, little research has been done in this part of the world about this highly important group. The present attempt is to collect information, opinion reactions, values, and beliefs of university students in Lebanon. This questionnaire will be distributed to samples of students in the four universities in Beirut. [BAU, the fourth university, did not participate in the study.] You were one of the students selected at random to respond to this questionnaire. Please remember that whatever information you give will be used to help the researchers to understand the role of university students as a group, and not about you personally. That is why it is *not* required that you mention your name. Nobody will see this information except the researchers.

The more accurate and precise you are in answering the questions, the more likely that our conclusions and generalizations will be valid. Remember, however, to answer according to your actual feelings and not according to what you think you should feel.

## I. General information

| (%) | AUB | SJU | LU |
|---|---|---|---|
| **1. Sex** | | | |
| Male | 68 | 72 | 76 |
| Female | 32 | 28 | 23 |
| **2. Marital status** | | | |
| Single | 91 | 95 | 95 |
| Married | 8 | 4 | 5 |
| **3. Nationality** | | | |
| Lebanese | 52 | 93 | 93 |
| Other Arabs | 48 | 7 | 7 |
| **4. Religion** | | | |
| Sunnite | 38 | 10 | 27 |
| Shi'ite | 6 | 4 | 15 |
| Druze | 3 | 2 | 5 |
| Maronite | 7 | 41 | 29 |
| Orthodox | 19 | 16 | 14 |
| Catholic | 8 | 20 | 6 |
| Others | 19 | 7 | 4 |
| **5. Where do you live at present?** | | | |
| At home with family | 53 | | 62 |
| University dormitory | 30 | | 0 |
| With roommate(s) in apartment | 8 | | 19 |
| Alone in an apartment | 1 | | 9 |
| With spouse in an apartment | 3 | | 5 |
| Other (please specify) | 5 | | 5 |
| **6. Are you on any kind of scholarship?** | | | |
| Yes | 41 | 14 | 51 |
| No | 56 | 83 | 47 |
| NR | 3 | 3 | 2 |

| (%) | AUB | | SJU | LU |
|---|---|---|---|---|

## II. Information about parents

### 1. Father's occupation

| | AUB | SJU | LU |
|---|---|---|---|
| Business | 11 | 29 | 8 |
| Professional | 17 | 15 | 8 |
| Clerical | 14 | 14 | 18 |
| Medium business | 29 | | 25 |
| Peasant } Manual worker } | 18 | 11 | 11<br>17 |
| Other | 11 | 31 | 13 |

### 2. Family annual income

| | AUB | SJU | LU |
|---|---|---|---|
| £L 5,000 or less | 11 | 7 | 26 |
| £L 5,001–10,000 | 17 | 14 | 26 |
| £L 10,001–15,000 | 15 | 22 | 18 |
| £L 15,001–20,000 | 11 | 14 | 11 |
| £L 20,001–25,000 } | 10 | 17 | |
| £L 25,001–35,000 } | 10 | 7 | 11 |
| £L 35,001–50,000 } | 7 | 6 | |
| £L 50,001 or more } | 11 | 5 | 5 |
| NR | 8 | 8 | 3 |

### 3. Subjective social class identification

| | AUB | SJU | LU |
|---|---|---|---|
| Lower class | 2 | 4 | 1 |
| Lower middle class | 17 | 21 | 11 |
| Middle class } | 66 | 62 | 61 |
| Upper middle class } | | 6 | 22 |
| Upper class | 13 | 2 | 3 |
| NR | 2 | 5 | 2 |

### 4. Education of parents

| | Father(F) | Mother(M) | F | M | F | M |
|---|---|---|---|---|---|---|
| Illiterate | 9 | 14 | 3 | 6 | 13 | 30 |
| Elementary | 24 | 29 | 32 | 40 | 49 | 47 |
| Secondary | 33 | 40 | 38 | 46 | 28 | 17 |
| University | 33 | 13 | 23 | 6 | 8 | 2 |
| NR | 1 | 4 | 4 | 2 | 2 | 4 |

| (%) | AUB | SJU | LU |
|---|---|---|---|

**5. Which of the following best describes your current relations with your parents? (Circle one.)**

| | AUB | SJU | LU |
|---|---|---|---|
| My parents and I are very close. | 43 | 23 | 47 |
| My parents and I are on good terms. | 44 | 56 | 42 |
| My parents and I are not close. | 5 | 13 | 6 |
| My parents and I do not get along. | 4 | 7 | 3 |
| Other (please specify). | 4 | 1 | 2 |

**6. Are you closer to:**

| | AUB |
|---|---|
| Your father | 11 |
| Your mother | 30 |
| Equally close to both | 50 |
| Neither | 5 |
| Other | 4 |

**7. What is the size of your immediate family (including grandparents if living with your parents)?**

| | AUB | LU |
|---|---|---|
| 3 or less | 8 | 3 |
| 4–5 | 27 | 25 |
| 6–7 | 33 | 24 |
| 8–9 | 15 | 23 |
| 10 or more | 14 | 17 |
| NR | 3 | 8 |

**8. In your case has your family been very strict with you and wanted to have a lot to say about what you do, or have they been pretty free with you and let you make your own decisions? Check one of the following:**

| | AUB | SJU | LU |
|---|---|---|---|
| Family has always been very strict. | 6 | 6 | 2 |
| Family has been strict most of the time. | 10 | 8 | 6 |
| Sometimes the family has been strict. | 38 | 31 | 41 |
| Family has been very free with me and I pretty much made my own decisions. | 45 | 54 | 50 |

| (%) | AUB | | | SJU | |
|---|---|---|---|---|---|
| | Self | F | M | Self | F |

**9. To what degree do you feel that religious faith has been an influence in your life; in the lives of your parents? (Check one for each.)**

| | | | | | |
|---|---|---|---|---|---|
| Little influence | 34 | 24 | 9 | 32 | 16 |
| Some influence | 40 | 38 | 33 | 36 | 34 |
| High influence | 20 | 34 | 55 | 30 | 41 |
| NR | 6 | 4 | 3 | 2 | 9 |

**10. Do you and your parents believe in God as a being who is responsible for the creation of the universe and to whom man is accountable after death? (Check one for each.)**

| | | | | | |
|---|---|---|---|---|---|
| Yes | 60 | 82 | 93 | 62 | 78 |
| Uncertain | 28 | 9 | 2 | 19 | 9 |
| No | 11 | 4 | 0 | 16 | 4 |
| NR | 1 | 5 | 5 | 3 | 9 |

## III. Your opinions about life in general and your beliefs

**1. Which of the following provides you with the greatest satisfaction? (Check one.)**

| | | |
|---|---|---|
| Artistic and intellectual activities | 26 | 52 |
| Political activities | 8 | 14 |
| Religious activities | 3 | 3 |
| Civic and social activities | 10 | 14 |
| Business and money-making | 6 | 6 |
| Sports, leisure time, and personal hobbies | 24 | 5 |
| Family relations and friends | 13 | 0 |
| Other | 10 | 6 |

|   | LU<br>Self | F | M |
|---|---|---|---|
| M |  |  |  |
| 8 | 33 | 11 | 6 |
| 30 | 36 | 31 | 22 |
| 56 | 23 | 53 | 69 |
| 6 | 8 | 5 | 3 |

87
5
2
6

41
19
5
22

1

7

0
5

| (%) | AUB Self | F | M | SJU Self | F |
|---|---|---|---|---|---|
| **2. Which of the following political positions best describes yourself?** | | | | | |
| Leftist, revolutionary, but nonviolent | 11 | | | 12 | 5 |
| Leftist, revolutionary, and recommend the use of violence, if necessary | 12 | | | 11 | 3 |
| Reformist, nonrevolutionary, moderate | 38 | | | 48 | 31 |
| Rightist, antirevolution and antileftist | 15 | | | 19 | 26 |
| Satisfied with the status quo and with no particular political position | 9 | | | 1 | 8 |
| Religious—would like to reform society on religious basis | 6 | | | 0 | 0 |
| Other | 9 | | | 9 | 27 |
| **3. Which of the political loyalties best describes yourself?** | | | | | |
| Arab nationalism | 33 | | | 14 | 15 |
| Internationalism | 23 | | | 19 | 6 |
| Lebanese nationalism | 25 | | | 52 | 59 |
| Syrian nationalism | 5 | | | 7 | 3 |
| Other (please specify) | 8 | | | 2 | 1 |
| NR | 6 | | | 6 | 16 |
| **4. Which of the following forms of government do you prefer for your country?** | | | | | |
| Communism | 4 | | | 5 | 2 |
| Capitalistic democracy | 17 | | | 14 | 19 |
| Liberal democracy | 42 | | | 50 | 45 |
| Socialist democracy | 28 | | | 23 | 15 |
| Other | 5 | | | 3 | 0 |
| NR | 3 | | | 5 | 19 |

| M | LU Self | F | M |
|---|---|---|---|
| 0 | 12 | 4 | 4 |
| 0 | 28 | 5 | 2 |
| 0 | 43 | 39 | 37 |
| 0 | 5 | 19 | 16 |
| 0 | 2 | 16 | 22 |
| 0 | 0 | 0 | 0 |
| 0 | 10 | 17 | 19 |
| 13 | 40 | 37 | 35 |
| 6 | 17 | 5 | 4 |
| 62 | 26 | 38 | 39 |
| 4 | 9 | 1 | 0 |
| 1 | 6 | 1 | 2 |
| 14 | 2 | 18 | 20 |
| 1 | 11 | 3 | 2 |
| 19 | 13 | 20 | 17 |
| 45 | 22 | 28 | 28 |
| 14 | 47 | 29 | 29 |
| 1 | 3 | 3 | 4 |
| 20 | 3 | 17 | 20 |

**IV. The following statements describe the feelings of some university students. For each statement please check the column which best describes the extent to which you feel this way . . . whether you strongly agree [SA], agree [A], disagree [DA], or strongly disagree [SDA].**

| (%) | AUB | | | | | SJU | | |
|---|---|---|---|---|---|---|---|---|
| | SA | A | DA | SDA | NR | SA | A | DA |

**1.** Politically I am something of a rebel.

| | 9 | 37 | 38 | 11 | 5 | | | |
|---|---|---|---|---|---|---|---|---|

**2.** I am satisfied with the political conditions of my country at present.

| | 6 | 15 | 41 | 36 | 2 | 7 | 21 | 39 |
|---|---|---|---|---|---|---|---|---|

**3.** There is a great need for radical, basic, and general changes in the political system of my country.

| | 43 | 38 | 15 | 2 | 2 | 18 | 27 | 26 |
|---|---|---|---|---|---|---|---|---|

**4.** I find myself in basic disagreement with the general political trends, policies, goals, values, and activities of my government.

| | 26 | 43 | 23 | 3 | 5 | | | |
|---|---|---|---|---|---|---|---|---|

**5.** The change that is required in political systems should be gradual and peaceful.

| | 28 | 51 | 12 | 5 | 4 | 33 | 43 | 12 |
|---|---|---|---|---|---|---|---|---|

**6.** I totally reject the basic goals for which my government stands and the values on which its politics are based.

| | 16 | 34 | 34 | 9 | 7 | | | |
|---|---|---|---|---|---|---|---|---|

**7.** What is needed is revolution, not reform.

| | 13 | 16 | 38 | 28 | 5 | 11 | 11 | 33 |
|---|---|---|---|---|---|---|---|---|

**8.** Our political system is not really democratic.

| | 28 | 48 | 12 | 3 | 9 | | | |
|---|---|---|---|---|---|---|---|---|

**9.** There is a great deal of corruption and favoritism in the political administration in my country.

| | 48 | 38 | 6 | 1 | 7 | | | |
|---|---|---|---|---|---|---|---|---|

**10.** The change that is needed is a change in mentality and not in the system itself.

| | 33 | 41 | 15 | 4 | 7 | | | |
|---|---|---|---|---|---|---|---|---|

**11.** It is possible to improve our political system by a series of nonradical and nonviolent reforms.

| | 21 | 51 | 17 | 5 | 6 | 30 | 43 | 16 |
|---|---|---|---|---|---|---|---|---|

**12.** Elections in my country do not make sense to me.

| | 40 | 30 | 17 | 6 | 7 | | | |
|---|---|---|---|---|---|---|---|---|

**13.** Free speech should be granted to everyone and every group without exception and regardless of views and goals.

| | 73 | 16 | 4 | 6 | 1 | 46 | 35 | 11 |
|---|---|---|---|---|---|---|---|---|

| SDA | NR | LU<br>SA | A | DA | SDA | NR |
|---|---|---|---|---|---|---|
| 29 | 4 | 10 | 27 | 33 | 30 | 0 |
| 25 | 4 | 53 | 29 | 11 | 7 | 0 |
| 5 | 7 | 21 | 37 | 22 | 19 | 1 |
|  |  | 32 | 29 | 29 | 10 | 0 |
| 36 | 9 | 29 | 21 | 27 | 23 | 0 |
| 8 | 4 | 22 | 44 | 17 | 15 | 2 |
| 5 | 3 | 31 | 39 | 21 | 8 | 0 |

| (%) | AUB | | | | | SJU | | |
|---|---|---|---|---|---|---|---|---|
| | SA | A | DA | SDA | NR | SA | A | DA |

**14.** Premarital sexual intercourse should be tolerated for girls.

| | SA | A | DA | SDA | NR | SA | A | DA |
|---|---|---|---|---|---|---|---|---|
| | 24 | 17 | 25 | 29 | 4 | 28 | 33 | 17 |

**15.** Atheists should have the freedom to express their opinions publicly against religions and prophets.

| | SA | A | DA | SDA | NR | SA | A | DA |
|---|---|---|---|---|---|---|---|---|
| | 54 | 24 | 9 | 11 | 2 | 35 | 36 | 18 |

**16.** Doing my duties to my family gives me a great feeling of pleasure.

| | SA | A | DA | SDA | NR | SA | A | DA |
|---|---|---|---|---|---|---|---|---|
| | 58 | 32 | 8 | 1 | 1 | 34 | 36 | 21 |

**17.** I would do anything for the sake of my family.

| | SA | A | DA | SDA | NR | SA | A | DA |
|---|---|---|---|---|---|---|---|---|
| | 41 | 47 | 7 | 3 | 2 | | | |

**18.** For reasons of my own, I do not feel that my family is of great value to me.

| | SA | A | DA | SDA | NR | SA | A | DA |
|---|---|---|---|---|---|---|---|---|
| | 7 | 15 | 29 | 46 | 2 | 7 | 7 | 42 |

**19.** I derive little satisfaction from my relationship with members of my family.

| | SA | A | DA | SDA | NR | SA | A | DA |
|---|---|---|---|---|---|---|---|---|
| | 10 | 26 | 32 | 30 | 2 | | | |

**20.** Faith is a very poor substitute for reason.

| | SA | A | DA | SDA | NR | SA | A | DA |
|---|---|---|---|---|---|---|---|---|
| | 27 | 26 | 17 | 27 | 3 | | | |

**21.** My religion gives me a lot of personal satisfaction.

| | SA | A | DA | SDA | NR | SA | A | DA |
|---|---|---|---|---|---|---|---|---|
| | 30 | 26 | 22 | 20 | 2 | 25 | 34 | 23 |

**22.** Religion is a barrier to advancement in my country.

| | SA | A | DA | SDA | NR | SA | A | DA |
|---|---|---|---|---|---|---|---|---|
| | 38 | 24 | 12 | 23 | 3 | 13 | 25 | 33 |

**23.** I reject the basic teachings of my religion.

| | SA | A | DA | SDA | NR | SA | A | DA |
|---|---|---|---|---|---|---|---|---|
| | 15 | 19 | 23 | 39 | 4 | | | |

**24.** The secret of happiness is not expecting too much out of life, and being content with what comes your way.

| | SA | A | DA | SDA | NR | SA | A | DA |
|---|---|---|---|---|---|---|---|---|
| | 17 | 16 | 34 | 25 | 8 | | | |

**25.** Making plans only brings unhappiness, because plans are hard to fulfill.

| | SA | A | DA | SDA | NR | SA | A | DA |
|---|---|---|---|---|---|---|---|---|
| | 6 | 36 | 25 | 32 | 1 | | | |

**26.** With things as they are today, one ought to think only about the present and not worry about the future.

| | SA | A | DA | SDA | NR | SA | A | DA |
|---|---|---|---|---|---|---|---|---|
| | 15 | 22 | 18 | 43 | 2 | | | |

**27.** I feel at war with my society.

| | SA | A | DA | SDA | NR | SA | A | DA |
|---|---|---|---|---|---|---|---|---|
| | 36 | 39 | 15 | 8 | 2 | 6 | 30 | 39 |

**28.** I am very satisfied with my society and have little to complain about.

| | SA | A | DA | SDA | NR | SA | A | DA |
|---|---|---|---|---|---|---|---|---|
| | 3 | 19 | 37 | 38 | 3 | 34 | 46 | 12 |

**29.** I reject the basic values, goals, and trends dominant in my society.

| | SA | A | DA | SDA | NR | SA | A | DA |
|---|---|---|---|---|---|---|---|---|
| | 32 | 40 | 17 | 7 | 4 | 6 | 30 | 34 |

| SDA | NR | LU SA | A | DA | SDA | NR |
|---|---|---|---|---|---|---|
| 20 | 3 | 13 | 26 | 32 | 27 | 2 |
| 8 | 4 | 32 | 38 | 18 | 12 | 0 |
| 6 | 3 | 38 | 43 | 11 | 4 | 4 |
| | | | | | | |
| 40 | 4 | 3 | 11 | 43 | 39 | 3 |
| | | 3 | 20 | 42 | 31 | 4 |
| | | 27 | 39 | 17 | 15 | 3 |
| 15 | 2 | | | | | |
| 27 | 2 | 28 | 30 | 27 | 15 | 0 |
| | | 14 | 17 | 38 | 32 | 0 |
| | | 5 | 17 | 43 | 36 | 0 |
| | | 2 | 13 | 47 | 38 | 0 |
| | | | | | | |
| 20 | 6 | 26 | 37 | 29 | 8 | 0 |
| 5 | 3 | 4 | 9 | 46 | 41 | 0 |
| 24 | 6 | 27 | 38 | 30 | 5 | 0 |

|      | (%) | AUB | |  |  |  | SJU | | |
|------|-----|-----|---|---|---|---|-----|---|---|
|      |     | SA  | A | DA | SDA | NR | SA | A | DA |

**30.** I am dissatisfied with my society, but I do not concern myself a bit with its problems and don't care what happens to it.

|  | 8 | 22 | 29 | 38 | 3 |

**31.** I have no strong and enduring loyalty to anything or anybody in my society.

|  | 18 | 24 | 20 | 35 | 3 |

**32.** I am dissatisfied with my society and I am involved in a lot of activities to change it into the image I prefer for it.

|  | 16 | 31 | 31 | 14 | 8 |

**33.** I am dissatisfied with my society, but I try to go along and try to make the best of it.

|  | 35 | 34 | 21 | 6 | 4 |

**34.** I don't feel very much at home in this world.

|  | 23 | 29 | 27 | 17 | 4 |

**35.** I wonder what the meaning of life really is.

|  | 38 | 28 | 19 | 13 | 2 |

**36.** I find life very exciting and rewarding.

|  | 23 | 45 | 23 | 8 | 1 |

**37.** Nothing is really worthwhile and life is absurd.

|  | 10 | 24 | 23 | 38 | 5 |

**38.** I feel I'm cut off from communication with others.

|  | 7 | 23 | 31 | 35 | 4 |

**39.** I'm indifferent to what goes on in the world.

|  | 9 | 17 | 25 | 45 | 4 |

**40.** I feel all alone in the world.

|  | 6 | 21 | 22 | 48 | 3 |

**41.** Under the present conditions, only traditional leaders have the chance of being elected to parliament or of occupying important political positions in my country.

|  | 37 | 38 | 12 | 5 | 8 |

**42.** Ultimately, private property should be abolished and complete socialism introduced.

|  | 7 | 14 | 46 | 30 | 3 | 10 | 11 | 26 |

**43.** The capitalistic system provides for the best possible distribution of wealth, human nature being what it is.

|  | 6 | 33 | 43 | 9 | 9 |

**44.** There is nothing fundamentally wrong with our society; all we need to do is to introduce a few reforms.

|  | 5 | 38 | 38 | 14 | 5 |

|       |     |     | LU  |     |     |     |     |
|-------|-----|-----|-----|-----|-----|-----|-----|
| SDA   | NR  |     | SA  | A   | DA  | SDA | NR  |
|       |     |     | 11  | 17  | 45  | 27  | 1   |
| 45    | 7   |     | 21  | 26  | 31  | 18  | 4   |
|       |     |     | 8   | 25  | 35  | 29  | 2   |

| (%) | AUB | | | | | SJU | | |
|---|---|---|---|---|---|---|---|---|
| | SA | A | DA | SDA | NR | SA | A | DA |

**45.** When a national government is incompetent, the use of force to remove it can be justified.

| | 16 | 46 | 27 | 5 | 6 | | | |
|---|---|---|---|---|---|---|---|---|

**46.** As a student, I think that school and politics do not mix.

| | 12 | 20 | 48 | 15 | 5 | | | |
|---|---|---|---|---|---|---|---|---|

**47.** Religion should be separated from the state and civil marriage should be introduced.

| | 40 | 39 | 11 | 6 | 4 | 51 | 30 | 8 |
|---|---|---|---|---|---|---|---|---|

**48.** I prefer to accept reality when it seems I cannot change it.

| | 11 | 36 | 37 | 12 | 4 | 14 | 34 | 29 |
|---|---|---|---|---|---|---|---|---|

**49.** It is only wishful thinking to believe that one can really influence our political system. People like me can do very little.

| | 7 | 31 | 43 | 12 | 7 | | | |
|---|---|---|---|---|---|---|---|---|

## V. Political views and involvement

| (%) | AUB | SJU | |
|---|---|---|---|
| | Self | Self | F |

**1. Indicate to what extent you personally and your parents are involved in politics.**

| | | | |
|---|---|---|---|
| Very active | 8 | 9 | 8 |
| Active | 20 | 32 | 23 |
| A little active | 22 | 40 | 43 |
| Nonactive | 40 | 18 | 18 |
| NR | 10 | 1 | 8 |

**2. Membership in political parties**

| | | | |
|---|---|---|---|
| Yes | 13[a] | 4 | 4 |
| No | 85 | 95 | 80 |
| NR | 2 | 1 | 16 |

**3. Participation in strikes**

| | | | |
|---|---|---|---|
| Always | 3 | 7 | |
| Often | 9 | | |
| Sometimes | 31 | 55 | |
| Rarely | 32 | 15 | |
| Never | 23 | 22 | |
| NR | 2 | 1 | |

[a]Belong to political parties and/or political groups.

| SDA | NR | LU<br>SA | A | DA | SDA | NR |
|---|---|---|---|---|---|---|
| 6 | 4 | 54 | 30 | 10 | 6 | 0 |
| 19 | 4 | | | | | |
| | | 0 | 11 | 51 | 37 | 1 |

| M | LU<br>Self | F | M |
|---|---|---|---|
| 2 | 14 | 8 | 1 |
| 10 | 41 | 13 | 4 |
| 48 | 25 | 23 | 24 |
| 33 | 19 | 45 | 63 |
| 7 | 1 | 10 | 8 |
| 3 | 9 | 3 | |
| 81 | 91 | 97 | |
| 16 | 0 | 0 | |
| | 21 | | |
| | 40 | | |
| | 19 | | |
| | 20 | | |
| | 0 | | |

| (%) | AUB Self | SJU Self | F |
|---|---|---|---|
| **4. Support for Palestinian commandos** | | | |
| Strong support | 40 | 23 | 8 |
| Support | 38 | 55 | 31 |
| No support | 22 | 22 | 27 |
| NR | 0 | 0 | 33 |
| **5. Preferred commando organization** | | | |
| Fateh | | 39 | 30 |
| PFLP | | 8 | 2 |
| DFLP | | 1 | 0 |
| Others | | 2 | 0 |
| None | | 23 | 21 |
| NR | | 27 | 47 |
| **Preferred solution of Palestine problem** | | | |
| Popular armed struggle | 34 | 21 | |
| Classical war | 18 | 10 | |
| Combination of both popular armed struggle and classical war | 12 | 9 | |
| Peaceful solution | 36 | 60 | |
| Other | 0 | 0 | |

**7. Here are four alternative statements. Check the statement that best or most accurately describes your feelings. (Check only one statement.) [Asked only at LU]**

**1.** In general, I am satisfied with my society, and I do not think it is suffering from any basic weaknesses that require any special concern as some people would like to imagine. As in the case of any other society, a few reforms may be needed, and that can be done from within the present order.

**2.** I am not satisfied with my society, but I believe at the same time that it is very difficult to change it, at present at least. Therefore, I prefer to accept reality and make peace with it as much as possible and as long as it seems difficult to change it.

**3.** I am not satisfied with my society, but actually I am indifferent and uninvolved in any activities directed at changing it.

**4.** I am not satisfied with my society, and I am actually involved in several activities directed toward changing it in the direction I prefer for it.

| M | LU Self | F | M |
|---|---|---|---|
| | 35 | | |
| | 54 | | |
| | 11 | | |
| | 0 | | |
| | 52 | | |
| | 15 | | |
| | 3 | | |
| | 6 | | |
| | 24 | | |
| | 27 | | |
| | 18 | | |
| | 18 | | |
| | 29 | | |
| | 8 | | |
| | 22 | | |
| | 21 | | |
| | 20 | | |
| | 38 | | |

# Notes

## 1. Introductory Statement: Youth and Change

1.      Guido Martinotti, "The Positive Marginality: Notes on Italian Students in Periods of Political Mobilization," in *Students in Revolt*, ed. S. M. Lipset and P. G. Altbach, pp. 167–201.

2.      Herbert C. Kelman, "In Search of New Bases for Legitimacy: Some Social-Psychological Dimensions of the Black Power and Student Power Movement" (unpublished lecture, 1969).

3.      Constantine K. Zurayk, "Student Revolt," *al-Kulliyah* (Summer 1968): 11.

4.      Friedrich Engels, *Germany: Revolution and Counter-Revolution*, trans. L. Krieger, p. 41, cited by Lewis S. Feuer, *The Conflict of Generations: The Character and Significance of Student Movements*, p. 69.

5.      See S. M. Lipset, "University Students and Politics in Underdeveloped Countries," in *Student Politics*, ed. idem, pp. 3–53.

6.      Ibid., pp. 11–13.

7.      See Arthur Liebman, Kenneth N. Walker, and Myron Glazer, *Latin American University Students: A Six Nation Study*, p. 137.

8.      See Anouar Abdel-Malek, *Egypt: Military Society*, trans. C. I. Markmann, especially pp. 22–26, 34–37; A. J. M. Craig, "Egyptian Students," *Middle East Journal* 7 (Summer 1953): 293–299; Tawfic al-Hakin, *Awdat al-Ruh* [Return of the spirit] (a novel in Arabic).

9.      C. H. Moore and A. R. Hochschild, "Student Unions in North African Politics," in *Students in Revolt*, ed. Lipset and Altbach, pp. 351–379.

10.     Liebman, Walker, and Glazer, *Latin American University Students*, p. 19.

11.     C. Wright Mills, "The New Left," in *Power, Politics, and People: The Collected Essays of C. Wright Mills*, ed. Irving Louis Horowitz, p. 256.

12.     Herbert Marcuse, *An Essay on Liberation*, p. 15.

13.     See Carl Oglesby, "The Idea of the New Left," in *The New Left Reader*, ed. idem, p. 18.

14.     Alain Touraine, *The May Movement: Revolt and Reform*, trans. L. Mayhew, pp. 39–41. It is noteworthy that an opposite point of view is expressed by the German sociologist Jurgen Habermas, who asserts that "students are not a class, they are not even the avant-garde of a class, and they are certainly not leading a revolutionary struggle" (*Toward a Rational Society: Student Protest, Science, and Politics*, trans. J. J. Shapiro).

15.     P. G. Altbach, "Students and Politics," in *Student Politics*, ed. Lipset, p. 86.

16.     Kevin Lyonette, "Student Organizations in Latin America," *International Affairs* 42 (October 1966): 657.

## 2. Reasons for Student Revolt: A Sociological Model

1.    Feuer, *The Conflict of Generations*, p. 3.
2.    Ibid.
3.    Ibid., p. 10.
4.    S. M. Lipset and P. G. Altbach, "Student Politics and Higher Education in the United States," in *Student Politics*, ed. Lipset, p. 216.
5.    Richard Flacks, "The Liberated Generation: Roots of Student Protest," *Journal of Social Issues* 23, no. 3 (July 1967): 52–75; idem, *Youth and Social Change*, Ch. 4.
6.    F. Solomon and J. R. Fishman, "Perspectives on the Student Sit-in Movement," *American Journal of Ortho-Psychiatry* 33 (1963): 873–874.
7.    Kenneth Keniston, "The Sources of Student Dissent," *Journal of Social Issues* 23, no. 3 (July 1967): 108–137; see also idem, *Young Radicals*. For another critical study of the generational conflict theory see S. Lubell, "That Generation Gap," *Public Interest*, no. 13 (Fall 1968): 52–60.
8.    George Kennan, *Democracy and the Student Left*, pp. 9–10.
9.    Charles Malik, "Student Activism," *Discourse*, no. 4 (1971): 4. Similarly, AUB president Bayard Dodge repeated in several contexts in *The American University of Beirut* that "propaganda leaders did their best to stir up the youth" (e.g., p. 68).
10.    Malik, "Student Activism," pp. 3–4.
11.    Zurayk, "Student Revolt," pp. 11–12.
12.    Constantine K. Zurayk, "Abiding Truths" (address delivered at the Founder's Day Convocation, AUB, April 28, 1960).
13.    Zurayk, "Student Revolt," pp. 10–12.
14.    For details of this conception of development, see Halim Barakat, "Socio-economic, Cultural, and Personality Forces Determining Development in Arab Society," *Social Praxis* 2, nos. 3–4 (1976): 179–204.
15.    See I. Wallerstein and Paul Starr, eds., *The University Crisis Reader*, vol. 1. See especially articles by Robert Paul Wolff, Senator William Fulbright, and Nobel Laureate George Wald.
16.    J. H. Skolnick, *The Politics of Protest*, p. 100.
17.    Habermas, *Toward a Rational Society*, pp. 1–4.
18.    Touraine, *The May Movement*, p. 29.
19.    Daniel Cohn-Bendit, Jacques Sauvageot, and Alain Geismar, *The French Student Revolt: The Leaders Speak*, trans. B. R. Brewster, p. 11.
20.    Quoted by Martinotti, "The Positive Marginality," in *Students in Revolt*, ed. Lipset and Altbach, p. 191.
21.    Dodge, *The American University of Beirut*.
22.    Zurayk, "Abiding Truths."
23.    Lipset, "University Students and Politics in Underdeveloped Countries," in *Student Politics*, ed. idem, p. 7.
24.    For a detailed description of this concept of alienation, see Halim Barakat, "Alienation: A Process of Encounter between Utopia and Reality," *British Journal of Sociology* 20, no. 1 (March 1969): 1–10.

## 3. Social and Political Integration in Lebanon: A Case of Stratified Social Mosaic

1.    For instance, the American sociologist Edward Shils describes contemporary Lebanon as "a happy phenomenon, unique in the Third World, a prosperous liberal country. It has

a parliamentary body freely elected in the competition of a plurality of independent political parties." (See E. Shils, "The Prospect for Lebanese Civility," in *Politics in Lebanon*, ed. L. Binder, p. 1.) Similar descriptions are made by the Lebanese intellectual Michel Shiha (see *Lubnan fi Shakhsiyyatih wa Hudurih* [Lebanon: Its personality and presence]); by K. S. Salibi (see "The Personality of Lebanon in Relation to the Modern World," in *Politics in Lebanon*, ed. Binder, and *The Modern History of Lebanon*); and by Elie A. Salem (*Modernization without Revolution: Lebanon's Experience*). Others, such as Michael C. Hudson, see Lebanon as a precarious rather than a happy phenomenon (see *The Precarious Republic: Political Modernization in Lebanon*).

2.   The 1943 National Pact was concluded between the top Christian and Muslim political elites and not by the peoples of both communities.

3.   W. A. Kornhauser, "Political Man," in *Sociology*, ed. L. Broom and P. Selznick, 3d. ed., p. 708.

4.   Y. Khal, "A Dialogue with Kamal Junblat," *al-Qadayah al Mu'asirah* 1, no. 2 (1969).

5.   See *an-Nahar*, August 5, 1970. (Translations are mine unless otherwise indicated.)

6.   Hudson, *The Precarious Republic*, p. 12.

7.   See *an-Nahar*, September 3 and 9, 1968; November 17, 1969.

8.   *An-Nahar*, November 30, 1969, p. 10.

9.   Fu'ad I. Khuri, "al-Wāqi' al-ijtimā'í lil-Nizam al-Ta'ifi fi Lubnan" [The social bases of the confessional system in Lebanon], in *Nizam al-Ta'ifiyyah al-Si'asiyyah fi Lubnan* [The political confessional system in Lebanon] (Kata'ib publication, 1968).

10.   Michel Shiha, *Lubnan fi Shakhsiyyatih wa Hudurih*, p. 185.

11.   Hudson, *The Precarious Republic*, pp. 17–46.

12.   Salibi, "The Personality of Lebanon in Relation to the Modern World," p. 268.

13.   Levon Melikian and Lutfy N. Diab, "Group Affiliations of University Students in the Arab Middle East," *Journal of Social Psychology* 44 (1959).

14.   Habib Hammam, "A Measure of Alienation in a University Setting" (M.A. thesis, American University of Beirut, 1969).

15.   Munir Bashshur, "al-Tarbiyyah wa-Ta'lim fi Lubnan" [Education in Lebanon], *Mawaqif* 2, no. 7 (1970): 85–118.

16.   Peter Dodd and Halim Barakat, *River without Bridges: A Study of the Exodus of the 1967 Palestinian Arab Refugees*.

17.   The formally recognized political parties which are part of the Lebanese political system are (1) the National Bloc (essentially a Maronite party) founded by Ex-President of the Lebanese Republic Emile Edde, its present dean being his son, Raymond Edde; (2) the Constitution Party (essentially Maronite), founded by Ex-President of the Republic Bisharah al-Khuri, its present president being his son, Khalil al-Khuri; (3) the Party of the Free Nationalists (Hizb al-Watani'een al-Ahrar, essentially Maronite), founded by Ex-President Camille Sham'oun, who continues to be its president; (4) al-Kata'ib (essentially Maronite), founded by Pierre Jumayel, who continues to be its president; (5) the Progressive Socialist Party (secular and socialist, yet largely a Druze party), founded by Kamal Junblat, who continues to be its president; (6) al-Najjadah Party (essentially Sunni Muslim), founded by Adnan al-Hakim, who continues to be its president; (7) the National League Party (Sunni Muslim), founded by a number of Beirut Muslim leaders, its present chairman being Amin al-Arisi; (8) the National Action Movement Party (essentially Sunni Muslim), founded by Uthman al-Dana, who continues to be its president; (9) the Arab Liberation Party (essentially Sunni Muslim), founded by Rashid Karami, who continues to be its president; (10) the Democratic Party, recently founded by a few liberal Christian and Muslim intellectuals, its president being Emile Bitar.

18.   These are the Communist Party, the Ba'ath Party, and the Syrian Social Nationalist Party (also known as PPS [Parti Populaire Syrien]). In August 1970, the Lebanese minister of

the interior, Kamal Junblat, announced that these three political parties were officially recognized.
19.     S. M. Lipset, *Political Man*, p. 12.
20.     Elie A. Salem, "Cabinet Politics in Lebanon," *Middle East Journal* 21 (Autumn 1967): 496.
21.     See *an-Nahar*, September 7, 1968.
22.     See K. S. Salibi, *"Al-Mawarinah"* [The Maronites], *Malaf an-Nahar*, no. 40 (January 1970): especially pp. 40–47.
23.     Salibi, "The Personality of Lebanon in Relation to the Modern World," p. 268.
24.     Ibid., p. 269.
25.     Michael C. Hudson, "Democracy and Social Mobilization in Lebanese Politics," *Comparative Politics* 1, no. 2 (January 1969): 256.
26.     Salibi, "The Personality of Lebanon in Relation to the Modern World," p. 266.
27.     Morroe Berger, *The Arab World Today*, p. 294.
28.     République Libanaise, Ministère du Plan, *Besoins et possibilités de développement du Liban*.
29.     See Bashshur, "al-Tarbiyyah wa-Ta'lim fi Lubnan."
30.     Ibid., pp. 90–91.
31.     During the academic year 1973–1974, the total number of students enrolled in universities, colleges, and other institutions of higher learning in Lebanon amounted to 50,469 (49.30 percent of whom attended BAU, 29.38 percent LU, 9.15 percent AUB, 5.93 percent SJU and 6.24 percent other institutions). The percentage of non-Lebanese students was 55.34 percent.

## 4.     Religion and Student Politics

1.     See P. G. Altbach, "Students, Politics, and Higher Education in a Developing Area: The Case of Bombay, India" (Ph.D. dissertation, University of Chicago, 1966).
2.     Liebman, Walker, and Glazer, *Latin American University Students*, p. 148.
3.     Myron Glazer, "Student Politics in a Chilean University," in *Students in Revolt*, ed. Lipset and Altbach, p. 438.
4.     Moore and Hochschild, "Student Unions in North African Politics," p. 368.
5.     F. Solomon and J. R. Fishman, "Youth and Peace: A Psychological Study of Student Peace Demonstrators in Washington, D.C.," *Journal of Social Issues* 20, no. 4 (October 1964): 54–73.
6.     Kenneth Keniston, *Young Radicals*.
7.     Flacks, "The Liberated Generation."
8.     R. Braungart, "Family Status, Socialization, and Student Politics: A Multivariate Analysis" (Ph.D. dissertation, Pennsylvania State University, 1969). Data on the influence of religion on politics in general are reported in such works as Gerald Lenski, *The Religious Factor*, and Lipset, *Political Man*.
9.     Theodor Hanf found (in 1971) that 51.3 percent of the Christian students and 18 percent of the Muslim students in the four universities in Lebanon opted for Lebanese nationalism ("Factors Determining the Political Attitudes of Lebanese University Students," unpublished manuscript, 1971).
10.     A survey study by Habib Hammam on a representative sample of all the students registered at AUB during the academic year 1967–1968 found that alienation from religion was more prominent than alienation from the university, the world, society, the self, and the family (there was no measurement of political alienation). Seventeen percent of the students showed high alienation from religion; 26 percent showed moderate alienation; 31 percent, low alienation; and 25 percent were well integrated into religion. The index of intensity of aliena-

tion from religion was based on seven items (see Hammam, "A Measure of Alienation," pp. 69, 146). In response to a question as to whether or not they believed in the existence of God, 57 percent said yes and 37 percent said no. As to the degree that they felt that religious faith had influence in their personal lives, 35 percent said it had little influence; 29 percent, some influence; and 34 percent, great influence.

My data collected about three years later on Arab students at AUB and students at SJU and LU show the following: at AUB, 15 percent strongly agreed that they rejected the basic teachings of their religion, 19 percent agreed, 23 percent disagreed, and 39 percent strongly disagreed. Sixty percent said they believed in the existence of God, 28 percent said they were uncertain, and 11 percent said no. As to religion's influence in their lives, 34 percent said it had little influence; 40 percent, some influence; and 20 percent, great influence. At SJU, 56 percent said they believed in the existence of God, 17 percent said they were uncertain, and 14 percent said no. Regarding religion's influence in their lives, 26 percent said it had little influence; 33 percent, some influence; and 30 percent, great influence. At LU, 14 percent strongly agreed that they rejected the basic teachings of their religion, 17 percent agreed, 39 percent disagreed, and 31 percent strongly disagreed. Sixty-six percent said they believed in the existence of God, 23 percent were uncertain, and 11 percent said no. Regarding religion's influence in their lives, 33 percent said it had little influence; 36 percent, some influence; and 28 percent, great influence.

11.    The question on Arafat, Habash, and Hawatmeh was used only in the Arabic version of the questionnaire that was used at LU; it is not included in the appendix.

12.    Theodor Hanf found in the aforementioned paper that the advocates of Lebanese nationalism were over-represented on his religiosity scales. The Arab nationalists and Lebanese nationalists showed a high degree of identification with their religions, while the Syrian nationalists, leftist Arab nationalists, and leftists showed a low degree of identification.

13.    S. M. Lipset, *Revolution and Counterrevolution*, p. 170.

14.    This wording was found only in the Arabic version of the questionnaire; a different version of the statement appears in the Appendix.

## 5.    Family and Student Politics

1.    Richard E. Dawson and Kenneth Prewitt, *Political Socialization*, p. 111.
2.    Liebman, Walker, and Glazer, *Latin American University Students*, p. 142.
3.    Ibid., pp. 143–144.
4.    Richard Flacks, "The Liberated Generation," p. 68.
5.    Herbert H. Hyman, *Political Socialization*.
6.    Kenneth P. Langton, *Political Socialization*, pp. 52–59.
7.    Liebman, Walker, and Glazer, *Latin American University Students*, p. 105.
8.    Langton, *Political Socialization*, pp. 52–59.
9.    Dawson and Prewitt, *Political Socialization*, p. 124.
10.    Langton, *Political Socialization*, pp. 52–68.

## 6.    Social Class and Student Politics

1.    Karl Marx, *Nachlass* I, p. 398 [*Correspondence of 1843*], quoted by Georg Lukács, *History and Class Consciousness: Studies in Marxist Dialectics*, trans. Rodney Livingstone, p. 3.
2.    Karl Marx, *The Holy Family*, quoted by Lukács, *History and Class Consciousness*, trans. Livingstone, p. 46.
3.    Karl Marx, *Selected Writings in Sociology and Social Philosophy*, ed. T. B. Bottomore and N. Rubel, pp. 231–232.

4. Ibid., pp. 188–189. See also Karl Marx, "The Eighteenth Brumaire of Louis Napoleon," in his *Selected Works* 1: 334; Marcuse, *An Essay on Liberation*. In the latter work, it is shown how the Marxian theory recognized that impoverishment does not necessarily provide the soil for revolution (p. 15). An interesting application of the Marxian theory to the Arab situation is found in George Habash, *Laborers and the Palestinian Revolution*.

5. "Karl Marx to S. Meyer and A. Vogt, April 8, 1970," in *Karl Marx and Frederick Engels on Britain*, p. 506.

6. Karl Marx and Friedrich Engels, *Basic Writings on Politics and Philosophy*, ed. Lewis S. Feuer, p. 458.

7. John C. Leggett, *Class, Race, and Labor: Working-Class Consciousness in Detroit*, p. 91. Similar results are also reported in Lipset, *Political Man*, Ch. 10; Mark Abrams, "Social Class and British Politics," in *Political Sociology*, ed. L. A. Coser, pp. 204–215; L. E. Hazebrigg, "Religious and Class Bases of Political Conflict in Italy," *American Journal of Sociology* 75, no. 4., pt. 1 (1970): 496–511; E. Allardt, *Patterns of Class Conflict and Working Class Consciousness in Finnish Politics*; M. Janowitz, "Social Cleavage and Party Affiliation: Germany, Great Britain, and United States," in his *Political Conflict*; M. Zeitlin, *Revolutionary Politics and the Cuban Working Class*, p. 65.

8. Data showing that leftists come from more privileged families than do rightists are reported by Flacks, "The Liberated Generation"; Keniston, *Young Radicals*; Braungart, "Family Status, Socialization, and Student Politics"; G. Lyonns, "The Police Car Demonstration: A Survey of Participants," in *The Berkeley Student Revolt*, ed. S. M. Lipset and S. S. Wolin; W. A. Watts and D. Whittaker, "Free Speech Advocates at Berkeley," *Journal of Applied Behavior Science* 2 (1966): 41–62; D. L. Westly and R. G. Braungart, "Class and Politics in the Family Background of Student Political Activists," *American Sociological Review* 31 (1966): 690–692.

9. Westly and Braungart, "Class and Politics," p. 692. They offer this explanation in the light of the status politics theory of Richard Hofstadter, "The Pseudo-Conservative Revolt—1955," in *The Radical Right*, ed. Daniel Bell, pp. 62–80.

10. Daniel and Gabriel Cohn-Bendit, *Obsolete Communism: The Left-Wing Alternative*, p. 13.

11. Cornelis J. Lammers, "Student Unionism in the Netherlands: An Application of a Social Class Model," *American Sociological Review* 36 (April 1971): 250–263.

12. See Frank Bonilla, "Students in Politics: Three Generations of Political Action in a Latin-American University" (Ph.D. thesis, Harvard University, 1959); R. L. Scheman, "The Brazilian Law Student: Background, Habits, Attitudes," *Journal of Inter-American Studies* 5, no. 3 (1963); D. Goldrich, *Radical Nationalism: The Political Orientations of Panamanian Law Students*; D. Nasatir, "A Note on Contextual Effects and the Political Orientations of University Students," *American Sociological Review* 33 (April 1968): 210–219; R. E. Scott, "Student Political Activism in Latin America," in *Students in Revolt*, ed. Lipset and Altbach, pp. 403–431; Glazer, "Student Politics in a Chilean University"; Liebman, Walker, and Glazer, *Latin American University Students*.

13. Nasatir, "A Note on Contextual Effects," p. 212, quoted by B. Berelson and G. A. Steiner, *Human Behavior: An Inventory of Scientific Findings*, p. 427.

## 7.   Some Correlates of Political Alienation and Radicalism

1. For details on this conception on alienation, see Barakat, "Alienation."

2. Mills, *Power, Politics, and People*, p. 253. For Mills's definitions of *right* and *left* see especially pp. 253–256.

3. Michael W. Miles, *The Radical Probe: The Logic of Student Rebellion*, p. 28.

4. Ibid.

5. See Ghassan Tueini, "The Constitutional Revolution," *an-Nahar*, January 30, 1973.

6. For the data on the relationship between religion and leftist-rightist orientations, see Chapter 4.

7. For the data on the relationship between family and leftist-rightist orientations, see Chapter 5.

8. For the data on the relationship between social class and leftist-rightist orientations, see Chapter 6.

9. Quoted by Richard Lichtman, "The University: Mark for Privilege?" in *The University Crisis Reader*, ed. I. Wallerstein and Paul Starr, 1: 119.

## 8. Search for National Identity: Early Stages in the Development of the Student Movement

1. The story of the 1882 revolt is found in the following sources: *al-Muqtataf* 7 (1882–1883): 2–6, 65–72, 121–127, 158–167; ibid. 9 (1884–1885): 183, 243–244, 468–472; "The Memoirs of Jirji Zaydan," *al-Hilal* 33 (1924–1925): 17–20, 153–156, 271–275, 373–376, 516–520, 637–640 (parts of these memoirs are also found in *al-Abhath* 20, no. 4 [1967]); Yusuf Quzman Khuri, "Dr. Cornelius Van Dyck and the Awakening of Syria during the 19th Century" (in Arabic) (M.A. thesis, American University of Beirut, 1965), pp. 122–137; Shafiq Jiha, "The 1882 Crisis and the Address of Dr. Edwin Lewis in the Syrian Protestant College in Beirut" (in Arabic), in *Kitab al-'Id*, ed. G. Jabbour (Centennial Publication of AUB, 1967); A. L. Tibawi, "The Genesis and Early History of the Syrian Protestant College," pt. 1, *Middle East Journal* 21, no. 1 (Winter 1967): 1–15, and pt. 2, ibid. 21, no. 2 (Spring 1967): 199–212.

2. Stephen B. L. Penrose, *That They May Have Life: The Story of the American University of Beirut, 1866–1941*, pp. 43–44.

3. See Jirji Zaydan's memoirs in *al-Abhath* 20, no. 4 (1967): 329, or in *al-Hilal* 33 (1924–1925).

4. For the complete text of this letter see *al-Abhath* 20, no. 4 (1967): 350–352.

5. Ibid., p. 352.

6. Ibid., p. 353.

7. The Board of Managers was composed of the American and British consuls at Beirut, the British consuls at Damascus and Jerusalem, four British businessmen, and several American and British missionaries stationed in the major cities of the Near East (see Dodge, *The American University of Beirut*).

8. *Al-Abhath* 20, no. 4 (1967): 339–340.

9. Ibid., p. 341.

10. Ibid., p. 355.

11. Ibid., pp. 343–346.

12. On the question of religious freedom, see A. L. Tibawi, "Genesis and Early History," pp. 199–212, and Penrose, *That They May Have Life*, pp. 46–58.

13. Quoted in Penrose, *That They May Have Life*, pp. 47–48.

14. Daniel Bliss, *The Reminiscences of Daniel Bliss*, ed. F. J. Bliss.

15. Penrose, *That They May Have Life*, p. 33.

16. Dodge, *The American University of Beirut*, p. 22.

17. Penrose, *That They May Have Life*, pp. 69–70.

18. Dodge, *The American University of Beirut*, p. 56.

19. Ibid.

20. Interview with Dr. Raif Abillama, *al-Kulliahah* (Winter 1973): 8–9.

21. Penrose, *That They May Have Life*, pp. 135–136.

22. Ibid., pp. 137–138.

23. Ibid., pp. 138–139.

24. Ibid., pp. 139–142.

25. Dodge, *The American University of Beirut*, p. 68.
26. Najm-ad-Deen Rifa'ci, "We and the West in the Future," *al-'Urwa al-Withqa* 10, no. 4 (June 1945).
27. Dodge, *The American University of Beirut*, p. 72.
28. Ibid., pp. 85–86.
29. Constantine K. Zurayk, "Participation of AUB Students in Palestine Struggle," in *AUB Campus Yearbook* (1971), p. 23.
30. See Najib Azzam, "The Student Council: A Short History," *Outlook*, December 7, 1971.

## 9.  Confrontation or Negation: Recent Developments in the Student Movement

1. E. Khuri, "Revolutionaries or Boy Scouts?" (unpublished manuscript, 1972).
2. For a condensed review of the ideas of the Wa'i Movement by one of its founders, see Isam Khalifeh, "The Lebanese University: A Distorted Body . . .," *an-Nahar Literary Supplement*, April 16, 23, and 30, 1972.
3. The League celebrates the occasion yearly in one of Beirut's luxurious hotels, and this celebration is often attended by the AUB president and vice-presidents, conservative professors, some members of the Lebanese cabinet and parliament, leaders of al-Kata'ib and the National Bloc, and former President of the Lebanese Republic Camille Sham'oun.
4. *Outlook*, November 24, 1970.
5. Ibid., p. 3.
6. Ibid.
7. Student leaflet in my possession.
8. Student leaflet in my possession.
9. *Al-Rabita*, no. 1 (1967–1968).
10. Ibid., Spring 1972, p. 28.
11. The description of strikes and demonstrations in this section is based on my personal observations at the time. Quotations are from student leaflets and other documents in my possession except as otherwise noted.
12. *An-Nahar*, April 23, 1972.
13. Ibid., March 21, 1973.
14. Najemy was killed in early 1976 by one of the expelled students.
15. AUB received $73,082,000 from the U.S. government between 1959 and 1971 (distributed as follows: $55,792,000 between 1959 and 1969; $10,990,000 in 1970; and $6,300,000 in 1971), and requested $6,000,000 for 1972. See *American Schools and Hospitals Abroad* (Washington, D.C.: U.S. Government Printing Office, 1972). The above amounts do not include U.S. government scholarships granted between 1952 and 1959, nor do they include research grants.
16. *Outlook*, May 17, 1971.
17. Ibid.
18. Ibid.
19. *An-Nahar*, October 12, 1971.
20. *AUB Bulletin*, Fact Sheet, March 20, 1974.
21. *An-Nahar*, April 20, 1974.
22. Ibid., April 21, 1974.
23. Ibid., April 23, 1974.
24. Ibid., April 6, 1974.
25. One of the suspended students killed two deans during the civil war.

26.	President Howard Bliss, quoted by Penrose, *That They May Have Life*, pp. 139–142.
27.	*AUB Bulletin*, October 14, 1971; *an-Nahar*, October 10, 1971.

## Epilogue. The Lebanese Civil War: Its Social Origins and Prospects

1.	Binder, ed., *Politics in Lebanon*, p. 1.
2.	Shiha, *Lubnan fi Shakhsiyyatih wa Hudurih*, p. 185.
3.	Salem, *Modernization without Revolution*, pp. 3–4.
4.	Ibid., pp. 144–145.
5.	See Iliya Harik, "The Electoral System and Voters' Attitudes in Lebanon" (unpublished manuscript). Another optimistic view of Lebanon is projected by David and Audrey Smock, *Political Fragmentation and National Accommodation: A Comparative Study of Lebanon and Ghana*.
6.	For both messages, see *an-Nahar*, June 26, 1976.
7.	Halim Barakat, "Social and Political Integration in Lebanon: A Case of Social Mosaic," *Middle East Journal* 27, no. 3 (Summer 1973): 301–318; originally published in Arabic in *Mawaqif* 1, no. 1, (1968). Chapter 3 of the present study is a revised version of this paper.
8.	Halim Barakat, "The Religious Factor and Voting Patterns in Lebanese Elections: A Tendency toward Sectarian Polarization," *Mawaqif* no. 19/20 (1972): 6–16.
9.	The leftist-nationalist camp has included several Lebanese parties and movements, such as the Progressive Socialist Party (of Kamal Junblat), Lebanese Communist Party, Syrian Social Nationalist Party, Arab Ba'ath Socialist Party, Communist Action Organization, Nasserites, and others. On the other hand, the rightist camp has included the Phalangists (Pierre Jumayel), Party of the Free Nationalists (Camille Sham'oun), Guards of the Cedar, Maronite League, Maronite Order of Monks, and other private militias, such as that of Ex-President Franjieh.
10.	See Iliya Harik, *Mann yahkum Lubnan* [Who rules Lebanon].
11.	See *an-Nahar*, January 8, 1973.
12.	*New York Times Magazine*, August 15, 1976.

# Selected Bibliography

Abdel-Malek, Anouar. *Egypt: Military Society*. Translated by C. I. Markmann. New York: Vintage Books, 1968.

Allardt, E. *Patterns of Class Conflict and Working Class Consciousness in Finnish Politics*. Helsinki: Institute of Sociology, 1964.

Barakat, Halim. "Alienation: A Process of Encounter between Utopia and Reality." *British Journal of Sociology* 20, no. 1 (March 1969): 1–10.

———. "Social and Political Integration in Lebanon: A Case of Social Mosaic." *Middle East Journal* 27, no. 3 (Summer 1973): 301–318.

———. "Socio-economic, Cultural, and Personality Forces Determining Development in Arab Society." *Social Praxis* 2, nos. 3–4 (1976): 179–204.

Bashshur, Munir. "Al-Tarbiyyah wa-Ta'lim fi Lubnan" [Education in Lebanon]. *Mawaqif* 2, no. 7 (1970): 85–118.

Bell, Daniel, ed. *The Radical Right*. Garden City, N.Y.: Doubleday, 1962.

Berelson, B., and G. A. Steiner. *Human Behavior: An Inventory of Scientific Findings*. New York: Harcourt, Brace and World, 1964.

Berger, Morroe. *The Arab World Today*. Garden City, N.Y.: Doubleday Anchor Books, 1964.

Binder, L., ed. *Politics in Lebanon*. New York: John Wiley and Sons, 1966.

Bliss, Daniel. *The Reminiscences of Daniel Bliss*. Edited by F. J. Bliss. New York: F. H. Revell Co., 1920.

Broom, L., and P. Selznick, eds. *Sociology*. 3d ed. New York: Harper and Row, 1963.

Cohn-Bendit, Daniel, and Gabriel Cohn-Bendit. *Obsolete Communism: The Left-Wing Alternative*. Translated by Arnold Pomerans. New York: McGraw-Hill, 1968.

Cohn-Bendit, Daniel, Jacques Sauvageot, and Alain Geismar. *The French Student Revolt: The Leaders Speak*. Presented by Hervé Bourges. Translated by B. R. Brewster. New York: Hill and Wang, 1968.

Coser, L. A., ed. *Political Sociology*. New York: Harper Torchbooks, 1967.

Craig, A. J. M. "Egyptian Students." *Middle East Journal* 7 (Summer 1953): 293–299.

Dawson, Richard E., and Kenneth Prewitt. *Political Socialization*. Boston: Little, Brown and Co., 1969.

Dodd, Peter, and Halim Barakat. *River without Bridges: A Study of the Exodus of the 1967 Palestinian Arab Refugees*. Beirut: The Institute for Palestine Studies, 1968.

Dodge, Bayard. *The American University of Beirut*. Beirut: Khayat, 1958.

Engels, Friedrich. *Germany: Revolution and Counter-Revolution*. Translated by L. Krieger. New York: International Publishers, 1933.

Feuer, Lewis S. *The Conflict of Generations: The Character and Significance of Student Movements*. New York: Basic Books, 1969.

Flacks, Richard. "The Liberated Generation: Roots of Student Protest." *Journal of Social Issues* 23, no. 3 (July 1967): 52–75.

————. *Youth and Social Change*. Chicago: Markham Publishing Co., 1971.

Goldrich, D. *Radical Nationalism: The Political Orientations of Panamanian Law Students*. East Lansing: Bureau of Political and Social Research, Michigan State University, 1961.

Habash, George. *Laborers and the Palestinian Revolution*. Beirut: Kitab al Hadaf, 1970.

Habermas, Jurgen. *Toward a Rational Society: Student Protest, Science, and Politics*. Translated by J. J. Shapiro. Boston: Beacon Press, 1971.

Hakim, Tawfic al-. *Awdat al-Ruh* [Return of the spirit] (a novel in Arabic). Cairo: Maktabat al-Adab, 1933.

Harik, Iliya. *Mann yahkum Lubnan* [Who rules Lebanon]. Beirut: Dar an-Nahar, 1972.

Hudson, Michael C. *The Precarious Republic: Political Modernization in Lebanon*. New York: Random House, 1968.

Hyman, Herbert H. *Political Socialization*. New York: Free Press, 1959.

Janowitz, M. *Political Conflict*. Chicago; Quadrangle Books, 1970.

Keniston, Kenneth. "The Sources of Student Dissent." *Journal of Social Issues* 23, no. 3 (July 1967): 108–137.

————. *The Uncommitted*. New York: Harcourt, Brace and World, 1962.

————. *Young Radicals*. New York: Harcourt, Brace and World, 1968.

Kennan, George. *Democracy and the Student Left*. Boston: Little, Brown and Co., 1968.

Lammers, Cornelis J. "Student Unionism in the Netherlands: An Application of a Social Class Model." *American Sociological Review* 36 (April 1971): 250–263.

Langton, Kenneth P. *Political Socialization*. New York: Oxford University Press, 1969.

Leggett, John C. *Class, Race, and Labor: Working-Class Consciousness in Detroit*. New York: Oxford University Press, 1968.

Lenski, Gerald. *The Religious Factor*. Garden City, N.Y.: Doubleday Anchor Books, 1961.

Liebman, Arthur, Kenneth N. Walker, and Myron Glazer. *Latin American University Students: A Six Nation Study*. Cambridge: Harvard University Press, 1972.

Lipset, S. M. *Political Man*. Garden City, N.Y.: Doubleday Anchor Books, 1963.

————. *Revolution and Counterrevolution*. New York: Basic Books, 1968.

————, ed. *Student Politics*. New York: Basic Books, 1969.

Lipset, S. M., and P. G. Altbach, eds. *Students in Revolt*. Boston: Houghton Mifflin Co., 1969.

Lipset, S. M., and S. S. Wolin, eds. *The Berkeley Student Revolt*. Garden City, N.Y.: Doubleday, 1965.

Lukács, Georg. *History and Class Consciousness: Studies in Marxist Dialectics*. Translated by Rodney Livingstone. Cambridge: MIT Press, 1971.

Lyonette, Kevin. "Student Organizations in Latin America." *International Affairs* 42 (October 1966): 655–661.

Malik, Charles. "Student Activism." *Discourse* (magazine published by philosophy students at AUB,) no. 4 (1971): 1–5.

Marcuse, Herbert. *An Essay on Liberation*. Boston: Beacon Press, 1969.

Marx, Karl. "The Eighteenth Brumaire of Louis Napoleon." In his *Selected Works*, vol. 1. Moscow: Foreign Languages Publishing House, 1962.

————. *Selected Writings in Sociology and Social Philosophy*. Edited by T. B. Bottomore and N. Rubel. London: Watts and Co., 1956.

Marx, Karl, and Friedrich Engels. *Basic Writings on Politics and Philosophy*. Edited by Lewis S. Feuer. Garden City, N.Y.: Doubleday Anchor Books, 1959.

————. *Karl Marx and Frederick Engels on Britain*. Moscow: Foreign Languages Publishing House, 1953.

Miles, Michael W. *The Radical Probe: The Logic of Student Rebellion*. New York: Atheneum, 1971.

Mills, C. Wright. *Power, Politics, and People: The Collected Essays of C. Wright Mills*. Edited by Irving Louis Horowitz. New York: Ballantine Books, 1963.

Nasatir, D. "A Note on Contextual Effects and the Political Orientations of University Students." *American Sociological Review* 33 (April 1968): 210–219.

Oglesby, Carl, ed. *The New Left Reader*. New York: Grove Press, 1969.

Penrose, Stephen B. L. *That They May Have Life: The Story of the American University of Beirut, 1866–1941*. Beirut: American University of Beirut, 1970.

République Libanaise, Ministère du Plan. *Besoins et possibilités de développement du Liban*. 2 vols. Beirut: Mission IRFED, 1960–1961.

Salem, Elie A. *Modernization without Revolution: Lebanon's Experience*. Bloomington: Indiana University Press, 1973.

Salibi, K. S. "Al-Mawarinah" [The Maronites]. *Malaf an-Nahar* (Beirut), no. 40 (January 1970).

———. *The Modern History of Lebanon*. London: Weidenfeld and Nicolson, 1965.

Shiha, Michel. *Lubnan fi Shakhsiyyatih wa Hudurih* [Lebanon: Its personality and presence]. Beirut: al-Nadwah al-Lubnaniyyah, 1962.

Skolnick, J. H. *The Politics of Protest*. New York: Ballantine Books, 1969.

Smock, David, and Audrey Smock. *Political Fragmentation and National Accommodation: A Comparative Study of Lebanon and Ghana*. New York: Elsevier, 1975.

Solomon, F., and J. R. Fishman. "Youth and Peace: A Psychological Study of Student Peace Demonstrators in Washington, D.C." *Journal of Social Issues* 20, no. 4 (October 1964): 54–73.

Tibawi, A. L. "The Genesis and Early History of the Syrian Protestant College." Pt. 1, *Middle East Journal* 21, no. 1 (Winter 1967): 1–15; Pt. 2, ibid. 21, no. 2 (Spring 1967): 199–212.

Touraine, Alain. *The May Movement: Revolt and Reform*. Translated by L. Mayhew. New York: Random House, 1971.

Wallerstein, I., and Paul Starr, eds. *The University Crisis Reader*, vol. 1. New York: Random House, 1971.

Zeitlin, M. *Revolutionary Politics and the Cuban Working Class*. New York: Harper Torchbooks, 1970.

Zurayk, Constantine K. "Abiding Truths." Address delivered at the Founder's Day Convocation, AUB, April 28, 1960.

———. "Participation of AUB Students in Palestine Struggle." *AUB Campus Yearbook* (1971).

———. "Student Revolt." *Al-Kulliyah* (AUB alumni magazine) (Summer 1968): 10–12.

# Author Index

# Subject Index

of, 26, 34, 36, 37, 38, 149, 165, 167, 191;
political parties in, 28, 30, 32, 34, 37, 158,
186, 223–224; political system of, 26, 29,
32, 34, 35, 62, 186, 187, 190, 191, 192, 193;
society in, 3, 10, 25–28, 41, 74, 118, 185,
186
leftists, 8, 10, 11, 14, 28, 59, 60–65, 67–70,
76–77, 80–84, 88, 96, 103, 104, 105, 106–
111, 118, 121, 122, 123, 132–139 passim,
158–159, 160, 161, 164, 176, 187, 188, 194–
198 passim
liberalism, 8–9, 11, 15, 81, 84–85, 102, 131–
133
liberals, 11, 15, 22, 28, 60–65, 72–77, 96, 122,
123, 124, 133, 134, 158, 159–162, 192. *See
also* reformists
liberation, 3, 4, 9, 10, 32, 50, 70, 78, 80, 104,
130, 139, 155, 159, 183, 197
LU. *See* Lebanese University

Marjayun, 35, 36, 38
Maronites, 26, 33, 35, 36, 38, 39, 44–45, 61–
69, 75, 118, 126, 127, 193, 198, 223
Marxism, 8, 103, 152, 226
Matn, 35, 36, 38
Mexico, 59, 80
Middle East, 40, 151, 154, 178, 180, 194,
196
minorities, 26, 28, 105, 198
missionaries, 40, 144, 146, 150
modernization, 33
Morocco, 7, 47, 60, 153
mosaic society, 3, 25, 27, 31, 35, 37, 41, 50,
59, 187, 188, 191
Mount Lebanon, 33, 36, 43, 144, 190
Muslims, 26, 28, 31, 32, 36, 37, 39, 40, 41, 42,
44–45, 51, 56, 60–78, 106–111, 115, 117,
118, 124, 125, 126, 128, 129, 131, 146, 149,
163, 187, 188, 190, 193, 197, 223

Naba, an-, 190
Nabatiyyah, 36, 38, 168, 169
National Bloc, 28, 160, 223, 228
nationalism, 5, 28, 29, 33, 34, 51, 66–67, 96,
115, 116–117, 135–137, 151, 187. *See also*
Arab nationalism; Lebanese nationalism;
Syrian nationalism
National Pact, 27, 28, 37, 223
Netherlands, 105, 226
New Left, 8
Norway, 94

Pakistan, 47, 48, 49
Palestine, 17, 31, 48, 49, 66, 68, 71, 74, 84, 88,
111, 116, 151, 152, 153
Palestinian resistance movement, 10, 31, 59,
66, 68, 71–72, 81, 84, 86, 88, 102, 111–114,
116–117, 138, 154, 158, 165, 167, 194–196,
197
Palestinians, 18, 34, 47, 70, 76, 124, 125, 152,
153, 154, 155, 159, 160, 170, 187, 190, 191,
195, 196, 197
Paraguay, 59
PFLP. *See* Popular Front for the Liberation
of Palestine
pluralism, 25, 27, 28, 31, 37, 50, 185, 186
Popular Front for the Liberation of Palestine
(PFLP), 72, 84, 86, 114, 154, 158, 177
Progressive Socialist Party, 28, 158, 223,
229
proletariat, 5, 103, 104
Protestants, 26, 44–45, 146
Puerto Rico, 59

radicalism, 7, 11, 16, 21, 22, 51, 55, 74, 76,
81, 105, 106, 121–139, 153, 161, 181, 183,
186, 192
Rashaya, 35, 36, 38
reference groups, 28, 39, 40, 197
reformists, 11, 60–65, 81–84, 104, 106–111,
121, 122, 123, 132–138 passim. *See also*
liberals
religiosity, 59, 60, 67–68, 80, 81, 85, 89, 90,
126
religious ties and cleavages, 9, 10, 17, 26, 27,
31, 32, 33, 35–44 passim, 50, 55, 56, 59–78,
104, 111, 118, 124, 125–127, 139, 187–188,
191, 193, 198
revolution, 30, 40, 59, 60–65, 81–84, 104,
105, 108, 110, 111, 120, 121, 122, 132–139
passim, 153, 155, 159, 161, 164, 166, 183,
186, 197
rightists, 10, 11, 40, 59, 60–65, 67–70,
76–77, 81–84, 96, 103, 105, 106–111, 118,
121–125 passim, 132–138 passim, 152,
159, 160, 161, 162–164, 172, 179, 187, 188,
195, 196, 197, 198
rural, 17, 50
Russia, 6

Saida. *See* Sidon
Saint Joseph University (SJU), 10, 11, 43,
44–47, 55, 56, 60, 61, 65, 67, 71, 94, 96, 97,